Schooling in a
"Total Institution"

Critical Studies in Education and Culture Series

Learning Work: A Critical Pedagogy of Work Education
Roger I. Simon, Don Dippo, and Arleen Schenke

Cultural Pedagogy: Art/Education/Politics
David Trend

Raising Curtains on Education: Drama as a Site for Critical Pedagogy
Clar Doyle

Toward a Critical Politics of Teacher Thinking: Mapping the Postmodern
Joe L. Kincheloe

Building Communities of Difference: Higher Education in the Twenty-First
Century
William G. Tierney

The Problem of Freedom in Postmodern Education
Tomasz Szkudlarek

Education Still under Siege: Second Edition
Stanley Aronowitz and Henry A. Giroux

Media Education and the (Re)Production of Culture
David Sholle and Stan Denski

Critical Pedagogy: An Introduction
Barry Kanpol

Coming Out in College: The Struggle for a Queer Identity
Robert A. Rhoads

Education and the Postmodern Condition
Michael Peters, editor

Critical Multiculturalism: Uncommon Voices in a Common Struggle
Barry Kanpol and Peter McLaren, editors

Beyond Liberation and Excellence: Reconstructing the Public Discourse on
Education
David E. Purpel and Svi Shapiro

Schooling in a "Total Institution"

Critical Perspectives on Prison Education

Edited by Howard S. Davidson

Critical Studies in Education and Culture Series
edited by Henry A. Giroux and Paulo Freire

BERGIN & GARVEY
Westport, Connecticut • London

31.95

To Rose Hodesson Davidson,
my mother

Library of Congress Cataloging-in-Publication Data

Schooling in a "total institution" : critical perspectives on prison
    education / edited by Howard S. Davidson.
        p.   cm.—(Critical studies in education and culture series,
    ISSN 1064–8615)
        Includes bibliographical references and index.
        ISBN 0–89789–347–6 (alk. paper).—ISBN 0–89789–426–X (pbk. :
    alk. paper)
        1. Prisoners—Education. 2. Education—Philosophy. I. Davidson,
    Howard S. II. Series.
    HV8875.S37 1995
    365′.66—dc20   94–36221

British Library Cataloguing in Publication Data is available.

Copyright © 1995 by Howard S. Davidson

Library of Congress Catalog Card Number: 94–36221
ISBN: 0–89789–347–6
        0–89789–426–X (pbk.)
ISSN: 1064–8615

First published in 1995

Bergin & Garvey, 88 Post Road West, Westport, CT 06881
An imprint of Greenwood Publishing Group, Inc.

Printed in the United States of America

The paper used in this book complies with the
Permanent Paper Standard issued by the National
Information Standards Organization (Z39.48–1984).

10 9 8 7 6 5 4 3 2 1

Contents

Series Foreword

Within the last decade, the debate over the meaning and purpose of education has occupied the center of political and social life in the United States.
Dominated largely by an aggressive and ongoing attempt by various
sectors of the Right, including "fundamentalists," nationalists, and political
conservatives, the debate over educational policy has been organized
around a set of values and practices that take as their paradigmatic model
the laws and ideology of the market place and the imperatives of a newly
emerging cultural traditionalism. In the first instance, schooling is being
redefined through a corporate ideology which stresses the primacy of
choice over community, competition over cooperation, and excellence over
equity. At stake here is the imperative to organize public schooling around
the related practices of competition, reprivatization, standardization, and
individualism.

In the second instance, the New Right has waged a cultural war against
schools as part of a wider attempt to contest the emergence of new public
cultures and social movements that have begun to demand that schools take
seriously the imperatives of living in a multiracial and multicultural democracy. The contours of this cultural offensive are evident in the call by
the Right for standardized testing, the rejection of multiculturalism, and the
development of curricula around what is euphemistically called a "common culture." In this perspective, the notion of a common culture serves as
a referent to denounce any attempt by subordinate groups to challenge the

narrow ideological and political parameters by which such a culture both
defines and expresses itself. It is not too surprising that the theoretical and
political distance between defining schools around a common culture and
denouncing cultural difference as the enemy of democratic life is relatively
short indeed.

This debate is important not simply because it makes visible the role that
schools play as sites of political and cultural contestation, but because it is
within this debate that the notion of the United States as an open and
democratic society is being questioned and redefined. Moreover, this debate provides a challenge to progressive educators both in and outside of
the United States to address a number of conditions central to a postmodern
world. First, public schools cannot be seen as either objective or neutral. As
institutions actively involved in constructing political subjects and presup-
posing a vision of the future, they must be dealt with in terms that are
simultaneously historical, critical, and transformative. Second, the relationship between knowledge and power in schools places undue emphasis on
disciplinary structures and on individual achievement as the primary unit
of value. Critical educators need a language that emphasizes how social
identities are constructed within unequal relations of power in the schools
and how schooling can be organized through interdisciplinary approaches
to learning and cultural differences that address the dialectical and multi-
faceted experiences of everyday life. Third, the existing cultural transformation of American society into a multiracial and multicultural society
structured in multiple relations of domination demands that we address
how schooling can become sites for cultural democracy rather than chan-
neling colonies reproducing new forms of nativism and racism. Finally,
critical educators need a new language that takes seriously the relationship
between democracy and the establishment of those teaching and learning
conditions that enable forms of self and social determination in students
and teachers. This suggests not only new forms of self-definition for human
agency, it also points to redistributing power within the school and between
the school and the larger society.

Critical Studies in Education and Culture is intended as both a critique
and as a positive response to these concerns and the debates from which
they emerge. Each volume is intended to address the meaning of schooling
as a form of cultural politics, and cultural work as a pedagogical practice
that serves to deepen and extend the possibilities of democratic public life.
Broadly conceived, some central considerations present themselves as defining concerns of the Series. Within the last decade, a number of new
theoretical discourses and vocabularies have emerged which challenge the
narrow disciplinary boundaries and theoretical parameters that construct
the traditional relationship among knowledge, power, and schooling. The
emerging discourses of feminism, post-colonialism, literary studies, cultural studies, and post-modernism have broadened our understanding of

how schools work as sites of containment and possibility. No longer content to view schools as objective institutions engaged in the transmission of an unproblematic cultural heritage, the new discourses illuminate how schools function as cultural sites actively engaged in the production of not only knowledge but social identities. *Critical Studies in Education and Culture* will attempt to encourage this type of analysis by emphasizing how schools might be addressed as border institutions or sites of crossing actively involved in exploring, reworking, and translating the ways in which culture is produced, negotiated, and rewritten.

Emphasizing the centrality of politics, culture, and power, *Critical Studies in Education and Culture* will deal with pedagogical issues that contribute in novel ways to our understanding of how critical knowledge, democratic values, and social practices can provide a basis for teachers, students, and other cultural workers to redefine their role as engaged and public intellectuals.

As part of a broader attempt to rewrite and refigure the relationship between education and culture, *Critical Studies in Education and Culture* is interested in work that is interdisciplinary, critical, and addresses the emergent discourses on gender, race, sexual preference, class, ethnicity, and technology. In this respect, the Series is dedicated to opening up new discursive and public spaces for critical interventions into schools and other pedagogical sites. To accomplish this, each volume will attempt to rethink the relationship between language and experience, pedagogy and human agency, and ethics and social responsibility as part of a larger project for engaging and deepening the prospects of democratic schooling in a multiracial and multicultural society. Concerns central to this Series include addressing the political economy and deconstruction of visual, aural, and printed texts, issues of difference and multiculturalism, relationships between language and power, pedagogy as a form of cultural politics, and historical memory and the construction of identity and subjectivity.

Critical Studies in Education and Culture is dedicated to publishing studies that move beyond the boundaries of traditional and existing critical discourses. It is concerned with making public schooling a central expression of democratic culture. In doing so it emphasizes works that combine cultural politics, pedagogical criticism, and social analyses with self-reflective tactics that challenge and transform those configurations of power that characterize the existing system of education and other public cultures.

Henry A. Giroux

Preface

Schooling in prison is stormy. I have never known it to be otherwise. Happenstance accounts for how most people find themselves teaching in prison. Frustration with doing little more than occupying prisoners' time or the ever present threat of cutbacks keeps teachers looking elsewhere for job opportunities. Student turnover is high for myriad reasons. In 1993, when the chapters in this book were written, sixteen state prison systems and the federal prison system in the United States had adopted mandatory education policies, and the number of jurisdictions considering compulsory schooling showed every sign of growing. Prisoners are being compelled to attend school for specified periods if they are designated functionally illiterate; depending on the jurisdiction, those who resist are denied parole hearings or prevented from participating in alternative forms of "treatment" until they comply. A similar story can be told about Canada. Yet, as literacy education expands exponentially, most of the prison higher education programs offered by approximately 300 colleges and universities across North America are being dismantled. In the United States, the major source of funding for higher education has been cut off by disqualifying prisoners from receiving financial assistance through federal Pell Grants. In Canada, the entire university level education program was cancelled in 1993 by a decision of the Solicitor General. Meanwhile, many basic education programs formerly operated by public school boards and community colleges are being privatized or operated with volunteer labor.

In public schools and university settings, change follows protracted struggles to reshape curriculum and alter teachers' working conditions. The struggles take time because these school systems are embedded in complex networks of social relations that slow processes of transformation. This is not the case for schooling in prison. By comparison, schooling in prison operates in isolation from the forces that impede radical change in public education. There are no teachers' unions or associations able to defend working conditions. Curricula change is not subject to intense debates among competing interests. There are no school boards prepared to fight for prison schools if the choice is between saving these schools and preserving more conventional programs. I have attended staff meetings where we were told without previous notice that at the end of the term (i.e., in a few months) the prison school would close; later the decision would be reversed. The experience is by no means unique.

Thus, when contributors to the literature on prison education are not writing for the converted about the benefits of certain teaching methods or materials, the tone of their discourse expresses a desire to justify their mission and, in doing so, attempt to create stability, even growth. If they are writing about crime as a consequence of cognitive deficiencies or educational disadvantage, the subtext aims to create a theoretical justification for their "profession" and presence. They aim to dampen criticism by making assertions about a positive relationship between schooling and reduced recidivism. The discourse could almost be described as polemical insofar as it provides educators with arguments they can use to justify their practice "in the trenches," and it creates a body of research promoters use when defending prison education to policy makers. In this context, "the critics" are the antieducational bureaucrat, the right-wing talk show host, the prison guard, and the conservative politician: those who think schooling prisoners is "coddling inmates" or, even worse, rewarding them with educational opportunities that are increasingly unavailable to law-abiding citizens. The prison educator is almost always fearful that conditions can turn against him or her; therefore, critique from within the ranks is distrusted and restrained lest it become their opponent's weapon.

While it is obvious from reviewing the literature that the vast majority who produce it remain hesitant or see no need to promote critical reflection, the sheer size of the prison education enterprise and the magnitude of frustrations experienced by many teachers and students when they try to make sense of their practices have created an audience for criticisms. Perhaps this audience knows that justifications alone do not protect them from adverse policy decisions, or perhaps a protracted economic depression has helped them to realize that new literacy skills are not enough to keep someone from criminal activity. Whatever the reasons, conditions in prison education have opened up possibilities for critical perspectives to be heard, and the history of prison education has created possibilities for such perspectives to emerge.

During the two decades in which prison higher education grew dramatically, an increasing number of sociologists and historians were brought into prison education as teachers for these university programs. Among them were teachers who were familiar with critical discourses. They found themselves in unexpected discussions with prisoners and unexpected conflicts with carceral authority. Those who bothered to notice saw that the prevalent discourse in prison education was out of touch with theoretical developments in sociology, history, and criminology. For the most part, however, they did not see themselves taking on the project of revising this discourse because they did not identify themselves as sociologists or historians of education, least of all prison education. When they took their prison experience back to their disciplines, it influenced their work in sociological theory, social history, and, in some cases, politics. If encouraged to do so, they could make significant contributions not only to the discourse on prison education per se but also to critical studies on education and culture in general.

The growth of literacy education in prisons has created another way in which prison education has come into contact with critical discourse. Among the many paid and volunteer educators teaching literacy are individuals who understand literacy in the context of more general questions about cultural practices and conceptions of language. Unlike the teachers in the university programs, these people identify themselves as educators. Where given the opportunities, these literacy teachers may be willing to challenge prevailing assumptions within prison education that represent literacy as a neutral technology that prisoners learn in order to get jobs and thereby avoid criminal activity.

The growth of prison education, both in higher education and in literacy education, has created possibilities for a critique to emerge which aims to interrogate ideologies, to revisit historical memories, and to reconsider how social conditions mold practices. In this volume I have brought together individuals who wish to see these possibilities for a critical perspective realized. Each has had direct experience with schooling in prisons either as a teacher or as a student. The teachers are historians, sociologists, criminologists, and educators who for the most part have taught university-level courses. The students have participated in both adult basic education and prison higher education programs. Our accounts are reflexive, even autobiographical, when we explore practices in which we have been personally involved. With a few exceptions, this is the first time these teachers and students have been encouraged to reconsider schooling in a total institution. In reply to this request, they have chosen to rely on critical reflection as a method which allows one to be explicit about the actual conditions in which schooling in prisons takes place.

This collection of essays is not my initial effort to foster critical perspectives on prison education. The first undertaking was to establish the *Journal of Prisoners on Prisons* (JPP) in 1988. The purpose of JPP has been to create a discourse on crime, punishment, and social justice constructed entirely by prisoners and former prisoners. Bob Gaucher, who has worked on the journal from its inception, describes it as the formation of a critical ethnography with political implications. He sees this development as having been made credible by the conjuncture of postmodernism and feminist theories which have opened the academy, if only slightly, to accounts of oppression by the oppressed (Gaucher 1994, 1). In 1993, JPP published a special issue on prison education, which created an opening for prisoners and former prisoners to speak to this practice. It also recognized the premise that critical perspectives on schooling in prison cannot develop without prisoners and former prisoners participating in the dialogues that construct these perspectives. That premise is recognized here.

The 1993 issue of JPP saw the beginning of what has become a continuous process of collaboration. The reader will notice that the contributors to this volume have drawn on research published in JPP for their own work. Essays appearing in the special issue on prison education by former prisoners Therasa Ann Glaremin and Juan A. Rivera were revised for inclusion in this volume. Moreover, creating JPP brought me to the attention of Elizabeth Barker, who made it possible for me to meet other contributors.

In 1989 Elizabeth Barker, founder of Boston University's prison higher education program, invited me to teach sociology at Norfolk and Bay State prisons for the summer session. I returned to teach again in the summers of 1990 and 1992. During the first visit, she introduced me to Dante Germanotta, who coordinated Curry College's program at Walpole Prison and was president and a founding member of the Massachusetts Council on Prison Education. Thanks to Professor Barker, I also met Peter Cordella, who had taught sociology for the Boston program. Julian Stone was my student in a course on the history of criminal justice that I taught at Bay State in the summer of 1992. He told me about the courses he developed to prepare jailhouse lawyers, which I asked him to write about for this collection. I met the historian Peter Linebaugh during that summer and learned that he too had taught in prison.

At the fourth International Conference on Prison Abolition held in 1991, I shared a session with Edward Sbarbaro. Drawing from submissions made to JPP, I spoke about prison writing as resistance. Ed spoke about Palestinians in Israeli prisons and how they transformed incarceration into opportunities for political education. Afterward we discussed possibilities for this book.

Robert P. Weiss and Karlene Faith first came to my attention through their contributions to *Social Justice*, a journal that has nurtured the development of critical criminology. During conversations with members of JPP's editorial board, I learned that they also had taught in prison. Jim Thomas and Michael Collins were known to me through their critiques of prison education published in *Adult Education Quarterly*.

As a group, we may differ on what constitutes a critical perspective. However, what sets us apart from the mainstream and forms a basis for unity is that we do not refer to ourselves as "correctional educators." We are not in the business of rehabilitating prisoners. We are not so unconscious of how structural conditions influence human agency as to claim that schooling alone is going to improve students' opportunities to get jobs and avoid being sent back to prison. We understand that education in any form is not a neutral technology that can be detached from the context in which it takes place. Yet we are not so obtuse to our own experiences and forgetful of our own histories that we would deny that education can make a difference. The operational definition for success accepted in the literature of "correctional education" is to reduce the rate of recidivism. This measure of success is not accepted here. Insofar as critical perspectives are about questioning presuppositions and avoiding reductionism, a definition of our success is one among many issues that remain subject to interrogation.

In closing these prefatory remarks, I want to acknowledge the work of a group of individuals whose assistance made this collection of essays possible. It is unlikely that this book would have come about without Elizabeth Barker. The program she established through Boston University has located in several prisons a place where teachers and prisoners could come together and learn from each other. She introduced me to these places and provided the opportunity for me to meet many of the contributors to this collection.

Michael Collins, Robert Hyndman, Robert Gaucher, Peter Linebaugh, George Melnyk, and Alice Pitt read various chapters and offered advice. Joanne McNabb's skills at word processing turned cut-and-paste manuscripts into drafts we could read. Thanks to Joanne, Warren Otto, and the staff of the Continuing Education Division, The University of Manitoba, I have been able to step back from my duties to devote time to this project.

Countless questions emerge when editing a collection of original essays. Very few were answered without depending on Marcia J. Stentz for her good judgment and generous spirit. Each contributor to this collection has benefited from the time she has taken to suggest modifications that would improve the quality of our writing. Our clarity owes much to her care.

1

Possibilities for Critical Pedagogy in a "Total Institution": An Introduction to Critical Perspectives on Prison Education

Howard S. Davidson

The story of deviance and social control is "a battle story" (Pfohl 1985, 3): a never-ending battle over social order. Winners gain control over the way people think about what is acceptable and normal (p. 3). Losers resist continuously and in doing so become outsiders: the rebels, the disordered, and the delinquents as defined by the winners. Winners determine the means to control, outsiders through a combination of strategies (e.g., execution, exile, shame, welfare, schooling, imprisonment, treatment). Imprisonment and schooling—schooling in prison—is the combination of strategies that concerns us here.

At this moment in the battle imprisonment is a preferred means of control. In the 1970s the state prison population in the United States was under 100,000. By the year 2000 it will exceed one million and it is predicted to reach 1.3 million by 2010 (Carter 1991, 18). But this is a fraction of the total number of people controlled by criminal justice systems. On any given day in 1991, one million people were in American prisons and jails and another 2.7 million were either on probation or parole (Breed 1991, 1). In Washington D.C., 42 percent of all males between 18 and 35 years of age—mostly blacks and Latinos—were either in prisons, on probation or parole, out on bond, or had a warrant against them.[1] Along with forced labor, schooling is a principal method for controlling prisoners and for their "rehabilitation." Various forms of compulsory education are already practiced in U.S. and Canadian federal prisons and many state and provincial prisons.[2] I shall return to the contemporary features of prison education.

North America is becoming a penal society. At 111 prisoners per 100,000 people (1990), Canada is among the five countries with the highest per capita incarceration rate in the world. The United States leads at over 400 prisoners per 100,000. For comparison, in 1990 the average per capita rate among 24 European countries was 75 per 100,000 (Christie 1991, 14). But per capita rates do not allow for an adequate appreciation of how poverty and racial subjugation are defining features of imprisonment. For instance, by 1991, the incarceration rate for black males in the United States was 3,370 per 100,000 (Mauer 1992). African Americans constitute 12 percent of the general population but over 40 percent of the prison population (Breed 1991, 6). Among Latinos the figures are 6 percent and 13 percent, respectively. In Canada, aboriginal people represent about 3 percent of the general population but 11 percent of federal and 15 percent of provincial prisoners (Stanford 1991, 21). The chapters by former prisoners Juan A. Rivera and Therasa Ann Glaremin illuminate how racism, poverty, and patriarchy define imprisonment in North America.

Deviants "are trapped within the vision of others" (Pfohl 1985, 3). When people are asked to describe the type of offender they envision when they think about crime and punishment, it is clear that they have in mind the violent criminal and that they vastly overestimate the percentage of people imprisoned for violent offenses (Doob and Roberts 1988). In fact, violent offenders are a minority. About 30 percent of the people held in provincial prisons are there because they cannot afford to pay fines—not because a court thought they presented a danger to society (Stanford 1991, 14). About 26 percent of Canadian federal prisoners were sentenced for violent crimes, compared to nearly 45 percent for property and drug-related offenses (p. 15). Similar figures for the United States led the National Council on Crime and Delinquency to observe that the majority of prisoners "did not require the security of a prison nor would [they] benefit by a lengthy prison term" (Breed 1991, 6).

Crime is frightening, harmful, and destructive; it is also about power and politics. Behaviors become crimes when they threaten the safety, prestige, and fortunes of those with sufficient power to influence the processes by which behaviors become crimes. The accused burglar and the drug pusher are incarcerated as criminals. The corporate executives who manipulate food prices or operate hazardous work places make profits (Reiman, 1990). The budgets for prison construction, services, and staff—$55 billion annually in the United States (Carter 1991, 15)—spurs the growth and political influence of criminal justice system bureaucracies. Private firms operating prisons and security systems profit from increasing prison populations and the fear of crime. Schooling in prison cannot avoid being caught up in the power and politics (i.e., the battle) of crime and social control. A central theme throughout this volume is that everything about schooling in prison is political.

The aim of this book is to advance the conventional discourse on prison education with the development of critical perspectives. The contributors have interpreted this aim as a call to write on prison education as political education: not just about the politics of schooling but about schooling for the politicalization of prisoners. Each chapter is not merely a contemplation of schooling in prison. Through case studies and critical reflections on their own experiences with prison schools as teachers and prisoner-students, the contributors have produced a discourse on the possibility of prison education as critical pedagogy.

Because the articulation of prison education as critical pedagogy is a central, compelling theme in the following chapters, I shall focus on this theme in these introductory remarks. Before doing so, I think it is essential that misconceptions about possibilities for critical pedagogies be averted. Therefore, I begin by describing the major contemporary features of schooling in prison as the context in which the possibilities for prison education as critical pedagogy are raised.

CONTEMPORARY FEATURES OF SCHOOLING IN PRISON

The ethos of prison education conceptualizes schooling as a means to habilitate/rehabilitate/reform prisoners by correcting functional learning deficiencies correlated to criminal activity, hence the term correctional education. Two schools of thought about what needs to be corrected dominate the discourse. One is rooted in a functionalist theory of social problems that became popular in the 1960s and 1970s. The prisoner is understood to be someone who lacks the academic, vocational, and social skills to achieve socially acceptable goals. This leads him or her to deviant or criminal behavior in order to achieve what cannot be gained legally. Meeting the prisoner's basic educational and cultural needs should correct criminal behavior by opening up job and social opportunities that allow one to achieve goals legally. Across North America this "opportunities model" is the explicit, official purpose of schooling, especially in the field of literacy education (Solicitor General 1990, 57; Schwartz and Koch 1992, 100).

The second school of thought emerges from a marriage between cognitive development theory—Piaget and Kohlberg—and neoliberal perspectives on deviance (Wilson 1983). It propounds that crime results from individuals making poor (i.e., criminal) decisions when faced with life's many problems. Out of neoliberalism comes the market metaphor, in which individuals make rational decisions based on calculating benefits against costs. Law-abiding citizens make socially acceptable decisions even when they face great adversity. They do so because their cognitive development is sufficiently mature to calculate into the cost/benefit equation potential punishment for wrongdoing, social costs, and moral and interpersonal considerations. Immature or deficient reasoners fail to calculate properly the true (instrumental, moral, social, personal) consequences of their choices. Thus, the proper aim of education is to promote cognitive development so that the person will calculate the real instrumental and social costs of resolving problems with criminal activities and will choose instead law-abiding alternatives. In the prison education literature, this is referred to as the moral development or cognitive development school. It enjoyed considerable support in the 1970s and early 1980s, especially among promoters of prison higher education (Jones and d'Errico 1994, 10; Morin 1981a), and it continues to have a considerable influence in some jurisdictions (Arbuthnot and Gordon 1988; Ross and Fabiano 1985).

A most significant influence of cognitive development theory on prison education was Lawrence Kohlberg's pedagogy for cognitive moral development (Morin 1981c). In Canada, Kohlberg's influence surfaced at the University of Victoria's (UVic) degree program in federal prisons. Stephen Duguid, one of the program's founders, promoted liberal arts education as a means for promoting moral development (Duguid 1981). Kohlberg aside, the UVic program attracted deserved attention for its scope, for the support it enjoyed among prisoner-students, for the research it generated, and for its progressive influence among people with an interest in the field. The full extent of its support became apparent in 1983 when Correctional Service of Canada (CSC) canceled the program to save money. To the Solicitor General's chagrin, the program's coordinators organized a protest that was "a truly impressive lobby effort, perhaps a classic example of [what] citizens can do when they have a cause and the motivation to pursue it" (Duguid and Hoekema 1986, 186). They forced the government to reverse its decision. It is worth noting that radical educators were drawn to support the UVic program because of a dramatic incident in 1981 in which prisoners defended the UVic facilities and library against violent protests by other prisoners during a prison insurrection.

In the United States, prison-based post secondary schools were first introduced in the late 1950s (Gaither 1982, 22; Silva 1994, 25). By 1966 the Office of Economic Opportunity funded the Newgate Prison higher education project based on the opportunities model of improving access to higher education and thereby improving job and social opportunities (Seashore and Haberfield 1976, 186). In the 1960s federal funding supported a growing number of colleges that were prepared to establish higher education programs.[3] Many of these schools provided programs free or with minimal costs for departments of correction. Small grants from liberal state governments made possible a wide range of creative programming (Cleveland 1989). How volunteer work and small grants kept an extensive feminist studies program alive during the 1970s is explicated here by Karlene Faith in chapter 12 of this volume. Gratuity or a small stipend allowed Peter Linebaugh to teach Marxism in four prisons from 1972 to 1981 (see chapter 5). Later, prisoners received student financial assistance under federal Pell Grants (Taylor 1994). Through to the late 1980s this funding became increasingly significant, especially as departments of correction began to withhold supplementary funds and universities faced tighter budgets.

Most liberal arts degree programs survived the 1980s, but as the decade came to a close it was clear that serious trouble lay ahead. In 1993 every university degree program in Canadian prisons was canceled by the Solicitor General. Just ten years earlier, when the CSC had moved against the UVic program, supporters stopped the CSC bureaucracy. When the program (which in the intervening years had been taken over by Simon Fraser University) was eliminated in 1993, little organized effort was made to restore it by the programs' coordinators. The prisoners, on the other hand, took the CSC to court. The program was lost, but not because the students did not try to defend it (*Williams Head Institution Inmate Committee v. Correctional Service of Canada*, 66 Fed Trial Report. 262 [1993]).

Meanwhile, in 1991, right-wing Congressional legislators in the United States began sponsoring bills to prohibit prisoners from receiving Pell Grants. If they succeed, as expected, every program will face major cutbacks and most will not survive. College programs will either close or run with volunteer labor, ridiculously low budgets for texts and materials, and virtually no student support services.[4] In chapter 2 in this volume, Jim Thomas spells out, in terms familiar to anyone who has participated in prison schools, just how limited the resources are and what toll this tendency has taken on the quality of teaching and the ability of students to produce good work. The program in which Ed Sbarbaro (chapter 6) taught his critical criminology course is already a victim of these cutbacks as is the Curry College program at Walpole Prison in which Dante Germanotta worked (see chapter 7).

Meanwhile, schooling in adult basic education (i.e., "literacy") has moved through this twenty-five-year period along a different path, and it has come into the 1990s facing a decidedly different future. In the United States, legislators who would prohibit prisoners' eligibility for Pell Grants have approved legislation (e.g., the National Literacy Act) that authorizes funds for projects that improve vocational and basic education programs in prisons (Schwartz and Koch 1992, 104–5). While there is some talk of cognitive moral development within this aspect of prison education, the opportunities model is the ideology driving the federal Office of Correctional Education (established in 1991): "Providing inmates with literacy training, marketable job skills, and life skills will enable them to be contributing citizens when they return to their communities" (p. 100).

During the 1970s, adult basic education was provided sporadically in state prison, while in county jails it was nearly nonexistent (Martin 1976, 44). But along with the dramatic growth of the prison population beginning in the late 1970s, interest in and support for literacy education programs increased. By 1982 the U.S. Federal Bureau of Prisons initiated a mandatory adult education policy which compelled all prisoners functioning below "grade six" to enroll in a literacy program for ninety days. Until prisoners passed the sixth grade standard, they "could not be promoted to prison jobs above the lowest grade" (McCollum 1989, 122). Four years later, in 1986, Virginia passed a "No Read, No Release" parole policy. By 1991 over ten states had mandatory literacy programs for prisons (DiVito 1991) and the federal system had increased mandatory participation to 120 days (Jenkins 1994, 27).[5] By 1994, sixteen states had mandatory programs, including New York State, and the American Bar Association had adopted a "model mandatory education statute" (p. 26). In some jurisdictions attendance is compulsory; in others, prisoners are denied access to work-release, furloughs, and treatment programs if they refuse to attend classes (Ryan and McCabe 1993, 134). Jenkins is lucid about the conditions supporting the mandatory movement. He states that the greatest incentive for prisoners is relief from boredom; the institution benefits by running programs that help to maintain order in the face of overcrowding and longer sentences; and society benefits because there exists a "very strong correlation between educational disadvantage and criminality" (Jenkins 1994, 27).[6]

In Canada the demand for basic literacy as mandatory education has moved at a slower pace but in the same direction. In the 1970s basic education is described as "patchy in operation, at times basically fumbling in implementation and existing in an atmosphere of half-hearted support" (Ontario Institute for Studies in Education 1979, 69). In 1987, the Solicitor General Canada announced his major literacy initiative. Prisoners who tested below a "grade eight level" were denied access to treatment and work placements until they completed a basic education program. Therasa Ann Glaremin (in chapter 3) describes how women experienced this shift in policy. In 1988, after years of women prisoners being denied equal access to basic schooling, "they [the CSC bureaucracy] sort of changed it all around. They started rounding-up people in droves and forcing them to go to school against their wills. They were saying that anyone who worked in these jobs had to have their grade nine education." In 1992, CSC raised the minimum literacy level to grade ten. In 1994 CSC planned to follow the American lead and make education explicitly compulsory.

Mandatory schooling can be expensive if the practice of using certified teachers from public school boards and community colleges is followed. To reduce costs, efforts are under way to privatize mandatory schooling by turning program contracts over to private firms. Students in prisons may notice little difference because certificated teachers working for school authorities made ample use of competency-based curriculum and computer programs to teach math and basic reading skills. Private companies offer similar services without the cost of hiring certificated teachers. With the introduction of GED and vague standards like "grade eight," prison authorities are free to use whomever they like to run programs. In fact, community colleges and computer companies are being replaced by volunteer tutors from local community-based literacy programs (Lawrence 1994, 46–47). The tutors may be supervised by a trained reading teacher or by "coordinators of educational services" who, as likely as not, are guards with minimum training in adult education. More "innovative" programs use prisoners as peer-tutors with trained teachers assigned to supervise them (Steurer 1991).

In chapter 4 of this volume, Michael Collins provides one of the few arguments against the pell mell introduction of competency-based schooling, the hallmark of mandatory programs. He sees it as designed to preclude independent expression and intended to place complete emphasis on "functional" literacy skills. This form of curriculum is broken down into measurable units for evaluation; hence, teaching prisoners to this or that grade level is more easily determined. Collins is able to show how these competency-based programs fit neatly into the predominant correctional models and provide for easy surveillance of the individual's behavior.

Schooling in the total institution has been a continuous, vicissitudinous feature of the penitentiary since its inception in the eighteenth century. It is not likely to disappear. The form it takes in the immediate future will be determined by the nature of the structural forces bearing down on these schools. We may assume that financial aid to prisoners for post-secondary education will be eliminated. Advocates of longer and harsher sentences may be sure that their political agendas will be well represented, as mainstream political parties continue their move to the Right. Authoritarian popularists are kept at bay by the more mainstream conservative parties incorporating the Right's agendas into legislation. Electoral support for anti-immigration and law-and-order legislation is relatively easy to achieve. If funds are increasingly taken from public schooling and post-secondary education, tolerance for prison education will be further eroded. The more correctional educators can represent schooling as quasi-punitive, the more likely it is that they will be spared severe cutbacks. Mandatory schooling couched in the language of behavior modification and "get tough" labels seems to be the chosen defense of a considerably influential sector within correctional education. Their defense may suffice. If literacy education can be reduced to a narrow, computerized, competency-based curriculum then costs can be kept to a minimum, especially when outside volunteers, or prisoners working under the supervision of an education officer/guard, meet the minimum requirements for a teacher. Supporting the movement in this direction are a growing number of software companies who see sizable markets in the expanding prison population if mandatory literacy programs continue to expand. Major initiatives in teacher education support competency-based curriculum and distance education formats that will provide the training needed to operate the computerized, packaged, functional programs (Eggleston 1992; Gehring 1992). Considerable funding ($8 million in 1992) for these programs, albeit with the greater amounts spent for juvenile programs, has been provided by the Office of Correctional Education (Schwartz and Koch 1992).

With forces bearing down on prison higher education and the notable push for mandatory literacy education as the two most prominent features of schooling in prison, arguments on behalf of prison education as critical pedagogy must surely be treated with scepticism. However, because these arguments are raised here, it is the issue to which I shall now turn.

CRITICAL PEDAGOGY: POSSIBILITIES AND VISIONS

What qualifies as critical pedagogy in this context is difficult to articulate, but articulate it we must if it is to be distinguished from any schooling that enhances critical thinking skills and promotes collaborative teaching methods. It is often said in the literature on critical pedagogy that it is about creating a "critical consciousness" that politicizes students versus education that domesticates them (Shor 1993, 25). It has been described as a pedagogy of resistance against oppression; indeed, a pedagogy for "transition to socialism and to radical change in the social relations of production" (Torres 1993, 130). Critical pedagogy is about insisting on consistency between democratic values and democratic practices in the classroom. For Shor, critical pedagogy is more than merely involving students and teachers in participatory decision making. It is a condition that can only be realized fully through the democratization of culture (Shor 1993, 26–27). The language of resistance, critical consciousness, democratization may have ideological appeal among some educators and prisoners—just as it may frighten (most) others—but beyond appeal, what practices can it name and inform in this context?

When Paulo Freire wrote that critical pedagogy "starts with the conviction that it cannot present its own program but must search for this program dialogically with the people" (Freire 1970, 118), I believe he is saying that he would refuse to articulate a reply to the above question. Freire does not provide a working definition of critical pedagogy, but a method for realizing its program within a particular context. We are advised to set aside the problem of articulating a program for prison education as critical pedagogy and to turn our attention instead to creating the conditions needed to "search for this program dialogically" with prisoners.

In the context of public schooling, Roger Simon sees the possibility for realizing a program when participants are encouraged to be conscious of the coercive forces which affect how they express themselves, imagine their futures, ask their questions, and weigh and judge the worth of their answers (1992, 20). Possibilities for critical pedagogy exist when students begin to recognize "those options available in a situation when one . . . takes into account both the 'coercive encouragement' of particular [social] forms and the limited range of capacities those forms encourage" (p. 21). Examining the contemporary features of these forms is important but insufficient because their contemporary features can appear as unalterable realities to which the individual must adapt. Recognizing the historicity of social forms is essential, because through historical consciousness we realize that forms are alterable. They are subject to struggles waged to change them. It matters who participates in these struggles and what these participants understand to be their true interests.

For instance, in chapter 3 Michael Collins observes that providers of literacy education *have opted for* curricula that reinforce a narrow function-alist perspective toward literacy. This emphasis on a dimension that corresponds to official objectives "serves to announce that the educational provision is not only accommodative to the system of surveillance and control . . . , [but] in fact, [it is] integral to the panoptican." Collins rejects the view that teachers in prison have few if any reasonable opportunities to resist adopting this curriculum. He challenges teachers to investigate the range of options for literacy education and to explore the conditions that influence how option selection takes place. In doing so, teachers may gain a far better appreciation for the coercive forces that actually impede any possibility to carve out and hold a space that permits a more learner-centered curriculum. In the context of mandatory literacy as a get tough policy, Collins reminds us that there are "seams in the system which can be exploited by life enriching alternatives."

In the context of a seminar on critical pedagogy, I once referred to the possibility of prison education as precursor to an intelligent riot. It was Roger Simon who encouraged me to give it more thought. Since then, I have asked myself if an intelligent riot denotes a link between education and revolution as critical mass action. In the context of the seminar room this formulation had some appeal. In the context of the prison, it strikes me as romanticism. However, if teachers and prisoners are aware of the depth of the tragedy that is the prison, and of the terrible barbarism to which it gives form, then it is not romanticism to propose that critical pedagogy as intelligent riot should articulate a vision of teachers and prisoner-students as "eternal protesters," who, in the words of Isaac Deutscher, work

to maintain the opposition to the powers that be, to militate against the taboos and conventions, to struggle for a society in which nationalism and racialism [and sexism] will at last lose their hold on the human mind. I know this is no easy way out; it may be distressing and hurtful; and for those who take it there can be no precise formulation of a set of precepts for action. But if we do not remain protesters, we shall be moving in a pernicious circle, a suicidal circle. (Deutscher 1968, 58–59)

The term "total institution" conjures up an image in which there is no place to hide, no possibility for argument, certainly no opportunity for "eternal protest" or "opposition to the powers that be." Why would anyone imagine there is space for critical discourse within a total institution when it is plausible to claim that protest informed by critique in the non-prison world has been made improbable with the materialization of modernism? If public spaces such as schools, parks, bars, media (as audiovisual space), and home have been colonialized by an ever encroaching technicism (driven by social relations conducive to massive accumulations of wealth), why even suggest that technicism is any less advanced in the prison and that protest may be articulated there? Indeed, the term total institution survives Goffman as sociological shorthand for domination by technicism. Goffman described one of its primary features as the "handling of many human needs by the bureaucratic organization of whole blocks of people—whether or not this is a necessary or effective means of social organization" (1961, 6). But I would argue, and I believe that the accounts produced for this book would defend my position, that prisons as total institutions are also "sites of opposition"—perhaps no less and no more constrained than other cultural and educational formations.

There is no need to romanticize this opposition, to portray prisoners as "primitive rebels" or "eternal protesters," or to see teachers as an "intellectual vanguard." The reality is more complex and not at all tidy.[7] In chapter 10, Peter Cordella sees among prisoners only a minority who are prepared to consider "the reality rather than the rhetoric of the atomized society because [they] have personally [experienced] its contradictions." Most want to take their place among those who compete successfully in an atomized world. Robert P. Weiss (chapter 8) sees most students as conservative, holding fast to the American Dream, and more inclined to attribute their personal failures to bad luck or to not knowing the right people than to blame structural inequality. On the other hand, there are the students, whom Cordella describes as "ideational." These students, who are "united in their commitment to the shared responsibility that defines persons in community," are the individuals who demonstrate "the potential for critical pedagogy in prison . . . education."

Unfortunately, the majority of teachers in prison schools strive to justify their practices not to criticize them, and they do this for a very good reason. As we have seen from the overview of contemporary features, educators are in constant danger of having their programs eliminated. As a consequence, unless political conditions directly threaten the existence of their programs, they display little interest in criticism lest it be turned against them. Nonetheless there is dissatisfaction. David Werner, for instance, has opposed a view of teachers as correctional educators, if for no other reason than desiring to be "well rid of society at large expecting them to do something of which they were never capable" (Werner 1990, 75). In its place he suggests that the "single goal to which prison education must strive is *individual empowerment*" (p. 156), which he later develops as "promoting the consideration of moral and ethical dimensions within every trade or academic subject taught in prison" (p. 159). Others have taken exception to the opportunities model (Jones and d'Errico 1994, 10–11; Lawrence 1994, 49). Lucien Morin, for instance, vehemently insists that education be accepted as a right "rooted in the concept of human dignity," pursued for the sole purpose of "human development" (1981b, 24).

However, this language of dissatisfaction proves to be disappointing because it is made on behalf of alternative means of correction and, Werner's criticism notwithstanding, not as a critique of prison education as correctional education (e.g., Duguid 1992; Werner 1990, 161). Still, it reminds us that there is an audience eager to hear what those who refuse to speak of schooling as correctional education have to say. The teachers who speak the language of dissatisfaction are ready to listen. It matters what they hear and how they are heard.

In this book they will notice that no one suggests that a causal relationship can exist between schooling and recidivism rates. This is not because we have no concern with crime and the harm it creates, nor is it a sign that we are callous to students' conditions and their desire to leave prison and live creative lives. One reason for dismissing the recidivism-education relationship is the reductionism implied by positing that relationship. Another is our position that the conditions that produce most criminal activity are eliminated not by the domestication of individuals, but by their politicalization: by individuals becoming conscious of themselves as historical beings who demand to create social forms that are conducive to genuine social justice. Germanotta argues in Chapter 7 that once "critical reflection begins, in the context of formal education being pursued in a prison setting, prisoner-students find their own life histories placed in a new perspective, and they begin to *see the possibilities of genuine personal transformation and eventually transformation of the world* [my emphasis]." Concrete examples of this critical reflection are documented by each contributor to this volume. It remains to be seen if it is possible for teachers and students to hold a space wherein students may continue to "see the possibilities of genuine personal transformation and eventually transformation of the world."

Because it is steeped in individualism, the tendency of liberal pedagogy is to personalize critique and to personalize politics. Typically, liberal pedagogy stops short of articulating how an individual's alienation relates to the dehumanization of the social sphere and how collective political action is necessary to recapture one's humanity. To distinguish themselves from being content with personalization, those who articulate and encourage a realization of critical pedagogy have committed themselves to realize their world view through collective action.

In his introduction to a collection of essays on *Critical Pedagogy and Cultural Power*, Livingston draws from Freire's remarks what he (Livingston) regards as the "essence" of efforts to provide a definition of critical pedagogy: "empowerment of subordinate groups through shared under-standing of the social construction of reality" (1987, 8). The concept of empowerment he admits is subject to much abuse; thus he cautions against "the intellectual conceit of equating the 'discovery' of social reality with its transformation" (p. 8). Nonetheless, Livingston does not abandon critical pedagogy as a useful term because it names a set of related educational practices connected to a common "historical project:" "to expose the dynamics of cultural power and to enable popular engage-ment in creating alternative futures" (p. 12). It is this commitment to "creating alternative futures" that sets those historical projects apart from liberal pedagogy.

In an extensive essay on the teacher as "transformative intellectual," Henry Giroux emphasizes throughout that critical pedagogy is not merely discovery or the ability to think critically. The educator is confronted with the concrete possibility for a "radical pedagogy as a form of cultural politics . . . understood as a set of practices that produces social forms through which different types of knowledge, sets of experiences, and subjectivities are constructed" (Giroux 1988, xxxv). The attention to produc-ing social forms brings forth the question of power, in other words, by what means is this production accomplished. In Giroux's terms:

a pedagogy of cultural politics presents a twofold set of tasks for critical educators. First, they need to analyze how cultural production is organized within asymmet-rical relations of power in schools. Second, they need to construct political strategies for participating in social struggles designed to fight for schools as democratic public spheres. (pp. 101–102)

It is clear that for these educators that critical pedagogy is not merely about personal growth but must express itself as "political strategies de-signed to fight" for a specified social transformation.[8] In the context of schooling in prison, it is necessary to ask how cultural production is organized within asymmetrical relations of power in prisons and the prison school; and to construct political strategies for participating in social strug-gles designed to fight for prisons and prison schools as democratic public spheres. If one agrees with this formulation, it is not difficult to imagine the courage required to strive for its realization. Is this courage futile in the total institution? There is ample evidence in the history of prisoners' struggles to indicate that it is not (Dunne 1993; Gaucher 1991).

On January 14, 1976 about 350 prisoners at Archambault prison (Quebec) began a work strike that lasted nearly fourteen weeks. The strike was for improved living conditions and in sympathy with striking prisoners at St. Vincent de Paul prison. As the strike progressed, mass action outside the prison supported the prisoners' demand that the authorities recognize the prisoners "as a valid partner in a valid dialogue" (Gosselin 1982, 179). By

February, the strikers produced a manifesto that contained a section on education. In this section they demanded the "immediate opening of a special class for illiterate prisoners. Other prisoners will run these classes, with a ratio of one prisoner to three prisoner-students" (p. 195). They demanded access to college-level courses and an end to discrimination against francophone prisoners, who received less educational programming than anglophone prisoners (p. 196). They prefaced these demands by articulating the following vision:

To us, talking about education means talking about the chance to acquire an intellectual and practical formation that increases understanding and decreases alienation from things, from reality and from life. A step toward a liberated spirit. (p. 195)

The strike at Archambault was not an isolated event. In chapter 5, Peter Linebaugh documents moments in which prisoners engaged in organized protests that are continuous with the struggle and the purpose of the Archambault strike. Karlene Faith (chapter 12) provides examples of women in the California Institute for Women (1972–1976) organizing protests to demand the reinstitution of the Santa Cruz Workshop after the project was barred repeatedly by prison officials. Prisoners have filed law suits to force departments of correction to provide post-secondary programs. In chapter 7, Dante Germanotta describes at length the legal battles undertaken by Richard Cepulonis to bring schooling into the Massachusetts prison system.

Another aspect of the influence of prisoners' struggles for education is registered here. During the 1970s, when prisoners' protests captured the attention of Marxists, feminists, anarchists, and liberal democrats, radicals and reformers were attracted to the prisons. Like Karlene Faith and Peter Linebaugh, they went inside as teachers for post-secondary programs sponsored by progressive universities and community colleges. They taught feminism, Marxism, and political organization. They demonstrated that prison walls could be breached by radical academics, artists, and Buddhist scholars. They lectured on the 1939 Mombasa General Strike in Kenya and criticized the *Communist Manifesto*. They organized classes on the politics of drug use, radical psychology, and ethnic studies. They taught alternative forms of healing. Their essays record what prison education has been in the past and beg comparison/connection with the present.

An essential message in the current conservative onslaught is to represent resistance, such as this occurring in the 1970s, as anomalies, discontinuous with the 1950s as a period of gradual (i.e., "normal") change. However, after reading the contributions by Therasa Ann Glaremin, Juan A. Rivera, and Julian Stone—or students' comments recorded by Edward Sbarbaro—it is clear that a significant minority of prisoners continue "to speak a language of possibility" (Aronowitz and Giroux 1991, 181) that prefigures a different world view. This vision is more continuous with striking prisoners at Archambault, Malcolm X's struggle to educate himself and his brothers at Norfolk prison, and women demanding the return of the Santa Cruz Women's Prison Project than conservatives would want to allow.

The concern with critical pedagogy as an "engagement in creating alternative futures" is clearly registered throughout this volume. My reason for reviewing the contemporary features of schooling in prison was to caution against misjudging the intensity of the coercive forces that resist creating alternative spaces for the realization of its program. One must also guard against the more subtle forms of resistance, especially co-optation.

In his critique on higher education programs provided by outside universities, Wayne Knights emphasized that "cultural autonomy within the prison can only be achieved if a degree of institutional autonomy is created and the opening for such a venture can be found within the operating principles of the prison" (Knights 1989, 76). Knights turns to Herbert Marcuse's notion of "repressive tolerance" in order to explain how a strategy that strives to preserve cultural autonomy can get caught up in defending the smooth running of the prison by diffusing criticism. Potential dissidents are also potential intellectuals who may gravitate toward the opportunity to participate in the alternative community. In doing so, these prisoner-students have something to lose by risking confrontation. The emphasis shifts toward contemplation and away from action. Teachers avoid confrontations that may threaten "the program" or their own participation in it. In the name of being reasonable and practical, the university [or any educational program which pursues the "island" strategy] risks becoming part of the carceral itself (p. 76).

This danger of co-optation does not give Knights reason to prescribe abandoning the prison. Instead, the "next stage of development," he writes, "lies in confronting the problem; and it will likely involve the transition to a new concept of correctional education rather than further justification of educative models" (p. 76). Knights is close to correct. His error, as I see it, is that one cannot avoid repressive tolerance when one identifies the objective as creating a "new concept of correctional education." If correctional education is still the vision, legitimating the prison, depoliticizing prisoners' experiences, and domestication cannot be far away. The "next stage" must begin with a more profound reconceptualization of prison education. It must be grounded in a consciousness of the histories registered here by Linebaugh and Faith and establish the need to fight for prison schools as democratic public spheres. It must connect the struggle to realize prison education as critical pedagogy to struggles for its realization universally. A conceptual framework appropriate to the realization of prison education as critical pedagogy must allow for an understanding of the connections between schooling in prison and schooling outside of prison, in contrast to the typical discourse that treats prison education as a form unto itself. This reconceptualization raises the question of how to create alliances for a struggle to realize critical pedagogy on several terrains.

ALLIANCES FOR CRITICAL PEDAGOGY

It is naive to assume or expect that every prisoner is a natural ally for critical pedagogy. Rivera, for instance, points out that prisoners who "have a defeatist attitude about challenging the status quo" and those who have "racist attitudes" create opposition to the development of the Nontraditional Approach. Weiss has described the divisions between prisoners who support INSIGHT INC. and those who explicitly resist it. Cordella, like Weiss, has observed that the majority of prisoner-students are conservative. Faith notes that one cannot assume that all guards want to see prison education squelched or reduced to a punitive form of education. Collins has not hesitated to point to the willingness of teachers to accept functionalist, competency-based curriculum that would leave no room for dialogue. Thus, one is not automatically an ally because one is a prisoner, guard, or teacher. Alliances must be made. Making them requires work that will be performed by those who recognize the necessity for building alliances.

On the question of allies, it is reasonable to hope that collectively these essays will open a clearer shuttle between the participants in prison schools and people who are looking at sites of opposition in education and culture generally. Aronowitz and Giroux see critical pedagogy ("at its best") as enabling "teachers and others to view education as a political, social and cultural enterprise. That is, as a form of engaged practice, critical pedagogy calls into question forms of subordination that create inequities among different groups as they live out their lives" (1991, 118). If this is the case, then to achieve "its best" it would seem imperative that schooling and culture in prison become part of any comprehensive view of education and culture. It is hoped that through these essays we have constructed a bridge to a site of subordination that remains insufficiently explored within the parameters of critical perspectives on education. If we have been even marginally successful in constructing that bridge, then it is possible that we are providing opportunities for educators who do not presently participate in the discourse on prison education to do so. This collaboration between prison(er) educators and students and educators and students working elsewhere is essential for a continuous development of critical perspectives that inform and are informed by critical pedagogies.

In the context of discussing collaboration, I want to discuss how it is that schooling in prison and schooling elsewhere are conjoined. The conjuncture is not apparent and should not be treated lightly. We are not speaking of the prison as metaphor but as actual, oppressive, dehumanizing experiences in which people are *cut off* from the outside and people on the outside may be barred from entering, with no better reason than an administrative decision that one could "disrupt the good order of the institution." A close reading of the essays by Jim Thomas, Therasa Ann Glaremin, and Karlene Faith provides the basis for a greater appreciation of "the good order of the institution" and the difference it can make between being a teacher and student in a prison school and participating in a program in a conventional setting. When that is understood and never forgotten, we may shift our focus from the conditions that keep these two forms of schooling apart as two distinct discourses and refocus on how these discourses relate.

It is the central purpose of critical perspectives to unmask ideologies in order to make apparent, through progressive stages of interrogation and discovery, actual social relations. The social construction of false distinctions (borderlines) that divide or fragment practices into fetishized categories keeps the discourse on prison education apart from a discourse on education and culture in general. As critical perspectives on schooling in prison proceed to unmask the social networks that constitute prison education, those who conduct these investigations will find themselves examining precisely the same social network that constitute schooling outside the prison. Therefore, what brings those engaged in the realization of critical pedagogy's program "inside" into alliances with those engaged in its realization "outside" is not idle curiosity or a sense of benevolence. Alliances are formed because insiders and outsiders discover precisely where and how their two practices conjoin.

Thus, at some point the two pedagogies (programs) merge, without obfuscating the conditions that make them particular. As such, critical perspectives on prison education may cease to exist as a distinct field of investigation because the false distinctions which at first *seemed* to exclude this social form from a wider discourse on education and culture are more fully understood. As this understanding takes place, one can expect considerable resistance from those institutions that have an interest in representing prison education as distinct from other forms of education. At one level, the hostility may express itself as a defense of professionalism. As educators/students question who is inside prisons and who is not, and how that distinction is constructed, sustained, and depoliticized they are likely to encounter serious resistance against much entrenched knowledge and power. Thus, it would require political as well as intellectual activity in order "to remain eternal protesters: to maintain the opposition to the powers that be, to militate against taboos and conventions" (Deutscher 1968, 58): I suppose this is why my vision of critical pedagogy incorporates the image of an intelligent riot.

Today, the task of making alliances for the realization of prison education as critical pedagogy begins with the efforts of the book's contributors to identify the multiplicity of forms that relate schooling in prison to a wider network of social relations. Michael Collins emphasizes this in the relationships between literacy education inside and outside. Common to both contexts is the reduction of literacy to functional skills and persuading adults that literacy means jobs, although it is clear that for both populations of students, literacy education is more about keeping busy and out of trouble. For Dante Germanotta the school is not located in prison; it is embedded in the state. What matters is not how "effective" education is at rehabilitating criminals, but the extent to which the state has lost faith in educational practice as a form of control. This same concern is foremost in the thinking of people constructing possibilities for critical pedagogy elsewhere.

In chapter 8, Weiss links a prisoners' educational-entrepreneurial program to corporate America where images of success are reproduced and reflected back to working people as *their* American Dream. How do prisoners as losers recapture the dream? How do prisoners reconstruct their self-esteem? What will allow them to shed the prisoner identity for corporate identity? Weiss discovers a strategy which the typical advocate for a critical pedagogy would hesitate to support because INSIGHT is an "independent program which embraces dominant conservative ideology and conventional values." But INSIGHT is also a transformative ritual, a means by which prisoners struggle to "renegotiate" themselves for corporate approval. Weiss also points to the contradictions and constraints acting on INSIGHT. He registers the resistance of guards and other prisoners toward INSIGHT's operation and purposes, and he notes the limits imposed on this effort to recapture the American Dream by the difficulty INSIGHT graduates will face during a protracted period of high unemployment.

For Juan A. Rivera and cofounders of the Nontraditional Approach in New York State, building bridges involves a struggle to become reconciled with one's community as a productive member of that community. At the same time, it involves a radical critique of conventional (i.e., Eurocentric) society, which promises inclusion but has never delivered on that promise except to offer inclusion by cultural suffocation. Their radical critique of traditional schooling interrogates traditional forms of education for the part they play in keeping prisoners embedded in prison and apart from their communities. For Rivera and his coworkers, Latino and African-American prisoners require a means that will help them see the direct relationship among where they are, where they have come from (in the fullest historical sense), and what they must do to reconcile their relationship with their communities, the ones *they* harmed. When it becomes clear that prisoner education as traditional schooling will not work for African Americans and Latinos, Rivera and his coworkers are able to offer schooling that they believe will.

The research note by Sbarbaro (chapter 9) reminds us of the links between prisoner-educators and the industrial union movement, the Black Power movement, and the Palestinian struggle for independence. Even if the state has succeeded in criminalizing resistance in the eyes of the public, the consciousness of people in these movements was not so easily distorted. Many of their comrades, in some cases the majority, have spent time in prison, time spent educating each other, spreading propaganda, and strategizing.

When they enter the prison, political prisoners do not leave the struggle but engage it on another terrain. The difficulty they face is the attempt by the state to depoliticize their imprisonment by criminalizing their activity. Political education inside the prison must accomplish two objectives: It must connect the political struggle inside with the struggle taking place outside the prison; and it must expand this struggle by politicizing prisoners who do not recognize the politics of crime and punishment. Political and politicized prisoners become prisoner-educators, as the examples of Malcolm X and Richard Cepulonis provided by Dante Germanotta make abundantly clear. When political prisoners are released, they rejoin the struggle outside the prison. If the time inside was productive, new alliances have been created with those who previously had no sense of the political implications of their criminal activity and the politics of punishment.

Sbarbaro suggests that, without a strong sense of how prisons and imprisonment can become an integral part of any organized resistance, struggles to expand sites of opposition will not survive as these struggles intensify to the point where the state recognizes a serious threat to its hegemony. At that moment the state increasingly turns to police power to suppress opposition. Educators who speak seriously of oppositional sites today have a responsibility to learn from and to critique the question of prison(er) education as critical pedagogy. Close attention to prison(er) education in current struggles (e.g., the *intifada*) and to the features of prison(er) education under present social relations in North America should warrant a privileged position in any discourse on resistance.

If the signs and symbols of radical ideology are too visible (a slogan on a book cover, hairstyle, fashion, skin color), the border between inside and outside can be made more secure; yet it is still not impermeable. Reading Karlene Faith's account on the creation and organization of the Santa Cruz Workshops in the 1970s (see chapter 12), I find it hard not to smile at the incredible chutzpah displayed by the teachers and coordinators when they crossed the borderline. What nerve! But had they been isolated from a network of feminists (who understood connectedness) and activists in the women's and anti-war movements (who had learned a thing or two about organizing people against a holocaust in Vietnam and insidious oppression much closer to home), all their chutzpah would have counted for nothing.

A truly critical perspective must ask questions about social structure and attend seriously to the interplay of the setting and the structural context in which it exists. A critical perspective must help to make apparent how the particular and varying features of specific practices are altered by patterns of social change. A prerequisite for illuminating this interplay is seeing practices not as isolated phenomena developing over time in response to internal dynamics but seeing practices as deeply embedded in larger contexts. The more views one has of this embeddedness, the more opportunities are available for further discoveries. More is at stake than good research agendas. A multiplicity of views well understood makes apparent a multiplicity of points of resistance.

ON FUTURE DIRECTIONS

From here we could explore any number of issues raised in the twelve chapters that follow. However, if the possibility for prison education being/becoming critical pedagogy is our concern, and if we understand that this possibility requires us to encourage recognition of and action upon the coercive forces that shape the formation of critical pedagogy's program, then the aim of future explorations should be to highlight particular and varying features of specific kinds of coercive forces (e.g., ideological, physical, or procedural) and the structural conditions that shape these forces. Along with temporal processes and context, diachronic studies must illuminate how location within particular historically constituted identities, such as, race and gender, affect how coercive force is experienced, what forces are applied, and to what end. I have already mentioned in passing some possibilities for future exploration. Several others come to mind.

I would privilege historical sociological studies on prisoners' schools. These are needed to avoid seeing the prisoners' schools examined by Julian Stone and Juan A. Rivera as isolated events. Bits of evidence I have collected indicate that schools parachuted into prisons by reformers were used to subordinate the schools prisoners had set up for themselves. One example is documented by a socialist imprisoned in Auburn Prison, New York, in 1914. This radical became a teacher. At once, he took advantage of the opportunity to turn the school into "a center of revolutionary Socialist and industrial union propaganda" (Legere 1914, 339). The Industrial Workers of the World (IWW) and the Socialists provided him with reading materials, and the classes buzzed. When a reformer well known and admired in the correctional education literature, Thomas Mott Osborne, took over the prison's management and established a self-government league, the radical was sent back to the prison broom shop. When that did not stop him, he was transferred out of the prison and granted a quick parole, presumably to eliminate any subsequent problems with socialist teachings. If it should come true that, in the immediate future, prisoners will be used increasingly as peer tutors, a policy enacted to save money could become an opportunity for prisoners to take control of their own education. This in turn could increase the possibilities for a critical pedagogy. If he were alive today, Legere might welcome as an opportunity what we currently see as a regression. Histories of prisoners' schools, beginning perhaps with Legere's school in Auburn, could help us to see these possibilities.

There is also a need for historical accounts of postsecondary and literacy schooling that are not content with attributing their inception to reformers' crusades. To date, historical accounts have not attended to the interplay of reformers' initiatives and structural context in order to make sense of the intended and unintended transformations of prison schools over the last 150 years. It is not an exaggeration to say that even the earliest gains made by revisionist historians in the 1960s—not to mention social histories and the work of historical sociologists—have had no appreciable influence on how practitioners of correctional schooling understand the history of their field of practice.[9] Work done on the genealogy of public schooling and adult education provide useful models of how this historical project could proceed (e.g., Ball 1990; Curtis 1988).

There are no accounts here of prison education in county jails in the United States or remand centers and provincial prisons in Canada, that is, about prisons where sentences may run anywhere from several weeks to two years. In the mainstream prison literature, jails and provincial prisons are also treated as exceptional locations. This tendency bears little correspondence to the actual configuration, either of the prison population or the presence of prison schools. In jails and provincial prisons, teachers teach students who may remain in their classes anywhere from several days to several months, depending on transfers and unexplained reasons (i.e., unexplained to the teachers). Teachers and students complain that nothing can be accomplished; however, the schools continue to function (Davidson 1988). The easy answer to what is happening here is that schools provide a means to keep prisoners occupied. This may be, but it begs the question: Why use schooling to fight idleness?

CLOSING REMARKS

Can a critical perspective be anything other than a mere contemplation under today's conditions? I think so. Schooling will be played out like most patchwork efforts to solve social problems. Those who want to discard schooling as "coddling" convicts will be pacified more or less effectively by policy makers and educators who are willing to support mandatory literacy programs (making education punitive). Action on the ground—where teachers and students actually mix and work—will produce varying practices unintended and perhaps disliked by policy makers. Under tight budgets and conditions of overcrowding, it may be easier for administration to let some things "slide by" than to hold to the letter of the law. The point is not to dismiss the consequences of policy and to speak naively about human agency overriding adversity. The point is to suggest that struggle takes a multiplicity of forms. It will matter greatly who are present to exploit contradictions as an oppositional force, and it will matter how skillful they are at devising strategies that do not compromise basic principles.

From the essays included in this volume we can learn something about strategies and principles learned through praxis. Germanotta sees for prisoner-students the potential for despair and disillusionment that can follow on the heels of moments of promise. Sbarbaro has discussed with his students the question of what can be done now that they have acquired a more critical understanding of crime and punishment. In the context of the present prison system, both authors are cautious about making unrealistic claims. Weiss has analyzed a program that should have the greatest opportunity for postrelease success and that provides sustained activities while its members are incarcerated. Nonetheless, he believes that since "upward mobility underpins the American Dream [the ideological heartland of IN-SIGHT] chronic recession is likely to bring on a 'crisis of belief,' breaking down the viability of symbols manipulated as rewards." Faith has explained what happened to a radical venture under conditions far more conducive to political education than those we may expect in the near future. Peter Cordella has good reason to ask whether, under present conditions, any program that supports communitarian world visions will survive for long.

However, we should not forget that there is a dialectic of disillusionment. A "crisis of belief" can produce greater consciousness about the function and purpose of penal reforms. If there is the likelihood that disillusionment will produce despair, there is also possibility for an emerging historical consciousness that draws on what was learned through disillusionment to tear down ideological veils and construct strategies for transforming social relations. Which synthesis emerges dominant—despair or historical consciousness—will depend on the quality of dialogical relationships which formulates the educational program.

Perhaps the problem of strategies and syntheses has to do with more fundamental assumptions about schooling than previously acknowledged. Do we need to be more critical about our presuppositions than we have ever been before? Perhaps we need to rethink the critical potential for programs which, at their core, rely on "outsiders" to provide the knowledge and power (including the funds and resources). Without romanticizing prisoners as primitive rebels, without dismissing the harm they might have done against members of their own communities (not the "ruling class"), can we envision a critical pedagogy that locates prisoners-students at the center and ourselves—today's teachers—in a supporting, but critical, role? What evidence can be offered to suggest the viability of this strategy as other than a romantic's vision? Julian Stone's law courses provide an example. The rigorous courses continue, and jailhouse lawyers continuously use their skills to demand the rule of law. Individuals who were convicted but are innocent have "found justice" through the efforts of these jailhouse lawyers. I suspect (and Stone would know) that jailhouse lawyers have been more successful at halting the worst that prison conditions have to offer than the initiatives of many outsiders. Certainly their struggle has been more sustained. If the state cannot deliver based on its own rules, these lawyers acting in their own collective interest will make sure that the contradictions are not expressed without considerable cost to state legitimacy.

Similarly, the founders and sponsors of the Nontraditional Approach did not wait for, nor did they want, teachers to organize a curriculum on their behalf. According to Rivera, it was only after the founding group had worked to develop a critical pedagogy to teach the "direct relationship" that educators and other outsiders were able to add their support.

Are these two examples actually models for a critical pedagogy that can survive, if not flourish, under present conditions? At the very least they suggest that we have much to discuss with students about possibilities and visions for prison education and a critical pedagogy.

NOTES

1. Survey of the National Center on Institutions and Alternatives reported in "Race—The Hidden Agenda of the Justice System." *Bars and Stripes*, 13(2), June 1994. It is worth noting that the increase in the prison population is not caused by a comparable increase in the crime rate (Lauen 1990; Stanford 1991, 6). It is directly attributed to changes in sentencing legislation, which send a higher percentage of persons convicted of crimes to prison and for longer sentences than ever before (Breed 1991, 6).

2. Unlike the United States with federal and state criminal codes, Canada has only a federal criminal code. Canadians sentenced to two years or less are imprisoned in provincial prisons (jails).

3. On Law Enforcement Assistance Administrative (LEAA) and private funding for prison higher education in the 1960s and 1970s see Silva (1994, 27–28) and Lawrence (1994, 35). Between 1968 and 1981, $260 million was allocated through the LEAA to about 3,000 prisoners for higher education (pp. 35–36).

4. For an account of the magnitude and significance of Pell Grant funding on prison higher education, including a discussion on possible consequences if (or when) it is eliminated, see Taylor (1994) and Silva (1994, 26–28).

5. Compulsory schooling is not new. In 1877 at Elmira Reformatory, prisoners were required to attend school until they achieved a grade eight level education (Silva 1994, 24; Eggleston 1991, 171).

6. In the discourse on mandatory literacy, education is justified as a form of behavior modification that will serve "as a focal point for modifying behavior and preventing deviant activity. The failure to incorporate the school and education system in crime prevention is to ignore a tool which has a great potential for success" (Lab [1988] quoted in Williamson 1992, 21; also see McCollum 1990, 163–164).

7. On teacher and student resistance to consistency between democratic values and democratic practice in educational activity—the "authority dependence" of

teachers and students—see Shor (1980). For references to a literature on authority dependence see Shor (1993, 28–29). For a literature on prisoner culture in the United States that is relevant to authority dependence see Johnson (1976) and, for Canada, Hartnagel and Gillian (1980) and Mann (1967). Also see the discussion by Thomas on the influence of gangs on prison higher education (chapter 2 in this volume).

8. On critical pedagogy as an explicit commitment to Marxism and revolutionary practice in Latin America, see Carlos Alberto Torres' "From the Pedagogy of the Oppressed to a Luta Continua" (1993). For a critique of Freire's ideas and pedagogy on the question of its relation to change within the existing capitalist state, see McLaren and Leonard (1993), da Silva and McLaren (1993), and Shor (1993).

9. Studies of the work of four or five male reformers (e.g., Zebulon Brockway and Austin MacCormick) are characteristic of correctional education historiography (e.g., Eggleston 1991). Silva attributes the history of prison education to the "systematic swinging" in "prison philosophy" toward prison education (1994, 28). Typical of the historical approach, Silva makes perfunctory references to the "swings" being "tied to political and economic factors" (p. 29).

2

The Ironies of Prison Education

Jim Thomas

At a recent college graduation ceremony, the graduates marched in wearing traditional caps and gowns, parents and faculty in the audience were teary-eyed, and even the official handing out diplomas and offering the ritual handshake was emotionally moved. After the ceremony, the father of one graduate, who traveled to Illinois from Virginia, warmly thanked me for contributing to the education of his son. The son, like the other graduates, was a maximum security prisoner; one of the presiding officials was a prison warden, and among the guests were faculty and individuals with an interest in college education. Seeing his son graduate, said the father, was the proudest and most exhilarating moment of his life. I thanked him, and I complimented his son, who was a fine student. I suppressed my deeper thoughts: "Prison education is half-sham, and your son was able to learn and graduate in spite of, rather than because of, the state's commitment to the college program."

Discussions with colleagues who teach college courses in prison reveal a consistent theme: They are all enthusiastic advocates of postsecondary education inside prisons, but they are frustrated by the discrepancy between what "progressive education" ought to be and what it really is in prison. In this chapter, it is suggested that the discrepancy is embedded in the nature of prisons, and that even the most creative and innovative programs will ultimately fail without a dramatic transformation of the current ideology and practices of punishment.

The problems described here will be familiar to those who participate in prison schools as teachers and students. Drawing on nearly a decade of experience as an Illinois prison instructor in a maximum institution and as a prison reform advocate, I can identify a few of the problems that place education, especially higher education, in opposition to the penal regime.[1]

Ideally, postsecondary education is an activity best pursued in an environment unconstrained by coercion, threats, and impositions on access to intellectual resources and ideas. Educational goals include self-directed learning, unrestricted information transfer, and critical thinking. While these ideals are rarely attained in colleges and universities, they are thwarted to a greater extent in prisons, where learning is subverted, resources are restricted, imagination and creativity are stifled, and critical thinking is suppressed. The accounts described in this chapter will demonstrate for those who are unfamiliar with teaching in prison how this takes place.[2]

WHAT IS PRISON EDUCATION?

The concept of education in U.S. prisons dates back to the Auburn model of the early nineteenth century, but its implementation as an integral part of the correctional goal of human management and rehabilitation is more recent (Jones 1992). The Auburn system of punishment, grounded in the Protestant ethic of developing disciplined work habits, emphasized religious instruction. In 1826 the Auburn chaplain and theological student-volunteers organized thirty-one classes attended by 160 prisoners (Sutherland, Cressey, and Luckenbill 1992, 512). However, well into the mid-nineteenth century few institutions provided even basic educational courses. The emergence of positivist criminology as the dominant model of corrections contributed to the growth of the rehabilitative ideal in the late nineteenth and early twentieth centuries. With its emphasis on an etiology of crime that focused on the individual and on an interventionist ideology, positivist criminology provided the foundations for policies and programs intended to rehabilitate while punishing.

Reaching fruition in the early decades of the twentieth century, the "Big House" model of corrections described by John Irwin (1980) incorporated a variety of educational, vocational, and industrial programs in the belief that hard work and personal growth might transform prisoners from "social deviants" into tractable citizens. By the 1950s, most progressive prisons in the United States offered elementary and high school programs (p. 46); by 1991, virtually all state systems offered Adult Basic Education (ABE) and the General Equivalency Diploma (GED). By 1994 two-year college programs existed in 90 percent of the state correctional systems, four-year college classes were offered in two-thirds of these systems, and graduate programs were available in 17 percent of them. It would seem that the philosophy of "improving" prisoners through education permeates the penal system (Bureau of Justice Statistics [BJS] 1992, 658–59); however, the image of nearly universal educational provisions is deceptive.[3]

Although all state systems currently offer some form of educational services, most staff and participants are clustered in the ABE and GED programs, ostensibly to meet the needs of the 38 percent of people in state prisons who enter with less than a seventh grade education (p. 660). This reputed need for "the basics" justifies the precipitous increase in mandating educational participation. In Illinois, for example, prisoners are tested for literacy upon entry to prison. If they cannot demonstrate a sixth grade reading proficiency, they are required to enroll in a mandatory ABE program for a period of ninety days. If they do not improve their proficiency during the period, they are recycled until they do. As a consequence, the number of participants in basic education programs, seemingly high, is the result of coerced participation. Meanwhile, postsecondary education is accessible to only a few. Again, in the case of Illinois, less than 7 percent of all prisoners participate in two-year college programs, and less than 1 percent in four-year college programs (Illinois Department of Corrections 1991, 43). The point here is that the notable increase in the number of prisoners registered in educational programs does not indicate a general commitment to education, as is frequently espoused when administrators refer to enrollment statistics to counter challenges to their commitment to education. What the statistics indicate is a questionable commitment to basic education, questionable because the institutions rely on coercion to ensure participation. If education fails to rehabilitate, the failure should not be attributed to some inability to stimulate the intellectual curiosity and cognitive development of the student. The truth may have much more to do with a series of problems inherent in the contemporary prison environment.[4]

SUBVERTING THE PROCESS

By their nature, maximum security prisons simply are not designed for delivering adequate, high-quality educational programs because too many obstacles subvert the learning process. Some of these are readily discernible and reflect the conditions of control; others are far more subtle. These obstacles range from overt hostility and disruption of classes by staff to broader sociostructural influences which intensify the discrepancy between educational goals and actual practice.

Staff Interference

Regardless of how well intended educational policies appear on paper, the behavior of prison staff can intentionally or inadvertently disrupt programs. Individually, these disruptions may appear to be little more than nuisance behaviors. In the aggregate, however, they increase the burden on instructors and students.

The Lockdown

Lockdowns are one of the most frustrating obstacles. Used as a security measure, a lockdown confines prisoners to their cells for an indefinite period.[5] During a lockdown, only those prisoners assigned to jobs critical for the maintenance of the institution are permitted to leave their cells. Prisoners involved in programs, nonessential job assignments, or other activities remain confined. Visits stop, meals are delivered to the cells, and most activity is curtailed. Lockdowns hinder teaching by preventing students from attending class, using the library, and using other resources to complete assignments. In my years as a prison instructor, classes averaged at least one lockdown in each sixteen-week semester. It is not unusual for some cells to be locked down and not others. This creates additional problems because one group gets ahead of the others. Some students work on their own trying to play catch-up under very difficult conditions. When a sizable number of students get behind, those who were able to attend class must wait while the instructor repeats course material for the benefit of those subject to the lockdown. Unlike campus courses, instructors cannot provide makeup sessions to students barred from class because inflexible prison routine does not allow for rescheduling or to provide makeup sessions for students who cannot attend.

The consequences of lockdowns are not limited to lost time. When lockdowns include searches of cells, classroom notes and papers in progress may be strewn about, destroyed, confiscated, or "lost." When this occurs, prisoners' assignments and projects are disrupted and the time required to construct or recover lost material significantly reduces class performance. More serious is the danger of confiscation of "contraband" class resources, especially if capricious staff judge that a prisoner possesses "too many books." Students have had books and other resources which were legitimately obtained for a class confiscated. Even if prisoners successfully petition for return of the material, the time-consuming process prevents use of the material for pressing assignments.

Confiscation is not restricted to lockdowns. Prisoners' books are confiscated because staff assume they were stolen or obtained without authorization. Books are confiscated because a student may have too many (i.e., actually "in excess" of the authorized number of books a prisoner is allowed to possess). Since confiscation of classroom material is within the "legitimate" range of staff discretion, staff hostile to educational programs have an effective means for abusing their authority "within the rules." Such abuse, while seemingly trivial, is a serious threat to any program. Availability of class resources cannot be guaranteed and assignments may be impossible to complete. There is little flexibility to counter these problems, which places instructors in a double bind: They must either grade students on the quality and content of the work produced regardless of the obstacles that might have caused an inferior product, or assume the work would have been better had a disruption not occurred. Either way, normal evaluation is impossible, the learning process is weakened, and the student suffers either through a lower grade or an inferior evaluation of her or his work.

Getting Fucked With

Another form of staff interference in prisoners' education is the "fucking with the prisoner (or instructor)" game. Staff are able to disrupt the educational environment by invoking discretionary authority in ways that disrupt a class, threaten students, and block access to resources. This reduces the instructors' teaching effectiveness and contributes to tension between staff and prisoners. Actions that are inconceivable in campus classes and that would cause an instructor to invoke university rules or summon security forces are routine in prison, and nearly always are perpetrated by line staff.

Disruption takes many forms and ranges from unnecessarily long delays when the instructor undergoes the routine search when entering the institution to excessive noise by staff outside the classrooms. As an example, in my first few sessions in one Illinois institution, guards noisily entered the classroom unannounced and called the name of a prisoner not enrolled in the class. Even though the prisoner was not present, they continued to call his name while looking at me. After this happened a second time, the students noticed my obvious discomfort. Several pulled me aside and informed me that as long as I appeared to be visibly rattled by the disruption, the officers would continue to come in.

That's how they fuck with us. Don't let them do that to you. Next week they're gonna pull the same shit. When it happens, take your chalk and turn to the blackboard and pretend to write something. Anything. Just ignore them, whatever you do, and keep writing and don't look at them. Turn your back to them and let us handle it.[6]

As predicted, three guards entered the following week. They opened the door, stomped in loudly, and shouted in the small class room: "Davis! Davis in here? Where's Davis?" I turned my back and began writing on the blackboard, and the students broke into feigned concern for "Davis": "Where's Davis?" they began asking each other. They looked under their chairs, in their pockets, and through their notebooks for Davis, asking in mock seriousness, "Gee, where's Davis? Anybody seen 'im?" Then they stopped, as if on cue, and turned their attention back to the blackboard and feigned note taking, ignoring the guards. Giving up, the guards stomped out, slamming the door. Although it was the last time they bothered me, it nonetheless demonstrated the mundane ways in which staff could intrude on classroom activities.

This incident illustrates a crucial characteristic of prison pedagogy. Instructors are not simply instructors; they participate in a game of status and control between staff and prisoners. Effective teaching requires more than preparing competent lectures and assignments. It also requires that instructors participate fully in resisting, defusing, and mediating among the tensions inherent in prison life. The delivery of quality education, therefore, is dependant not so much upon an instructor's knowledge of course material and ability to deliver it, but upon interactional skills in a cultural war between groups competing for status and control.

Staff can also impede an educational environment by using subtle threats to "fuck with" prisoners. Although they have no power to sanction an instructor, they can indirectly attempt to control and manipulate her or him to do their bidding. In one situation, I had kept a prisoner after class to discuss an assignment. Although I heard the guards call his cellmates to stand in line for the march back to their cells, the student remained with me and was a minute or two late. An angry officer approached and berated him for his minor tardiness. I attempted to intervene by explaining that the fault was mine and that although I had heard the "line call" a few minutes earlier, I did not inform the prisoner. An attempted apology was met with a stronger verbal attack directed toward the prisoner, including threats of disciplinary segregation. Although the guard was ostensibly referring to the prisoner, he was looking at and talking to me. His ploy made it clear that while he had no control over me, he had considerable power over the prisoner, and if my behavior was not to his liking, he would retaliate against him.

The power of staff to discipline prisoners illustrates another problem for education. Prison punishment is meted out primarily for minor offenses (Thomas et al. 1991), and some prisoners are targeted not so much for their behaviors as for their proscribed actions. For example, one student, an active jailhouse lawyer who consistently challenged prison policies with lawsuits, was sent to disciplinary segregation frequently and for minor offenses. The power of staff to punish disproportionately students, who under more normal circumstances may be rewarded for their scholarship and activities, effectively removes them from a course for a semester or more unless an instructor can find creative means to deliver and receive course material in the segregation unit.

In a third example, I brought a class of fifteen on-campus students into the prison for a mixed prisoner/nonprisoner session. Half of the outsiders were women. After the class, on-campus students were engaged in academic discussions with prisoners. Several officers walked over and began hustling the women. The prisoners attempted to preserve the intellectual focus of the discussion, but the officers used their authority to coerce and threaten the prisoners off the scene which enabled them to return to their hustling. This incident reflects more than an exhibition of male dominance games. It indicates how asymmetrical power relations between staff and prisoners can be used in humiliation rituals that reduce the status of the subordinate participants to the advantage of the dominant ones. A simple competition for the women's attention functioned to remind prisoners and outsiders of the subordinate and stigmatized status of prisoners. The officers' ploy shattered a dynamic intellectual experience. Discretionary practices by correctional officers can undermine even creative teaching strategies.

Disciplinary Constraints

Staff discretion also can subvert academic freedom by imposing a priori constraints on pedagogical strategies and course content. Sometimes these limitations are imposed with the assistance of prisoners. In one instance, a conservative student complained to staff that I had assigned to the class Karl Marx's *The German Ideology*. He argued that because Marx was a "communist revolutionary," assignments and lectures could have an adverse effect on prison security and control, presumably because the assignments would incite the prisoners to rebel against their keepers. A prison educational administrator complained to my university that I was a potential "troublemaker." I was called into a university administrator's office to discuss the matter. Although the administrator made it clear that he would support me, he also advised caution about course material. In this case, the prison official was acting on his own authority without consulting his superiors. Had he approached the prison warden, it is very unlikely that this arbitrary attempt at censorship would have been condoned. Indeed it should be emphasized that neither the warden nor his immediate subordinate ever acted in any way to obstruct my teaching activities. They were, in fact, consistently cooperative and encouraging, even exceptionally amenable to suggestions for creative course delivery. For that matter, only a relatively small number of line staff were ever abusive or caused problems. Most staff attempted to do their jobs fairly and humanely. This is precisely the point. This incident, like others described here, illustrates the complexity of the context in which prison schooling takes place. The problem is not simply staff interference; the reality is a complex drama played out by a large cast of supporting/subordinate players. For example, few of the conventional norms which protect the concept of academic freedom from arbitrary attacks are accepted in prison. Unlike her or his counterparts on a university campus, the teacher in prison must negotiate between satisfying capricious whims of staff and protecting course integrity. Nor can one naively assume that all prisoners share mutual interests and oppose those of staff. Despite the most well-intended official policies, staff and even prisoner discretion can undermine the professed goals of educational programs (Thomas et al. 1991).

Discretionary interference has several deleterious consequences. First, as Arcard and Watts-La Fontaine (1983) argued, the goals of prison security and the ideal of academic freedom often conflict. On occasion, it may be necessary to strike a balance between them. But, capricious staff behaviors can make this balance difficult, if not impossible. Second, when staff use their position to disrupt a class or to create obstacles to course delivery, resources, or participation, learning is threatened. There is no buffer that eases the burdens for staff or instructors, and appeals to a higher authority risk creating new and more intense disruptions that appear in other forms. Finally, regardless of whether the students or instructors are the target, some instructors decide that enduring such behavior is simply not worth the hassle, and they withdraw from prison teaching. During my years of prison teaching, fewer than five university instructors (out of over 2,000 eligible) were willing to teach in the maximum security prison regularly. This reduced the range of courses offered and restricted the diversity of intellectual perspectives essential for quality education. Even if other types of delivery problems were surmounted, hostile staff can effectively destroy the quality of college education.

The Social Organization of Prisons

No prison environment is pleasant, and the "dreadful enclosures" that we call maximum security prisons are especially debilitating. The control orientation of prisons creates not only difficulties for student performance, but also contributes to administrative problems that add to student frustration. Among the most serious is the threat of potential conflict, even violence, with other prisoners or with staff. Prison norms differ dramatically from those found among on-campus students, and the potential for disputes and the means for resolving them are somewhat more severe and direct. The social order of prisons does not stop outside the classroom door, and this has several consequences for educational programs.

Even when an instructor has the support of university and prison administrators to define course content in accordance with intellectual norms, content can still cause problems. For example, social science and humanities courses often address controversial topics that stimulate thinking and class discussion. In prisons, some topics, such as race, gay rights, women's rights, or deviance, must be presented with caution to avoid potentially volatile dialogue. In classes/prisons where one racial group is a significant minority, there is the risk of one group dominating the discussion while the other remains intimidated, angry, and silent. Or, a discussion risks becoming a strident and nonintellectual verbal free-for-all, which negates its intellectual value.

Class disputes may carry over outside of class, and personal hidden agendas, such as animosity toward specific individuals, groups, or prisoner factions, exacerbate the problem. Potential gang influence can intimidate individual students and undermine the class. One prisoner, who held the responsibility of student-clerk, placed himself in protective custody because of threats when he attempted to assign students to classes according to their needs and educational backgrounds rather than by the customary criterion of gang affiliation. Isolated gang members had been using classes to socialize, and his new policy disrupted their activities. Assigning students to classes on the basis of favoritism, rather than on the basis of meeting established prerequisites, risks populating classes with students who may be unprepared and who have a secondary interest in the program.

To illustrate the problematic nature of something as seemingly commonplace as a class discussion, one student reported that he was no longer able to attend my class because another prisoner took exception to something he had said during a discussion.

I got in a fight with some of the gang-bangers. They thought I was saying something about one of them, and I had some words with one. . . . He came to my cell later and came inside the door a bit. Four other fellows pushed their way in behind him . . . and they stood there. . . . The fellow pulled a lead pipe out of his shirt and raised it up like he was going to hit me.

The student was transferred to another institution that lacked a viable educational system, but this was preferable to the perceived risks he faced.

If prisoners cannot obtain courses for their program in one prison, they must either contrive reasons for transfer or do without the courses. One white prisoner explained how by manipulating staff willingness to protect whites from blacks, he could use the "race game" to obtain a transfer to a prison with an educational program he wanted.

Whites find it easy to get transferred if they say they are afraid for their lives from blacks. I'd like to go into some form of electrical or mechanical engineering when I get out, but they don't offer those kinds of courses. . . . If I don't get parole, I'll have myself beat up by a couple of brothers and get put into protective custody, then transfer out to wherever I can get the math courses.

Nor are prisons conducive to study. They are chaotic, noisy, and stressful. They have no "silence zones." Although some prisons attempt to keep college students celled together or in close proximity, spatial constraints and overcrowding make this difficult. Students may share a cell with others who prefer loud music to quiet reading. Whistles, bells, guards and prisoners shouting back and forth, poor lighting, no study space in cells—fifty square feet in floor space, which may contain two or more people—exacerbate the difficulties of reading, writing, and completing assignments. One student explained what for him was the greatest detriment to studying:

Just the people coming in [to the cellhouse and his cell]. It depends if you're in a cell by yourself, if you've got cellies. If you've got cellies, then you've got to contend with radio and television, with different types of conversations that might not be a part of you, or that you might not be interested in. Or you might have a problem with not being able to study late at night, or not being able to study early in the morning, or you might have a problem getting to sleep, or you might want to go to sleep at a certain time, and somebody just wants to be up all day and all night. So you run into different types of personality clashes within the institution that you have to adjust yourself to. Or you might come into a house where a couple of the officers, or maybe the captains or the supervisors [hassle you]. . . . This stresses you out.

Another student explained why his assigned paper was late:

Now, the only thing I had to write up was the [paper] summary. And they [the guards] moved me out of [my cell] at seven o'clock, and I get up—and they moved me out of the cell I was in. . . . There was nobody in the cell but me, and they came in and now put me in the cell with three other guys, and they all come in the cell new together, and they was arguing, and they started pulling me off into the argument, and I start arguing with them. Now, we got one guy in the cell who has an assignment, and he goes to work at five o'clock in the morning. And he wants the lights out at nine o'clock, and I told him I got to do work, and he says, "Hey, I gotta go to work at five o'clock in the morning," and so I shut off the lights, and we, me and the other guys, we get to arguing in the dark, and this goes on until two o'clock in the morning. And the other guy, the guy who has got to go to work in the morning, he gets mad, and he cusses us out. OK, so another guy, he's a Muslim. And this is Ramadan period. So they got to get up to eat before the sun comes up. So at three o'clock, four o'clock in the morning, they [the guards] come and pick them up and take them out to chow so they can eat. Now, I'm in bed and hear this and I think they're coming to get me, you know what I'm saying, 'cause that's how they do. They come early in the morning and get you [for disciplinary punishment], and I was thinking they're coming to get me. . . . So I lay back down. Now, my cellie wakes me up when he leaves, so I can go on sick call, and when I come back, they move another guy in. Yeh, five [in the four-man cell]. They move some other guy in. And he decides he can't move in, he moves out, and they move another guy in. And the police [correctional officers] come, and we said, "Hey, you can't move five in, 'cause there ain't no bed, and we ain't gonna put another bed in." So he moves out. The other guy, he decides he don't want to move in with these other guys. So he wants out, 'cause they was arguing—all night long. All day long, guys was coming in the cells, guys is coming back to the cells, guys is looking for cells. And that's why I didn't do my paper.

The humor of this narrative masks the ongoing frustration typical among students who must accommodate the chaotic and unpredictable environment of prison on the one hand and fulfill their educational responsibilities on the other. Constant noise, head counts, and other disruptions during sleeping hours reduce attention span during the day. Adapting to these tensions and navigating through the clashing "dual realities" of prison and class dramatically interfere with academic life.

Prisoners face other unique problems that jeopardize their abilities to function in a classroom. These include devastating emotional hardships. For example, one exceptionally good student failed to complete a major assignment and became lethargic during class. It was clear that he was not doing his work. He refused to speak during class discussions, and finally he decided to drop out of the college program. His documents revealed that he had been denied parole a few days earlier and had slipped into deep depression. Although he was persuaded to remain in the class, his experience illustrates the special emotional difficulties with which prisoners must cope while in school.

The social organization of prisons also shapes emotions, and these are rarely conducive to learning. Unexpected emotional disruption can occur when students have visitors on class days. They may be distracted if the visit will occur after class, or they may be angry if a preclass visit was unpleasant. There are no learning support services or psychological counseling centers. Ironically, it falls on instructors to work around these problems as best they can. Creative strategies to obtain resources, counsel students, deal with their on-campus bureaucratic problems, and compensate for unavoidable delays in meeting assignments can confer upon instructors reputations as troublemakers among staff.

STRUCTURAL IMPEDIMENTS

Even if all prison staff supported educational programs and the prison environment were made less intolerable, factors exist beyond the control of participants that jeopardize program delivery. Some of these factors shape classroom performance and attitudes, and others shape course content and programs overall.

Fiscal Problems

Some critics of prisoner education correctly note that many prisoners eligible for programs decline to participate. This, it is judged, indicates a lack of prisoner interest or initiative to take advantage of available resources. However, prisoners who decline educational opportunities offer another explanation. Prisoners are paid the minimum monthly stipend of about $15 a month. This sum can be supplemented by working at prison jobs. Thus prisoners, many of whom are indigent, cannot afford to take classes when they can make more money by participating in prison industry or some other enterprise. Many prisoners attempt to send some money home to family, and those who do not still find it difficult to provide a modicum of comfort for themselves on such a small stipend. The lack of compensation for participating in educational programs becomes a disincentive to all but the most committed students.

Fiscal problems also have an impact on the physical conditions in which classes are conducted. Most Illinois prisons set aside a specific area shared by all educational programs. These range from a few rooms to special buildings that house GED, secondary, and college facilities. At Stateville, classes are held in a large cinder block building partitioned off to divide secondary and college courses. Lighting is marginally adequate, and ventilation is poor. In summer, the cinder blocks function as an oven and keep heat in; in winter, they serve as an icehouse and heat is rarely adequate. Ventilating fans are noisy, which makes lecturing difficult. Minimum and medium security prisons built in the past decade have been designed to eliminate many of these problems, but the four Illinois maximum security prisons, built between the Civil War period and 1925, remain primitive. The conditions of nineteenth-century penitentiaries create a surreal atmosphere for those attempting to move education into the twenty-first century. The conditions of the classroom drain participants, reduce the attention span of students, and continually remind prisoners that prisons are for punishment, not for learning. This classroom ecology is the outcome of the fiscal crisis of the Reagan-Bush years. Reductions in corrections' budgets have forced cost cutting that has resulted in curtailment of programs, overcrowding, and other strategies to house a prison population that, in the United States, increases by almost 10 percent annually. Some well-intended administrators have attempted to make improvements, but they lack money and political and public support to make a significant impact.

Fiscal restraints interfere with course offerings in several ways. When Northern Illinois University (NIU) was delivering courses to Stateville Correctional Center, it divided curricular responsibility with a local community college. NIU offered third and fourth year courses, and the local college offered first and second year courses, many of which were prerequisites. NIU instructors had no control over the delivery of these prerequisites. When fiscal problems kept the college from delivering them, NIU instructors either allowed rule bending and accepted students without the prerequisites, or they played catch-up by adding prerequisite material into an advanced course. Typically, NIU administrators and instructors opted for the latter, but courses required for a major or for graduation could not be waived. In some cases, required courses were not only delayed but eliminated. This type of situation creates uncertainty over the possibility of completing degree requirements once the investment of time has begun, which discourages potential students from enrolling or prompts enrolled students to drop out.

Fiscal restraint also affects the ability of a program coordinator to maintain a viable pool of instructors willing to teach in prisons. In Illinois, the host universities are at least an hour away from their institutions; however, travel expenses and time are not paid, nor are instructors compensated for the extra work required to prepare course materials. At my institution, instructors are paid about $2,400 a course, providing little financial incentive to attract new instructors. In my experience, few teach in prisons for money, and that may be why so few want to teach. In addition, young, untenured instructors lack the time; other faculty find conventional courses outside prisons to be easier, less threatening, and less of an emotional strain. Without a variety of teachers with varying intellectual perspectives and styles, any college experience remains incomplete. The lack of fiscal resources prohibits course and instructor diversity and devalues the education received in comparison with the on-campus experience.

A flip side of fiscal restraint is the impact it has on popular perception of prison education. The complaint I hear most often from critics is: Why should prisoners get a free education when I have to pay through the nose to send my kids to school? On-campus education is, of course, heavily subsidized by the state. All students, including prisoners, who can provide evidence of need, have been eligible for financial aid (e.g., federal Pell Grants). In Illinois, tuition covers only 16 percent of the total university operating revenue; the rest comes from state funds. However, on-campus students receive significant benefits for their tuition that prisoners do not. In fact, one could argue that prisoners are being "ripped off." They do not have access to campus facilities, extracurricular events, or resources such as learning centers, libraries, and laboratories. They do not receive the same quality health care for their tuition, and they lack access to instructors outside of class.

In Illinois, books are provided by the Department of Corrections. Instructors are limited to about $25 of books per student, although the amount is flexible by about 20 to 30 percent. As the price of texts rises, course content is shaped by the limited use of texts and other resources. Prison libraries do not carry journals or academic volumes, which means that course materials must be imported by the instructor from the outside. And while students are often able to retain their books after completing a class, the official policy is that the books are to be returned to the Department of Corrections. Books are often shared by students as a collective resource for other classes and papers in an attempt to create a modest pool of readings that most on-campus students would take for granted. When books are confiscated in a shakedown or the official return policy is arbitrarily enforced, even these attempts at self-help are destroyed. This places prisoners in a double bind. If materials are not available because the institution will not or cannot provide them, the student loses. If a student can afford to purchase outside materials or devise other ways to collect them, the institution restricts such purchases, and if the restriction is not enforced, the prisoner runs the risk of having material confiscated in a shakedown. Thus in all cases, the student loses. In times of fiscal crisis, it becomes more difficult to obtain books, to photocopy articles, and to supplement class material. If creative solutions are found, they can be thwarted by hostile line officers.[7] Moreover, during state budgetary crises, prisoners are especially vulnerable. The reduction in financial aid to students has affected prisoners as severely as nonprisoners. But few, if any, prisoners can afford to pay for courses without assistance, and they do not have opportunities to supplement decreasing aid with paid work. As available aid evaporates, students are threatened with the possibility that they either will not be able to enroll in classes, or if they enroll, will be unable to complete their degrees because of the uncertainty of continued funding for their tuition or for course offerings.

When critics grouse about the "fairness of giving convicts a free education," they fail to realize that prisoners, regardless of their own hard work, initiative, and ambition, are receiving only partial value for tuition expenditures. In short, prisoners receive no special financial support simply because they are prisoners, and there is clear evidence that, compared to their counterparts on campus who receive the same grants, prisoners receive much less.

Administrative Problems

Prison policies and university policies do not exist harmoniously. The regimentation and tightly controlled nature of prisons often conflicts with the flexibility required for effective pedagogy. Restrictions on prisoners' movement throughout the institution, while necessary, nonetheless limit contact with other students and interfere with the use of resources. Restrictions also limit the amount of time instructors can advise individual students, because instructors can meet with students only during class hours. A variety of restrictive policies block the free flow of information, which is the cornerstone of any educational process. Instructors must be sufficiently flexible to take these handicaps into consideration when delivering and evaluating material. If instructors become too flexible in their standards, courses are watered down; if they bend the prison's rules too far in order to visit students or provide resources, they risk being barred from a prison and removed from the program.

Furthermore, university bureaucracies operate on the premise that students are sufficiently mobile to come into university offices to resolve problems, to use the telephone to obtain information, and otherwise are free to navigate through bureaucratic entanglements. For prisoners, these premises do not apply. Grade appeals or disputes with instructors are not readily resolved because the methods for processing them require procedures not easily carried out from prison. Checking on enrollment or graduation status, adding or dropping classes, and numerous other minor details that on-campus students resolve routinely become for prisoners a major enterprise. University procedures designed to reduce the barriers created by lack of mobility and accessibility to school officials only partially address the problem. What may seem like a minor inconvenience in problem resolution can take on a significance that typifies the barriers inherent to prison education.[8]

SYMBOL OR SUBSTANCE?

The problems of prison education render it largely a symbolic prop in the drama of rehabilitative services. When critics point to the lack of evidence demonstrating the effectiveness of education in reducing the recidivism rate or breaking the "cycle of crime," one might respond: "How do we know? We aren't fully implementing education, and what little there is becomes subverted." Some students obviously excel in college classes, and I have had former prisoners enroll and perform well in my on-campus classes. I have found prison students to be, in the main, better motivated and more interested in course material than their nonprisoner counterparts. Most, however, are victimized by the obstacles, and their educational experience suffers accordingly. Students' hard work and instructors' commitment to teaching fail to compensate for the deprivation of a complete educational experience. The tragedy of prison education is that programs cannot fully develop the potential of the vast majority of competent students who would benefit from an authentic educational experience.

For too long, many of us have believed that the answer to transforming prison educational programs from symbol to substance lies in reforming the programs or methods of delivering them or in soliciting the support of sympathetic administrators (Goldin and Thomas 1984; Thomas 1983). However, refining program delivery is not an answer. This strategy has failed. Prison education cannot be fully implemented without a dramatic transformation of the philosophy of punishment in North America and without rethinking how, as a society, we ought to define and respond to criminal offense. Nothing that even approximates the Enlightenment values of "an ideal education" can be attained in prison systems with dramatically increasing populations and disastrously decreasing educational resources. The vast discrepancy between the symbol and the reality cannot be reduced without a full-scale assessment of the social forces that create it.

Some think that there is no "prison crisis" but rather an "administration crisis" (DiIulio 1987). In this view, prison security, programs, and prisoners' well-being would coexist if prison managers would simply do their bureaucratic jobs properly. Prison education would be improved merely by improving the administrative methods for delivering it. "Bad prisons," so the argument runs, are primarily the consequence of incompetent administrators and meddling outsiders. Unfortunately, adherents to this view forget one crucial factor: Prison staff manage a contradictory set of ideological, practical, and normative precepts. The rules that establish the prison mandate and the policies that implement this mandate are ostensibly rational, humane, and binding. Despite acknowledgment and symbolic adherence to these rules, the practices of prison staff and administrators are often irrational, ideological, and context bound. This contributes to the uncertainty, unpredictability, and general chaos of life in maximum security prisons. As a consequence, prison education cannot be improved simply by rule following and better administration. The modest goal of this chapter is obvious: to get progressive prison educators to stop talking about reforming programs and to begin working to reform prisons.

NOTES

I am indebted to Robert J. Skorczeski, Jr., Carol Goldin, Howard Davidson, and the numerous prisoners who shared what they had, asking nothing in return.

1. Perhaps it is unnecessary to add that if a critical pedagogy is difficult to attain in the most conventional settings (Moton, Aylward, and Thomas 1985; Shor 1980), then I would argue that it may be virtually impossible in the dreadful enclosures of contemporary prisons.

2. While there is room for honest disagreement concerning the content of curriculum and the outcomes of education in conventional settings (e.g., Bowles and Gintis 1976; Karier, Violas, and Spring 1973; Spring 1972), the collusion between prison policies and practices and prison education undeniably subverts the best that conventional education has to offer.

3. The lopsided emphasis on ABE is also represented in Canadian federal prisons. For example, in 1981–1982, Correctional Service of Canada reported 1,737 prisoners "employed" in education; by 1988–1989 "the average number" of full-time students in ABE was 3,171 (Solicitor General Canada 1990, 58). Since 1993 this number has continued to increase; meanwhile, the postsecondary college degree programs offered on-site in federal prisons were canceled in 1993 [ed].

4. The prevalence of mandatory education serves to remind us that "correctional institutions" were never designed to rehabilitate (Irwin 1980, 47); indeed, among the functions served by prison education not the least of them is an adjunct form of control, an alternative means of surveillance (MacLean 1992).

5. Lockdowns can last a few hours or years, which has occurred at the level-6 federal maximum security institution in Marion, Illinois. Citing security problems, Marion administrators placed the prison on lockdown in October 1983. For a summary of the events leading to the lockdown, see Gonzales (1986) and John Howard Association Report (1986).

6. The data and examples were taken verbatim from transcribed, tape-recorded field notes and interviews with prisoners in Illinois prisons.

7. As an example, when a colleague once donated six large boxes of social science books to the student library these mysteriously disappeared while in staff possession.

8. Sometimes, broader social issues can lead to policies that virtually destroy a program. The national "war on drugs" provides an example. In the late 1980s, the Illinois Department of Corrections required drug tests of all new employees, including instructors who for years had been involved in the prison education programs. NIU, responsible at that time for delivering college courses to two institutions, argued that drug testing violated instructors' rights and academic freedom. The university refused to deliver courses as long as the policy remained in effect, and to date the policy has not been rescinded. The drug testing policy appears to have been a symbolic gesture with no great practical significance because there is no evidence of decreased drug use in prison; nevertheless, the policy demolished the college program.

3

On Prison Education and Women in Prison: An Interview with Therasa Ann Glaremin

Gay Bell and Therasa Ann Glaremin

INTRODUCTION

Therasa Ann Glaremin was released from Kingston Prison for Women after six years inside that institution and eleven months inside a provincial institution.[1] She was on day parole and was living in a halfway house in Kingston, Ontario. That was the fall of 1991 when I did a radio interview with her which was published in the *Journal of Prisoners on Prisons* (1991), for a special issue on prison education.

The radio interview was aired on CKLN-FM, a community radio station operating out of Ryerson Polytechnical Institute (Toronto, Ontario). It was aired during National Student Week (October 14–18, 1991). I thought it might give listeners a glimpse into the lives of prisoner-students. I also wanted the text of it printed in the *Journal of Prisoners on Prisons* in order to encourage prison activists on the outside to get community radio interviews with their contacts.

Subsequently, Therasa Ann was returned to the Kingston Prison for Women for another year. In June 1994, she was out again and living in the Kingston community; at that time, the interview was updated. She was asked to describe her current life.

I'm on Mandatory Supervision, living under heavy restrictions. I'm revising my play, *The Hanging Sheet*, for workshop performances in Toronto on Prisoners' Justice Day (August 10th), and working on another play and a novel. I'm one of three external coordinators for the Special Peoples' Olympiad at Collin's Bay Penitentiary. I did an hour-length TV show on Mother's Day about mothers in prison.

My husband, Roy, is in Collin's Bay Institution. We met through courses provided by Queen's University. We graduated together on June 5th, 1993.

INTERVIEW

Gay Bell: Would you like to tell us about your educational history?

Therasa Ann Glaremin: When I went into the system I had only a grade six education, and while I was at the Provincial [jail], it was pretty hard to really get anything because they had no programs at the Provincial. They had some limited programs through the Ministry of Education but as far as the school and that goes, there wasn't really anything. You were dependent on the postal service for your books and your courses.

When I was transferred from the Provincial in 1986 to the Federal system at the Prison for Women [P4W], I found that the educational program was enlarged. That is, they had a school there for prisoners, so I wanted to upgrade myself from my grade six level to the ABE level.

Gay: That's Adult Basic Education?

Therasa Ann: Yes, that's right. That's to grade nine level. But when I got there, it was a different thing. The Work Board[2] at that time, even though they were pushing to get you to your ABE, needed people to work in the institution in laborious positions—like in dining, kitchen, cleaners, laundry; they needed people to perform laborious functions to keep the institution tidy. They put me in the kitchen, apart from the fact that I wanted to go to school. They said that I wasn't going to need my education when I got out, that I would probably get a job in a restaurant or as a cleaner, if I wasn't a housewife.

So what I did was work in their kitchen serving food to the prisoners and cooking and cleaning and washing pots; but on my downtime, the time that was my own, I got my Ministry of Education courses, and I moved forward. I set a goal for myself and I wanted to achieve it. I wanted something more than being dependent on a man for something because I didn't have the education to move forward. So, when I got to my ABE level I was really happy and really satisfied. When I got my certificate I was really proud, and then I decided that I wanted to move on, forward.

I wanted my high school diploma; so I set my sights for my high school diploma. But the institution had other jobs for me to do. They sent me to microfilming. For about two years I was going outside the institution during the day as a technician doing microfilming. It was a monotonous job. Everything was mundane.

Gay: Is prisoners' labor contracted out?

Therasa Ann: Yes, prison labor is contracted out. Women working there receive the wage of the pen. and not the wage of the street. It [the microfilming] was run by an independent business which ran sweatshops with no advancement for people in its employment. The microfilming program has since been closed off to women and has found a place within the walls of Kingston Prison [for men]. It is a form of slave labor and offers no opportunities on the street as jobs of this nature aren't available.

So, as I was saying, when I came back to my cage I continued with my studies. There was a period when I couldn't get certain courses through the Ministry of Education. I had to go and see the Warden and threaten to expose what was really going on with these programs that we were supposed to be getting. The administration was making a big deal about education: "Oh, the education is great inside!" But we weren't getting any benefits from that. They just wanted us to clean, and if you were a good stool pigeon you might get into the education program.

Gay: What does that mean?

Therasa Ann: That means that you inform on other prisoners about their activities in order to get favors from the administration.

Gay: If you inform you might get something?

Therasa Ann: Yes, but I got nothing because I didn't care to talk about other prisoners' business. So I had to fight and put in grievances in order to get some time at the school to take required courses for my diploma, which I couldn't get through the Ministry.

I won my grievance, and the Warden went to bat for me and put me in school for about eight months. I got my high school diploma in June of 1988.

I was the Valedictorian and I gave a very emotional speech about the value of education. I spoke about how we are all at this stage in time and none would move forward if we didn't use this time that we were given as a punishment for being women—that's how I looked at it because I'm not guilty of what they say I've done; so I look at things in a different way.

There was a high percentage of women in prison at that time, in 1988, who did not have an education. As a result of the consciousness-raising efforts of myself, Gayle Horii, Jo-Ann Mayhew, and Fran Sugar, we got things moving towards getting more educational programs for the women. Men have those shops [vocational education courses] where they can get trades at the federal institutions. We didn't have that. We still don't in 1994, by the way, not if the Parole Boards can help it.

Gay: What do you mean?

Therasa Ann: In the federal pens, one has the option of learning a trade. P4W has no programs whereby a woman can leave with a license.

The Parole Board makes the decision as to whether a woman can go into the community or not. Men can leave prison with their papers to do wood-working, barbering, electronics, mechanics, etc. Women have John's Beauty Parlor, which is as bad as microfilming. Men can get limited parole to work outside of prison. Women are barred [from limited parole to work] because of their lack of training.

Education is the only certification a woman can bring with her and she has to be allowed, by decision of the Board and the Warden, to attend a men's prison to get that education because these university programs are offered on a larger scale to men. They are only offered to a limited number of federal women prisoners.

Gay: So, there's education for trades in the men's prison, but there's nothing for women.

Therasa Ann: Nonexistent; and that's why Gayle Horii, Jo-Ann Mayhew, Fran Sugar, and I were speaking on behalf of the federally sentenced women, by sitting on panels and task forces to decide what was the best thing we could do for the women. We believed that what the women wanted, their consensus, was to have trades. They wanted to leave with certificates, something they could have that would enable them to get jobs when they got out so they wouldn't have to be lower class citizens. They had three strikes against them: they are women, they are in the prison system, and they are uneducated. When they came in most of them were below the ABE level like myself—maybe grade eight or nine. About 7 or 8 percent of the women had high school, university degrees, things like that. In the crowd that I hung around with, 75 percent of the women had less than a Grade Nine education.

    What was being taught inside and outside were two totally different concepts. So the chance of a woman coming out with her hairdressing diploma and using it to get a job on the streets was very marginal, unless she fell down on her hands and knees and begged the employer to please let her have a job, or did something drastic. She would never get it on the merits of that hairdressing diploma because it was so poor in quality. And women never had the chance to leave prison with a mechanics certificate, or a certificate from a shop, or for barbering or anything.

    Anyway, through the efforts of me and my fellow sisters, we endeavored to start programming at the Prison for Women; and indeed programming did start—tons of programming through the ABE. But once again only those chosen few could go into the ABE. Then toward the end of 1988, coming into 1989, they sort of changed it all around. They started rounding up people in droves and forcing them to go to school against their will.[3] Something had to have come down from the upper echelon of power that Corrections [Correctional Service of Canada] works through because they took people out of their jobs and put them in school. They were saying that anyone who worked in these jobs had to have their Grade Nine education. The jobs had been done by women who didn't have their Grade Nine education and were doing quite well. That didn't matter. Now, they wanted them all to go to school in order to qualify for the same job.

Gay: How did the women feel about that?

Therasa Ann: It really confused the women. They were pissed off. Some of them didn't go to work, some of them withdrew, some of them turned to substance abuse. That didn't matter.

Gay: Tell me about the Queen's University Correctional Project?

Therasa Ann: It was a program headed by Queen's University and Correctional Service of Canada.

    As late as 1980, the high school diploma was the highest degree you could earn in the prison system. A fine lady named Darryl Dolen was a prisoner and had a high school diploma. She fought really hard to continue her education and challenged the process that eliminated women. As a result she was allowed to study in the Queen's program, which opened the doors for other women prisoners, like myself, to continue our education. She got her degree in Theology, and she instigated the Queen's Correctional Law Project.

Gay: So, that's how you started at Queen's?

Therasa Ann: That's how I started doing it. This system was put in place by Darryl Dolen and it seemed that all we had to do was take the bull by the horns—if you'll excuse the rude expression, I don't want to grab any bulls by their horns—and move forward with it. But it wasn't as easy as all that. When I and the women involved in the program wanted to move forward with it, we found that we couldn't.

As it stands now, there are no programs at the P4W that enable women to become better equipped for the workforce when they are released. The education program was the most beneficial program to the women, but courses were limited in number and women were chosen not because of their desire to attend programs, but by the Work Board and Warden, who decided which women should go.[4]

Whatever programs are offered at the federal level to women, they cannot even compare to what men in the system receive. Women are still not seen as the "breadwinners" in our present class structure. Therefore programs offered to them, when they come into conflict with the law, reflect and reinforce the patriarchal system by offering programming of a personal, psychological nature rather than affirmative action programs which would enable entry into the workforce.

Gay: Are women prisoners continuing to attend the Queen's courses?

Therasa Ann: They've pulled the university programs from the prisons [in 1993], so women are further barred from gainful employment and successful reintegration. They've pulled a very resourceful program that would've helped the women become contributing members of society, in keeping with the mandate of Correctional Service of Canada. Money should be spent for educational purposes rather than for healing or addictions—healing in prison is ridiculous! And you're forced to take the addictions programs once you get to a halfway house anyway.

Gay: So what are you doing now that you have your degree?

Therasa Ann: The Parole Board has decided I didn't do good time. They have blocked me from going to Toronto by refusing to increase my radius so I could follow up job opportunities elsewhere. My degree is in Drama. There are only a couple of theaters in Kingston, so I'm stuck. They won't even let me go to the Thousand Islands Theater. Now that I've graduated, I'm still fighting to get them to recognize my achievements. What's the point of being free if you're still treated like a fucking criminal!

Gay: So what do you see a woman prisoner's rights to education as being?

Therasa Ann: For those locked away, entry into a university program or an educational program, as opposed to correspondence courses, should be a right and not a privilege at the Warden's choice. As long as Corrections is treating women prisoners like children then Corrections has become a "bad parent" when it comes to the education of women prisoners in its care. Parents are liable to go to jail for not providing education to their children.

Gay: How can women prisoners protest when their rights are not respected?

Therasa Ann: By calling their local MPs and politicians in Ottawa, by addressing these issues with the Commissioner of Corrections (who makes the policies for Corrections), and by contacting Claire Culhane at the Prisoners' Rights Group (303–2075 E. 12th Ave., Vancouver, BC, V5N 2A9) and Prison News Service (PO Box 5057, Station A, Toronto, ONT, Canada M5W 1W4).

Gay: Thank you, Therasa Ann, for sharing your experiences and knowledge with us.

NOTES

Therasa Ann Glaremin and Gay Bell wish to thank Zoltan Lugosi for his help in preparing this interview for publication. Zoltan and Gay are both members of the Prisoners' Justice Day Committee, which is a day when Canadian prisoners fast and refuse to work in order to remember their fellow prisoners who died from murder, neglect, and suicide and to draw attention to conditions inside Canadian prisons. The PJD Committee is seeking to publicize this day, August 10th, every year and to make it an international memorial day. We can be reached c/o A Space, 183 Bathurst St., Toronto, Ontario M5T 2R7.

1. In Canada, persons serving a sentence of longer than two years are sentenced to federal prisons; a sentence of less than two years is served in a provincial jail. However, with only one federal prison for women, women may be sent to provincial jails to serve their sentences.

2. The Work Board is a panel of department heads (e.g., the head of school, head of laundry, head of social development) which assigns prisoners in the federal system to work placements. A prisoner must work in the board's placement in order to be paid a wage. There are five levels of pay, and one must stay in a job placement for fourteen weeks before receiving a wage increase or obtaining a job transfer. These placements are satisfactory only to the Work Board: They are never the choice of the prisoner.

3. Parole boards began asking prisoners why they did not get an education while inside and refused parole until prisoners at least finished ABE.

4. Zoltan Lugosi adds that women are chosen for courses if they seem to be able to carry the extra workload because it keeps the scholastic achievement statistics on the rise, thus making the program coordinators look good to senior management.

4

Shades of the Prison House: Adult Literacy and the Correctional Ethos

Michael Collins

> Shades of the prison-house begin to close
> Upon the growing boy

These lines from William Wordsworth's poem "Intimations of Immortality from Recollections of Early Childhood" (Wordsworth 1902, 831) invoke the utter starkness associated with our impressions of life in prisons. At the same time, the metaphorical intent of Wordsworth's depressing image obliges us to acknowledge how aspects of prison life are manifested in everyday experience on the outside. The prison is not such an isolated institution as many people on the outside, from a conventional bourgeois perspective, like to think.

Insights about the pervasiveness of prisonlike experiences in the everyday life of ordinary men and women are not startlingly original. It is important not to overstate them. Clearly, instances of repression, hostility, and anomie are experienced in prison on a more regular basis and with greater immediacy than is typically the case in other communities. Yet "shades of the prison house" do extend into outside communities, so it is appropriate in the context of this chapter to suggest that teachers of adult literacy in prisons share a common vocation with their counterparts working on the outside. Prison students usually come from similar backgrounds and can be identified as having the same kind of learning needs as adult literacy students on the outside. In this regard, prison teachers and teachers of adults on the outside serve the same constituency. Teachers in both contexts are faced with an orthodoxy that views illiteracy as a problem to be addressed by fixing individual deficiencies through further schooling for adults who have not managed themselves to make the grade.

It is fallacious, then, to imply that the differences between teaching literacy in the prison and teaching literacy on the outside completely outweigh the similarities. For teachers of adults on the outside, especially those concerned with adult literacy, the prison school can provide some useful insights into the nature of their chosen field of practice. Accordingly, teachers of adults on the outside are well advised to consult journal articles and texts that deal with prison teaching.[1]

APPROACHES TO LITERACY EDUCATION IN THE PRISON

At a fundamental level, the provision of adult literacy programs in prisons can be justified simply on the grounds that it provides prisoners with another chance to learn to read, write, work with numbers, and converse with a reasonable degree of assurance. This straightforward rationale is also tied to a notion that adult literacy adds a much needed aesthetic dimension to prisoners' experience and constitutes one of the few prison activities in which civil discourse might be fostered. Further, while prison service authorities are not inclined to promote educational initiatives that deal with issues of social justice, it is possible to address such concerns in the context of adult literacy without undue interference from official authority. The possibility seems to be present for teachers of literacy in the prisons to influence curriculum content despite typical complaints from the prison school about unnecessary interference by the guards. A notion that prison higher education alone constitutes the relevant pedagogical context to challenge conventional ideas is misleading. The misconception may have a lot more to do with the fact that providers of prison higher education have shown little or no interest in the potential of literacy programs to foster critical thought.

Yet the adult literacy curriculum most likely to find favor with official authority comes in the form of standardized modules. Modularized curriculum formats tend to find an ideal haven in the prison setting given their emphasis on prescriptive guidelines and orderly, sequentialized progression.

So even in the regimented environment of the prison it becomes appropriate to ask, "Which literacy is to be provided?" In posing this question, the possibilities for options emerge. Sensible options can only be conceived, however, through an understanding of the pedagogical perspectives that currently shape the discourse on literacy in prisons. These perspectives have been respectively defined in conventional literature on corrections education, and in a manner useful for our purposes here, as *the medical model*, *the opportunities model*, and *the cognitive deficiency model*. Each of these models provides a rationale from which teaching literacy to prisoners is legitimized. However, it should be borne in mind that in actuality these models represent overlapping concepts. Their perspectives on the schooling needs of prisoners are not entirely separate.[2]

The Medical Model

Through the medical model, correctional education is manifest in such a way that the prisoner-student is diagnosed as a mental patient requiring treatment. In effect, the curriculum from this perspective serves to pathologize further the lives of prisoner-students.

Although the medical model no longer goes unchallenged as a guiding paradigm for prison school programs, its influence is still very pervasive. This pervasiveness should come as no surprise. The medical model fits in nicely, and helps to sustain the notion of criminology as a professionalized discipline. The professionalized discourse has tended to identify criminality with individual, psychologized deficiencies that are amenable to treatment by behavior modification or *normalizing techniques*. Psychologistic labeling that defines the prisoner in terms of his or her personality disorders is a primary characteristic of the medical model. And this model's psychologized concepts have been reified to an extraordinary degree within the overall official discourse on corrections. Criminology as a discipline, the emergence of the modern prison as an institution for corrections, and the medical model are closely interrelated developments. They constitute an ideology in which literacy training is viewed as a means to bring about a reduction in the rate of recidivism by reshaping prisoners for rehabilitation.

The adult literacy programs that best exemplify the medical model are rigidly functionalist in design. The processes of learning to read and write are reduced to a form that is observable as measurable changes in behavior. Hence, standardized pretests and posttests, as well as in-between tests, become major features of a highly prescriptive curriculum design. The curriculum materials are typically prepackaged as learning modules which require the student to circle or underline the answer, fill in the blanks, or provide short written answers predefined by tightly set parameters. (Clearly, this kind of curriculum format is readily amenable to computerization and paves the way for international business corporations to stake out a claim in literacy training.) Emphasis is placed on the ability to read and respond to short written statements rather than on writing for free expression. Since students' learning needs and their learning objectives are already programmed into the curriculum design, the literacy teacher is redefined as a "facilitator" or "manager."

Undoubtedly, some functionalist curriculum designs that adhere to the medical model attempt to be somewhat more flexible than described in the previous paragraphs. In this regard, designers recognize the artificiality of their curriculum formats, and the claims of critics, by introducing further segments—virtually, more of the same. At best, such modifications can be viewed as variations on the functionalist theme which serve to underscore the shortcomings of psychologized reductionist approaches to teaching literacy. Certainly, these variations in the form of "add-ons" do not represent a turn toward alternative perspectives. The medical model, in all its manifestations, defines literacy training according to a behavioristic paradigm which legitimizes mechanistic, serialized, and regulatory forms of curriculum design.

These restrictive characteristics are clearly discernible in the so-called competency-based education (CBE) curriculum formats, which have been deployed in many adult literacy programs during the past decade or so.[3] A prime example of CBE in adult literacy is the Adult Performance Level (APL) curriculum initiative, which places a heavy emphasis on the acquisition of functional literacy skills.[4] The APL scheme defines the entire adult population according to three clear-cut categories. Category APL 1 includes adults whose income is below the poverty level; who have eight years, or fewer, of schooling; and who are unemployed or are employed in a low status job. APL 2 adults are described as having no discretionary income although they are above the poverty line. They have nine to eleven years of schooling and work in menial jobs. Finally, APL 3 describes adults who enjoy high levels of income or varying amounts of discretionary income. They possess a high level of formal education—high school completion or above—and occupy high status jobs.

Adults classified as APL 1 are labeled as "functionally incompetent." APL 2's are competent. They function at a "minimum level." The APL 3's are designated as proficient since their mastery of competency objectives is related to their success in terms of income, occupation, and level of education. Clearly, the prisons are overly represented with adults in APL 1.

The APL Model of Functional Competency is a grand curriculum scheme which *captures* within its categories the entire adult population. For a while it was enthroned as the exemplar of competency-based literacy training in North America. Curriculum packages, including easily administered pretests and posttests, were designed according to the rationality defined in APL's overarching categorical scheme.

This chapter does not afford the space for an examination of the empirical survey from which dubious claims about APL's generalizability were advanced.[5] What can be noted here, however, is that the APL in its quest to universalize a functionalist paradigm of curriculum design, epitomizes the medical model orientation toward adult literacy. As such, APL inevitably is particularly suited to those who view curriculum from a predominantly management perspective. Accordingly, APL and the clones it inevitably spawned in the field of curriculum design carry a certain appeal to prison administrators who can more readily endorse schooling in the form of education and training programs that fits in tidily with an overall system of surveillance and control.

The Opportunities Model

The advent of the opportunities model, which many mistakenly believe has more or less replaced the medical model, allows for greater flexibility in the design and teaching of adult literacy.[6] From the opportunities model perspective, adult literacy in prisons is tied to a notion that prisoners should be given a wide range of educational and training opportunities while they are incarcerated. The need to invoke reduction in the rate of recidivism as a primary criterion for educational programming is deemphasized. There is, therefore, less pressure to justify adult literacy programs in terms of their rehabilitation potential, though the notion that a reduction in recidivism can be realized through training is implicit.

Despite the greater flexibility which opting for the opportunities model can entail, teaching adult literacy still remains essentially accommodative to the purposes of institutional maintenance. The curriculum is envisaged as keeping prisoners "meaningfully busy." At the same time, it is apparent that the concept of "opportunities" has an extremely narrow purview. The deliberate linking of literacy to job training, or to "job readiness skills," does not really widen the scope of employment possibilities. Educators and prisoners alike are aware of the economic circumstances that determine this reality. These unfavorable circumstances are reinforced by the ex-con status and stigma from which former prisoners are not allowed to escape (MacLean 1991).

Learning to read, write, and do arithmetic to become a better worker is clearly undermined by the fact that marketing prisoners' production on a relevant scale cannot be permitted since it would involve competing with businesses on the outside. Further, and more important, the continuing economic downturn means that job opportunities to match expectations emanating from the opportunities model are just not readily available to former prisoners.

In these regards, the rationale for the opportunities model is flawed. However, it serves an important role in accommodating curriculum to the overall purposes of the institution, accentuating a sense of busyness and a purposeful educational endeavor. It is not difficult to understand how readily applicable the opportunities model is for literacy programs on the outside which cater to welfare recipients.

Ultimately, the distinction between the opportunities model and the medical model is a matter of degree. Both perspectives envisage the application of a "fix" to the individual and are legitimized within conventional corrections discourse on reduction in recidivism. The opportunities model places a mediator (prospects for a good job) between treatment of the individual (prison schooling) and the adoption of attitudes which define "good citizenship." With the medical model, the sequence and emphasis are as follows: Criminal mind (pathological deviancy) . . . treatment (literacy) . . . "good citizenship" (behavior).

The Cognitive Deficiency Model

With the cognitive deficiency model, literacy is enjoined to promote moral development through education. This model offers an optimistic viewpoint that envisages a more central role for education. While it is formulated in liberal humanistic terms, the cognitive deficiency model assumes that shortcomings in the prisoner's ways of knowing and acting are associated with the perpetration of misdeeds that harm others.

There is more than a touch of religious fundamentalism underpinning this model which merits closer scrutiny than is possible in this chapter. Behind the secular-humanistic rationale is a notion that the wages of sin are imprisonment, and that through education to eradicate character deficiencies there is a way to redemption.

Even though the cognitive deficiency model is invoked in curriculum formation outside of the prison, it is very much at home in the prison where it places special emphasis on the moral dimension of education. The model provides a practical alternative to the fixing techniques of the medical model and to the preoccupation with technical vocational training which characterizes the opportunities model.

From the cognitive deficiency point of view, adult literacy is conceptualized as a means for developing practical reasoning skills.[7] Practical reasoning in this regard is about moral development, and the liberal arts are identified as the primary source around which relevant practical reasoning skills can be effectively acquired.

It is important here to distinguish between Lawrence Kohlberg's developmental stage theory (after Jean Piaget) and the way it has been invoked, virtually "correctionalized," within even the most sophisticated commentaries on cognitive and moral development in prison education curriculum (Duguid 1986; Ross 1981). For Kohlberg, it is not individual deficiencies but the conditions experienced by the individuals that constitute the ultimately relevant source of retardation in cognitive and, hence, moral development. In this view, the prisoner is more deprived of opportunities to promote moral reasoning beyond the preconventional concrete stages (Kohlberg 1984) than deficient. Only by transforming prisons into democratic settings where prisoners have authority over significant aspects of administration through community decision making is it possible to create conditions for cognitive moral development. In the absence of these conditions, the cognitive conflict and the self-understanding it engenders for moral development are scarcely attainable.

Further, although Kohlberg's developmental stage theory provides the theoretical touchstone for advocates of a cognitive deficiency model, Kohlberg never claimed that an improvement in moral, or practical, reasoning would necessarily lead to a higher level of ethically informed action. Kohlberg, and those who worked closely with him, never forged the link they wanted to make between moral action and reasoning. Rather they argued that higher stages of reasoning were imbued with a consciousness of social circumstances. Accordingly, a person operating from a higher stage of reasoning is less likely to engage in egocentric (idiosyncratic) behavior for her or his own benefit but can still commit crimes from morally and politically informed interests. Any claim that a higher stage of moral reasoning *determines* moral (i.e., noncriminal) action is not confirmed by Kohlberg's research. In fostering a notion that cognitive and, hence, moral development can and should be increased in order to reduce recidivism, advocates of the cognitive deficiency model have dropped the crucial distinction Kohlberg made between moral (practical) reasoning and moral action.

ADULT LITERACY AND THE PANOPTICAN

In his influential book *Discipline and Punish: The Birth of the Prison*, Foucault (1977) reconstructs Jeremy Bentham's concept of the panoptican. Bentham conceived of the panoptican as the most effective design for modern prisons by which prisoners and staff could be kept under continuous surveillance. The significance of Foucault's analysis of the concept is in showing how the techniques of surveillance, normalization, and power relationships embodied in the modern prison also serve to shape—less emphatically but just as surely—everyday living on the outside. Foucault expresses the connections as follows: "In concrete terms: the more one analyses the process of 'carceralisation' of the penal practice down to its smallest details, the more one is led to relate them to such practices as schooling, military discipline, etc." (Foucault 1981, 7).

The adult literacy provision in prisons is enacted in full awareness of constraining panoptic conditions. On the outside, it is possible to underestimate the full force of constraining conditions and to talk naively about adult literacy as a means to empower the oppressed or the underprivileged. Hence, the circumstances in prison are significant for a critical understanding of the social context in which various forms of literacy projects are undertaken. The effects of disciplinary technology which seem to be more apparent in the prisons are at work on the outside. In this regard, the following interpretation of Foucault's insight by Rabinow is particularly instructive.

The aim of disciplinary technology, whatever its institutional form—and it arises in a large number of institutional settings, such as workshops, schools, prisons, and hospitals—is to forge a "docile body that may be subjected, used, transformed and improved" [citing Foucault]. This is done in several ways: through drills and training of the body, through standardization of actions over time, and through control of space. (Rabinow 1984, 17)

From this analysis, the way in which a panoptic viewpoint is systematically embodied in a conventional curriculum design becomes apparent. A clear-cut emphasis on the correctional dimension of adult literacy initiatives serves to announce that the educational provision is not only accommodative to the system of surveillance and control—correctional education is, in fact, integral to the panoptican.

Adult literacy projects conceived within the medical model are most closely tied to a panoptic scheme. The activities of students and teachers are continuously monitored within the parameters of standardized curriculum formats. These formats are filled out with a pedestrian content which steers students toward predictable responses. Critical discourse is precluded since it cannot be steered within predetermined limits. Creative initiatives on the part of teachers, which can be disconcerting for management, become redundant. This tendency is relevant because deskilled teachers are easier to keep in line.

For teachers whose level of performance and commitment is not impressive to begin with, standardized learning materials can be reassuring. Teacher preparation requirements are minimalized, and the deployment of learning packages enables less committed teachers to distance themselves from their students. The medium is the message (invoking Marshall McLuhan 1967). Students are to be kept busy rather than have their imaginations excited by energetic teachers.

In recent years, fanciful pedagogical notions, such as self-directed learning and individual paced learning, have been incorporated into the discourse around functionalist literacy curriculum. Unfortunately, these concepts only serve to mask the prescriptive and coercive nature of curriculum such as APL, and other variations on the competency-based education theme, rather than effecting any move toward learner and teacher autonomy. The curriculum packages still contrive to manage the "self-directed," "individually paced," learner within institutionally normed parameters. Teachers as "facilitators" of the curriculum continue to be deskilled. Accordingly, even when the self-directed learning strategy is invoked in legitimizing a functionalist standardized approach to literacy, the curriculum design endeavors to steer the entire educational enterprise and defines how the world *should be* read by adult learners.

If literacy curriculum, according to the medical model, is most closely aligned with the correctional ethos and the panoptican, approaches legitimated by the opportunities model fall within the same bailiwick. The interconnections among literacy, notions of useful work, and life skills, which the opportunities model specifies, is very relevant for institutional maintenance. Literacy programs in this mode receive official support in terms of their capacity to keep prisoners "meaningfully busy" and teachers in a predominantly accommodative role. While the teacher usually has more scope in designing the learning context and in determining content, literacy curriculum defined from an opportunities perspective is intended to promote an atmosphere of busyness and to serve the "good order" of the institution.

Literacy initiatives that claim to inculcate moral development according to the cognitive deficiency model reclaim a more central role for teacher and learners in the educational process. Unfortunately, the instrumentalization of literature as a primary source for literacy education in prisons seems antithetical to liberal tendencies which endorse the humanities. It is difficult to escape questions of ethical import about a "hidden curriculum" (Knights 1981) that co-opts the humanities for correctional pedagogy in the service of the panoptican. Shades of the prison house indeed.

Panoptic techniques and the correctional ethos in literacy curriculum are most likely to be discerned in prison settings. That is why the prison as a totalizing institution constitutes a critical context which can tell us much about the social control aspects of adult education and conventional schooling on the outside. The idea of panopticism, and its manifestation in prison schooling, is that ordinary men and women will, in effect, condition themselves according to institutionalized rules of conduct without bringing these norms into question.

ADULT LITERACY AS A DETOTALIZING (DECONSTRUCTIONIST) PEDAGOGY

For those who view adult education as a movement for progressive social change, it is tempting to overstate the extent to which alternative curriculum approaches can empower students through bringing into question the present structure of power relations.[8] However, as all who work in prisons understand, the panoptican is not monolithic. The system of surveillance and control may be all pervasive, but it is not sufficient to suppress all countervailing initiatives within the prison walls. By the same token, it is possible to engender approaches to teaching literacy which are neither totally constrained by the panoptican nor essentially accommodative to a correctional ethos. And even if the formal educational provision were to be shut down, research has demonstrated that individual and group learning projects of one kind or another are bound to occur.[9] We can look to the prisons for substantial evidence that self- and group-initiated human learning is ultimately more pervasive than the panoptican.

In the case of formal prison literacy initiatives, there are already instances in which prisoners are being taught how to write, to read, to discuss, and to appreciate literature without recourse to functionalist curriculum design and the constraints of a correctional ethos. Such instances in themselves represent a critical pedagogy. And while they may not be inclined to characterize their practice in this way, the teachers concerned are often guided by carefully worked out moral and political commitments.

Perhaps the most remarkable evidence of prison literacy initiatives relatively unencumbered with the correctional ethos comes in the form of publications—poetry, essays, plays, newspapers. Often the contributors are prisoners who were illiterate, certainly in APL terms, when they entered prison. The point about literacy initiatives which eschew concerns about fixing prisoners through education is that teachers and students simply focus their attention on writing, reading, and self-expression. Yet the role of the educators becomes more difficult, and more skilled, in such circumstances because they are obliged to work out students' needs for themselves (no APL 1, 2, 3) and prepare for each class in order to let learning take place.

With prison literacy projects that are dependent for their design, and day-to-day delivery, on the competence of committed teachers, it is often the authorities who tend toward accommodation. A sensible recognition that the panoptican is not all-encompassing leads to official sanction, even in the absence of enthusiastic management support, where prisoners with status endorse the value of an educational program.

To the extent that prisoners are not regarded as part of the mainstream population, there is sometimes an opportunity for their teachers to evade the conforming curriculum that is pressed on students in educational institutions on the outside. In this regard, prison educators may find themselves in the same position as teachers of marginalized groups on the outside.[10] Teachers of students from marginalized groups are often able to experiment with curriculum and teaching strategies because the authorities simply do not think it matters, provided such students are kept "meaningfully busy." Accordingly, many adult literacy teachers of prisoners and people from marginalized groups have more room to try out creative approaches than they care to acknowledge. Such acknowledgment entails extra work. It is far easier to opt for a standardized, prepackaged curriculum and insist that "they [officialdom] will not let us" attempt other approaches. Nevertheless, it is possible to witness prison-based adult literacy projects which, in terms of creativity and commitment, make some institutionalized adult literacy programs for "disadvantaged" people on the outside appear pedestrian by comparison. In any event, there is an ironic but relevant sense in which the panoptic effects on prison literacy are less compelling than they are for institutionalized literacy initiatives on the outside. Conscientious literacy teachers of prisoner-students, and of the population groups on the outside from which many prisoners originate, can take advantage of these laxer circumstances to create alternative curriculum and teaching strategies.

From a theoretical perspective, the prison significantly encapsulates the controlling influence of a powerful "systems world" described in the fundamental investigations of Max Weber and Jurgen Habermas.[11] Of these two eminent social theorists, it is Habermas who suggests convincingly that there are seams in the systems world which can be exploited by life-enriching alternatives. The systems world, supported by the expanding manifestations of technical rationality, cannot be rolled away but it can be resisted. Its harmful consequences for the way we experience everyday life can be offset through interactive, hence educative, processes derived from practically oriented, community-based values. In pedagogical terms, the chief concern becomes one of enhancing communicative competence in place of a preoccupation with incorporating narrowly defined, predetermined learning objectives.

Though a pedagogy derived from a notion of communicative competence may not seem entirely feasible, it is apparent that alternatives to its antithesis—educational programming steered by an overarching technical rationality—are achievable even within the prison walls.

PROSPECTS FOR ALTERNATIVES

Prospects for alternative approaches to teaching literacy in the prisons are already discernible in creative initiatives to encourage writing, reading, and discussion around topics of critical import. Such initiatives can flourish where the teacher prepares for every class unhindered by the narrow prescriptiveness of functionalist curriculum design and heavy-handed notions about the correctional aspects of what is to be taught.

The prison walls, while enclosing an inhospitable environment, have provided a productive haven to literate prisoners who are already inclined to write and read. In this regard, the names of Antonio Gramsci and Rosa Luxemburg spring readily to mind. The number of distinguished writers who produced a significant part of their work while in prison are legion. The point to be made here is that the means for enlarging meaningful adult education through the literacy provision in prison are at hand. Further, it would appear that the obstacles—as in "they won't let us"—to creative literacy teaching initiatives are overstated and can be tested by committed educators. To invoke Gramsci again, the section on "Organic Intellectuals" in his *Prison Notes* (Hoare and Smith 1975) points to ways in which educators as intellectuals can clarify their roles within the prevailing complex of power relationships and structures of repression. And to invoke another prison writer, somewhat more dramatically, there are ways in which teachers of literacy can create a pedagogy of hope *In the Belly of the Beast* (Abbot 1990).

Despite the overt, and perhaps overly optimistic, revolutionary implications of Paulo Freire's approach to literacy, his problem-posing pedagogy can be instructive for teachers in prisons. The main difficulties await the Freirean approach in prison as prevail on the outside. The approach can be too readily accommodated within a nebulous pedagogical strategy to instill critical thinking skills that lack a critical edge. Yet with an eye to the kind of analysis Gramsci prefigures for organic intellectuals in *Prison Notes*, prison educators can usefully adopt a Freirean viewpoint by posing to themselves the very problem entailed in its incorporation to a prison setting.[12]

It is through participatory literary practices in community-based settings and some educational institutions that the closest approximations to Freirean pedagogy have emerged. A central tenet of participatory literacy initiatives is that students, together with their teachers, will have a say in the formation of curriculum and the selection of relevant texts. The pedagogical intent is to counteract functionalist orientations by ignoring, as much as possible, conventional curriculum parameters and enabling participants to express themselves. Accordingly, the "voices" of the learners and their life stories become primary material for the learning process. Literacy in these terms is not so much about focusing on the need to read as on attending to the needs of people who cannot read.

The critical discourse around participatory literacy struggles with the issues of co-optation and compromise. These issues exist for alternative initiatives that seek some measure of official sanction—usually for funding purposes. Alternative approaches that work purposefully within such constraints are exemplified in *Participatory Literacy Education* by Fingeret and Jurmo (1989).

Clarity about the social conditions that continue to oppress their students enables teachers involved in participatory literacy to create more meaningful learning situations. Yet such an understanding also requires a willingness to address the contradictions participatory literacy practices entail. Literacy teachers inside and outside the prisons confront the same challenges when they endeavor to evade the correctional ethos and panoptic intent of functionalist curriculum. In order to maneuver intelligently (avoiding complete co-optation) and foster a relevant level of genuine participation, a careful critical analysis of what is at stake becomes an imperative. However, there is undoubtedly much more room for committed literacy teachers to maneuver, both within the prison and on the outside, than has yet been realized. The existence of this unclaimed space for progressive educational initiatives within the panoptican is largely confirmed in the pedagogy of Paulo Freire.

CONCLUSION

The authorities in Poland announced (March 1993) that the nation's prison system must be substantially expanded, and in a hurry. A relaxation in the kind of social controls that sustained the previous regime has been accompanied by a very dramatic increase in the number of criminal convictions. With "democratization" Western style comes the necessity, it seems, of reinforcing the panoptic influence of Poland's prisons. The rising flood of Polish prisoners, for which prison officials are planning correctional programs to go with the new prison cells, are drawn from the most disempowered sections of society. They represent people whose real needs can be addressed through the participatory approaches of Freirean pedagogy.[13] At present, however, the innovative Polish correctional project seems to be focused on a "fix alcoholics" rationale.

The profile of the burgeoning prison population in Poland is manifest elsewhere. Here is what a prominent observer of modern life in Canada had to say on the matter: "People who can't read come readily to view themselves as worthless junk, and many feel they must grab what they can out of life. Canada's prisons are full of men and women who can't read" (Callwood 1990). Yet the mainstream educational response in Canadian prisons, as in Polish ones, is to reproduce under the rubric of "correctional"—a functionalist design of literacy that necessitates passive acceptance of officially constituted information and behavior.

Fortunately for those educators who espouse a more meaningful notion of prison house literacy, the deployment of functionalist curriculum is not unassailable. A functionalist orientation to literacy permits alternatives if only because the correctional ethos really masks a widespread indifference about the welfare of prisoners. It suffices if prisoners are seen to be kept "meaningfully busy" and out of harm's way, while incarceration serves as a salutary lesson to the population from which prisoners are largely drawn of what can happen if one does not behave.

Meanwhile prison education that creates alternatives to functionalist curriculum design can counter the correctional ethos in the very heart of the panoptican. Participatory literacy projects for prisoners, though subject to systematic constraints, cast hopeful prospects for modern adult education practice beyond the prison walls.

NOTES

1. Instances of such sources abound within conventional literature on schooling in the prisons. See the *Journal of Correctional Education* (Washington, D.C.: Correctional Education Association) and the annual *Yearbook of Correctional Education* (copublishers: the Correctional Education Association, U.S.A., and the Institute of the Humanities, Simon Fraser University, Burnaby, BC, Canada).

2. It is also worth noting that the models, and the perspectives they represent, parallel theories of deviance in sociology and criminology. Though it is not feasible to enlarge on these connections here, teachers of prison literacy can gain important insights into the influence of deviancy theory from Stephen Pfohl's *Images of Deviancy and Social Control* (1985). The chapters on "The Pathological Perspective: Deviance as Sickness" and "The Critical Perspective: Toward a Power-reflexive Understanding of Deviance and Social Control" are particularly instructive in regard to the concerns of this chapter.

3. The emergence of the CBE phenomenon during the past two decades or so has provided a curriculum model that virtually embodies the functionalist approach to educational planning. CBE is characterized by systematic attempts to break down curriculum into measurable components. By learning the behavior prescribed in each component, one acquires "competence." Thus, for a CBE unit on "Occupational Knowledge," a student is required to indicate the appropriate letter, on a separate form, in answer to the following question: Faith Greer needs 400 hours of on-the-job training to get her license. If she works 25 hours a week, how many weeks will it take her to get her license?

4. For a positive report on APL by a leading advocate, see Norvell Northcut (1976). A summary of APL with critical analysis appears in Collins (1987).

5. An instructive empirical study on the Adult Performance Test demonstrates that APL measures do not even account for the dubiously established learning objectives of the curriculum model. Hence the APL system is not internally consistent. See Ronald Cervero (1980). For a fairly comprehensive coverage of the debates around CBE, see Collins (1983). Also see James Parker's response to Collins's critiques (1984) and Collins's reply (1984).

6. This programming flexibility, however, is likely to be determined by the requirements of a designated ("opportunities model") trades program. For example, Prince Albert Penitentiary in Canada was able to have Adult Education Grade XI recognized as an acceptable entrance to its Radio/TV Service (Electronics) Program, which required Grade XII on the outside. See Michael Collins' *A Report on Two Post-Secondary Education Programs: The Radio/TV Service [Electronics] Program at Prince Albert Penitentiary and the University Level Program at Collins Bay Institute* (1987, 5) Prisoners completing the program earned the same certification and licensing credentials as students on the outside.

7. A carefully worked out rationale for the cognitive deficiency model is presented by Duguid (1981, 1983). Here again, the parallel with criminology is worth noting (see note 2). The work of Clark and Cornish (1983) is especially illuminating in this regard. They describe the influence of the *medico-psychological model*. The primary assumption of this model is that prisoners obviously make bad choices because of some cognitive deficiency. Accordingly, treatment teaches them to make the right choices, while the social conditions they experience are engineered to shape the choices they make.

8. Paulo Freire's work still holds prominence wherever the issue of problem-posing pedagogy with oppressed people is addressed. See *Education for Critical Consciousness* (New York: Continuum, 1981), *Pedagogy of the Oppressed* (New York: Continuum, 1970), *Pedagogy in Process: The Letters to Guinea-Bissau* (New York: Seabury Press, 1978), *The Politics of Education: Culture, Power, and Liberation* (South Hadley, MA: Bergin & Garvey, 1985). However, with regard to prospects for social

change, it is important to bear in mind the realistic limitations of prevailing curriculum discourse around "perspective transformation and collective learning as social change" specified by Colin Griffin (1991, 268). This concern is echoed in H. Davidson's (1993, 25) observation on how leading critically oriented adult learning theorists posit human transformation in a way that reverts to a personalized (individualized) focus on transformation.

9. See, for example, the research of adult educator Allen Tough (1981).

10. The tendency toward allowing teachers greater control over curriculum where students are defined as "failures anyway" is addressed by C. Buswell (1980).

11. A thoroughly analyzed notion of systems-world vis-à-vis the life-world is central to the work of Jurgen Habermas, a leading contemporary exponent of the Frankfurt School Critical Theory. See, in particular, *The Theory of Communicative Action*, vols. 1 and 2, edited and translated by T. McCarthy (Boston: Beacon Press, 1984 and 1987). The Critical Theory of Habermas is of immediate relevance to educators concerned with the emancipatory potential of their work, especially in regard to the enhancement of communicative competence. Educators can look to his Critical Theory for an explanation of why the normative claims of Paulo Freire for an emancipatory pedagogy are rational.

12. For a recently published and sensible text on the application of Freire's pedagogical approach in conventional educational settings, see Ira Shor's *Empowering Education: Critical Teaching for Social Change* (1992). Chapter 2 deals with problem-posing strategies.

13. It is possible to distinguish between true and false needs through a problem-posing pedagogy where needs are defined along the lines set out by Herbert Marcuse. For Marcuse, "The insistence on operational and behavioral concepts turns against efforts to free thought and behavior from the given reality and for the suppressed alternatives" (1966, 16).

5

Freeing Birds, Erasing Images, Burning Lamps: How I Learned to Teach in Prison

Peter Linebaugh

I taught in four prisons: Concord State Prison, New Hampshire (1972–1973); Massachusetts Correctional Institution at Walpole (1973); the Federal Penitentiary at Marion, Illinois (1972–1974); and the New York Correctional Facility at Attica, New York (1979–1981). The prison teaching thus fell into two periods, one at the beginning of the 1970s, just after the holocaust at Attica while the Vietnam War was still in progress, and the other period at the end of the decade when Ronald Reagan was elected president and the massacre at the New Mexico State Prison seemed to spell the suicide of the prisoner movement.

At Attica I was paid for the work. Genesee Community College, which administered the consortium of western New York colleges contributing to the educational program at Attica, paid me $295 per credit hour per semester plus $75 to cover the expenses of travel, a total of $960. At Marion there was no direct payment, but there was some compensation by Franconia College in alleviation from other teaching duties. The teaching at Concord and Walpole was also unpaid, at least unpaid in money. Certainly, it was a rewarding experience. In many ways I was the student, learning to teach.

Each phase of prison teaching was in counterpoint to teaching at an outside institution. At the beginning of the decade, I taught at the experimental Franconia College, in the beautiful White Mountains of New Hampshire. At the end of the decade I taught at the University of Rochester which lies on the white bank of the Genesee River joined to the African-American side only by a disused railway bridge upon which a learned wit had painted the Langston Hughes line, "I've known rivers." The students at Franconia were countercultural, young, and inexperienced: dreamy, dopey, and disturbed. The prisoners I met were older; many were Vietnam veterans. They were both cynical and hopeful. They wanted to learn. As students these prisoners were accustomed to discipline; and they learned by challenging discipline. The students at the college were unaccustomed to discipline, many of them had to learn how to sit still and other habits of study. At the end of the decade, both students inside and outside were different. At Rochester they were competitive, "smart," and narrow. They tended to avert eye contact and already walked with a slight stoop. The prisoners tended to revert to ethnocentricism. While the political atmosphere of the earlier prisoner movement had dissipated, the students in prison were alert, wary, and curious.

Pablo Neruda compared thinking to freeing birds, erasing images, and burning lamps. In prison at the beginning of the decade, the job was to free birds. At the end, it was to burn lamps. At the university the job of both a teacher and a scholar were to erase images.

The experiences at Concord and Walpole were pedagogical but brief. The guards, when not actively hostile, could be surly, insolent, or officious. Teaching was either a mass encounter or strictly one on one. The pedagogical situation arose in conditions of tension—strikes by guards or riot by prisoners. In these circumstances, learning took place rapidly and on both sides. By way of contrast, the teaching at Marion and Attica was institutionally approved, and in this sense it resembled schooling. Approved teaching was less threatening to the guards' self-interest, and individual officers could be actively cooperative. Much in the situation, for example, syllabi, multiple written assignments, grades, and, at Attica, even a bell to ring the beginning and ending of class, would be familiar to students and teachers in schools and universities in the free world.

What drew me to prison teaching? There were personal, educational, scholarly, and political reasons. Personally, I had long admired rebels and outcasts. Educationally, much as I am sometimes reluctant to admit it, religious training came into play. I had read the Paul and Silas story, a story of self-activity by prisoners. The Lord's Prayer says the Kingdom of Heaven is to be on earth, which seemed to fit in just fine with the radicalism of the time. Jesus taught basic human solidarity, "For I was hungry, and ye gave me meat; I was thirsty, and ye gave me drink: I was a stranger, and ye took me in: Naked, and ye clothed me: I was sick, and ye visited me: I was in prison, and ye came unto me" (Matthew 25:36–37). I did not feel I was on a saintly errand. Still, years later when I was vulnerable to attack for teaching in prison, I knew it was right.

The scholarly reason was this. I was a Ph.D. student at the University of Warwick in England studying with a collective of social historians, under the guidance of E. P. Thompson, who was a dissident, erudite, and radical historian of great intellect and comprehension. He expected us to *know* what we were talking about. Since my research concerned historical definitions of criminality, it behooved me to know something more about the subject than could be gained by wandering around in library stacks, or gathering dust in archives. I was influenced by the American ethos of authenticity which said that you gotta walk the talk. There was the methodology of knowing the pear by tasting the pear which Mao Tse-tung wrote about in "On Liberalism." It should also be said that, while few people wanted to go to prison even on a visit, the address was respected, and you could get a hearing if you had been.

Politically, I was drawn to prison teaching because I admired Malcolm X, whom I chose to see less as a black nationalist than as living proof that egotistical criminality could lead to collective leadership for revolutionary social change. He was a righteous brother. He embodied and summarized a profound part of the African-American experience that linked the plantation to the prison and slavery to the prison population. He taught lessons of history that were deliberately untaught in the schools. Readers of his autobiography know the decisive importance of his educational experience in the print shop at Concord State Prison in Massachusetts. We wondered aloud whether one of his teachers, or older companions in prison, had not himself been in contact with, if not himself a member of, the Industrial Workers of the World, the IWW, or Wobblies.

> The sab-cat purred and twitched her tail
> And winked the other way;
> Our boys shall never rot in jail,
> Or else the Plutes will pay.[1]

This was recognized in the Black Panther newspaper in such slogans as "The Spirit of the Panther Is Stronger than the Man's Jails," or "Jails Are the First Black Concentration Camps" (*The Black Panther: Black Community News Service*, May 18, 1968). In October 1966 the Black Panther Party adopted a Ten-Point platform and program whose fifth point simply said, "We want education for our people that exposes the true nature of this decadent American society. We want education that teaches us our true history and our role in the present day society."

DIABOLICAL AND HYSTERICAL METABOLISM IN THE NEW HAMPSHIRE STATE PEN (1972)

I returned from England to begin teaching at Franconia College in the fall of 1972. The college was led by the young, brilliant conductor and violinist, Leon Botstein. He supported the lessons I taught. For instance, I pointed out that the students in the lycée in Hanoi during the Christmas bombing read

Michelet's account of the battle of Valmy, the turning point in the defense of the French Revolution. Goethe was a witness to the battle among the defeated counterrevolutionaries. Since I thought the United States was in a similar position, I quoted Goethe to my students, "From this place, and from this day forth, commences a new era in the world's history; and you can all say that you were present at its birth." We knew that young northern Irish people involved in the struggle for civil rights and expulsion of British troops from Ireland read James Connolly, and here in the States James Connolly was not even in print! It was clear we had to free some birds.

My colleague, Gene Mason, author of *The Politics of Exploitation*, had recently been released from a short bid in a Kentucky State Prison where he had been sent as part of a frame-up against his candidacy for Congress. While in prison he had learned of a dastardly hombre named Stagolee from fellow prisoners.

> It was back in the time of nineteen hundred and two,
> I had a fucked-up deck a cards and I didn't know what to do. My woman
>   was leavin', she was puttin' me out in the cold.
> I said, "Why you leavin' me baby?" She said, "Our love has grown cold."
> So she kept packin' the bags, so I said, "Fuck it," you know.
> So I waded through water and I waded through mud
> And I came to this town called the Bucket of Blood.
> And I asked the bartender for something to eat,
> He give me a dirty glass a water and a tough-assed piece a meat
> I said, "Bartender, bartender, don't you know who I am?"
> He said, "Frankly, my man, I don't give a goddamn."[2]

On the toast went, cold-blooded murder most foul, foul language getting only worse, and hideous misogyny. I was repelled and fascinated. Gene taught correspondence courses to prisoners and got me to do the same. We held a conference, a "Bolshevik Bandit Conference," and launched the New England Prisoners' Association. We definitely had the glint in our eye.

Our goal was to abolish prisons. We believed that prisons made criminals. They confirmed people in their wicked ways. Moreover, we thought that the wrong people were in jail, the poor and the weak. The wave of prison rebellions and strikes and riots from the mid-1960s had a qualitatively different content from the wave in the postwar period or that wave preceding the Great Depression. It was estimated that the American prison population declined from 120.8 per 10,000 in 1961 to 96.7 a decade later, owing to early releases based on probation and parole. Hence, the demand for the abolition of prisons corresponded to an actual tendency in Corrections, even if it was not accepted as an explicit policy of liberation. People were getting out all the time, and this made it easier to know what was happening inside. It was not long before we were invited to the New Hampshire penitentiary.

I thought about it a lot ahead of time. This was my first time going into prison. I was going to be surrounded by criminals! Wasn't I afraid? I fell back on formal rules of courtesy. I was not going to ask what crimes people had committed that had put them into prison. When Bertolt Brecht's powerful robbers came to the door, he helped them enter, and therefore he became available for miraculous transformations.

The first meeting at the New Hampshire penitentiary in Concord brought together a large number of prisoners and only two or three of us teachers. The students or prisoners who attended were serious indeed. A prisoner asked us what we thought of "Comrade Stalin's laws of dialectical and historical materialism?" One of us had to answer, and since I was teaching Karl Marx at the time, it seemed I should be the one to answer. But what were these laws?

Stalin's pamphlet, *Dialectical and Historical Materialism*, had made its way into the New Hampshire State Prison in picturesque Concord. It was published in 1940, after the purges and before the invasion of the Soviet Union. It had a worldwide circulation promoted both by Moscow and by Peking. Many prisoners were veterans of the war in Vietnam, which had provided them with direct experience of anti-imperial struggle. "Ho, Ho, Ho Chi Minh Is Going to Win" was a powerful slogan in the antiwar movement at "home." General Giap, Mao Tse-tung, and Joseph Stalin had become the logical recourse for those students who, having mutinied against imperial service, were looking for an alternative. Stalin's pamphlet seemed to be anti-imperialist. Hence, the prestige of the dictator. By contrast, Stalin had no prestige in academic circles where Marxism, to be acceptable, had to exist as a theoretical project, a project that stressed ideology, hegemony, or culture. The Frankfurt School stressed ideology; the Italian revisionist, Gramsci, stressed hegemony; and the English New Left stressed culture. Stalinist interpretations of Marx were anathema to all three. All three traditions disdained to investigate wages and hours. Of course, Stalin did too. But that did not matter in prison where wages were slavish, and there were no free hours anyway.

I was able to answer the question, muttering about "the unity of opposites" and "the transformation of quantity into quality" in order to gain time. But now as I review the pamphlet I find that Stalin's first example of the application of these laws to human history is instructive indeed. "The slave system would be senseless, stupid and unnatural under modern conditions. But under the conditions of a disintegrating primitive communal system, the slave system is a quite understandable and natural phenomenon, since it represents an advance on the primitive communal system." Stalin thus finds slavery to be a historical system of labor that *followed* communism, whereas in America so many consider slavery a stage of history that *preceded* capitalism. Stalin wrote this as he was constructing the gulag. The system of forced labor accompanied industrialization in

Russia as surely as it had in the United States, and like in the United States, though the XIIIth Amendment explicitly permits it, everyone pretends slavery does not exist. It does not seem quite so funny, as it once did, to call the pamphlet "Diabolical and Hysterical Metabolism." I was beginning to erase an image.

Neither our mass meetings inside the prison nor our individual correspondence with particular students was to last long. Low-level guerrilla war broke out over food and drink. The guards refused to bring food. ("They were going to throw it at us when we went by," whimpered one.) There was a Tobacco Rebellion to force the prisoners to beg for smokes. The administration turned off water to the prison. A guard was suspended who carried a German Luger into work in the kitchen. Ringleaders, including some of our students, were transferred to federal penitentiaries—Leavenworth, Marion, and Lewisburgh. Warden Vitek explained, "The Whole thing is psychology. They use it on us, we use it on them." The warden locked down the whole prison. We wrote *The New Hampshire State Prison Lock-Up and Shake-Down, March and April 1973*, and demanded the presence of citizen observers in the prison, circulating a demand of Massachusetts prisoners. At New Hampshire, during the lockup, one man was put in the hole. Yet they had to feed him. He was stripped naked. He threw his feces at the guards. We realized a person is never without a weapon.

I was deeply moved. Two unexpected feelings struck me. Whenever I entered prison and the gates clanged shut behind me and after I entered the society of the prisoners, I felt welcomed and every effort was always made to make me feel at home. Indeed, the prison *was* home to hundreds or thousands of men. Of course, I felt fear, but that fear left when I left the guards. The guards live in fear; it is a part of their working conditions. The second feeling I had was this. Although this was home to a mass of uniformed people whose individualities in clothing, grooming, behavior, and body language were severely curtailed, I had never been so struck by individualities as I was struck by them in prison. For good or evil, the inside shone out.

HARVARD AND WARWICK RESEARCH METHODS AT MCI WALPOLE (1973)

The Massachusetts Corrections Institution at Walpole was the maximum security joint. For more than a month in 1973, it was controlled by the prisoners. At Walpole the appointment of a liberal administrator, John Boone, provoked the guards and state police into a strike whereby they ceased all duties with the exception of "the guns and the keys," as was said at the time. This left the internal management of daily life—food, laundry, the workshops—entirely under the control of the prisoners. It was self-government, if not direct democracy. The Nation of Islam had long been an organized autonomous presence inside with connections outside. It forced other groups to organize—gangsters, Irish, Italians, Chicanos, and poor whites—just as in the Renaissance the formation of one nation-state encouraged the formation of others. Under some circumstances, these ethnic divisions ceased to be the basis of control. They could be turned upside down to become a problem to the penal system and the state. Thus the black vanguard forced others to organize. A council governed the inside; it immediately established relations with the outside, and it was not long before a system of twenty-four-hour citizen observation teams was organized among outsiders. The National Prisoners Rights Association (NPRA) was in command.

Michael Ignatieff, the young Harvard historian, who joined one of these teams, described the situation:

Into overcrowded facilities have been cast a new generation of prisoners, more insistent on their rights than any in recent memory. In response to these pressures, reform-minded administrators have liberalized the security and custody of many institutions, arousing intense antagonism and overt opposition among guards. This combination of population pressure, public disillusionment, fumbling reform, prisoner militancy, and guard intransigence has broken the fragile order inside the prison. (Ignatieff 1978, xi)

How did the experience affect, if it did, Michael's research work, which like mine, concerned crime and punishment in the industrial revolution? He had different assumptions. "It is easy to take prisons for granted for those who stay out of trouble." This assumed that trouble did not sometimes come in at the door without knocking. A second assumption was expressed thus: "Force being necessary to the maintenance of any social order, what degree of coercion can the state legitimately exert over those who disobey?" (p. 207). Many people in prison would assent to this, since people lived in a milieu of force and coercion. Nevertheless, the birds we were freeing, the lamp we wished to keep burning, did not exalt "social order." This indeed was the watchword of everything that was conservative, reactionary, and backward. Not that we proposed "disorder." On the contrary, in speaking of "community," as we tended to do, the main problem was not disobedience but cooperation.

At the conclusion of his book on prisons, Michael wrote, "It is tempting to look upon the history of prison reform as a cycle of recurring ironies" (p. 207). It is a temptation that we resisted because to us reform did not happen as a result of what reformers did: Reformers responded to what prisoners were doing. If irony summed up Ignatieff, self-activity was our methodological slogan. We investigated the connections between prisoners' struggles and struggles in the free world. His emphasis was on the state, rather than class relations. Our emphasis was on production and reproduction, rather than law and order. He tended to assume that prison contained the criminal class, or mainly bad people who could be rich or poor, while we thought it contained the working class or mainly poor people, who were good and bad. We were engaged in a war of ideas.

In Walpole I was locked up in protective custody, or the Hole, with a very big man. We had to share a tiny cell. He wanted to know whether I had $5 on me. I said no. Did I have any money? No. Would I promise to get him a portable radio when I got out? He was scary, and he knew it. He said he could hurt me. There was no point in denying it. Resigned to a beating, I replied, "So." We fell silent, he to his thoughts, me to my fear. I had to be in this man's cell for several hours. He had been placed there by the NPRA for an assault he had committed in the general population, and I, as a citizen observer, had been placed there by the shift organizers of the NPRA whom I now silently cursed. Any inclination to perpetrate further mischief on me was restrained when I asked him about the NPRA. He began to speak reluctantly and with suspicion, and then with a little warmth; soon with big eyes, he spoke about how the NPRA constitution worked in prison, speaking about how the prisoners had *to work together*, and how the NPRA council was chosen from *all the prisoners*, and how they were taking care of themselves. Cooperation. In turn, I heaved a sigh of relief, my fears and doubts disappeared, and I told him about the *Communist Manifesto*. The hours vanished in a twinkling.

I was looking for the Church of the New Song. In Walpole I found it, with its millenarianism, its obvious relation to the legal victories of the Nation of Islam, its theology that bore a relation to the liberation theology of Latin America, and with its echoes of the hopefulness of the antinomian spirit arising from the left-wing of the English Revolution of 1649. A votary of the Church guided me in the general population, explaining how the democracy and self-management of the prison operated. Before I departed, he pressed upon me a fistful of loose sheets containing handwritten notes on the sermons of Harry Theriault, the founder of the Church. He had given me a precious gift, and I despaired of having nothing to offer in return.[3]

The New England Prisoners Association (NEPA), under the direction of Randall Conrad, made a movie of this extraordinary episode when the prisoners controlled everything but the "guns and keys" in the prison. It was called *3,000 Years and Life*. I showed it in Geneva, Switzerland, May 1975. We showed the film in Padova, Italy, in June 1975. We showed it in Milan too, at the Parco Lambro, during the 5th Festival of Proletarian Youth, a countercultural and autonomist gathering, an Italian Woodstock. In consequence of taking the film around, we learned about the prisoner movement in Europe. Rotte Hilfe or "Red Help," a 1920s German organization, provided legal aid and help for family members of political prisoners. The German prisoner movement tended to divide between those who limited their support to the political prisoners and, after 1973 especially, those supporting all the prisoners. These "spontaneists" in 1974 led work stoppages and hunger strikes. Prisoner councils formed in Frankfurt exposed prison scandal. At an international gathering of European activists, I heard parts of the women's movement forsake prisoner work, and to declare their refusal to clean up the mess the men had made "once again." Harsh as this sounded at the time, it was a message that I received and filed away. Our movie was criticized because it was brushed by the workers' control ideology. Rather than abolish prisons, it called for prisoner self-determination, and since this seemed a concession to the structure of repression making prisons necessary in the first place, this part of the film received considerable criticism in Padova.

We had to explain about the power relations inside. Nobody could do this better than Bobby Scollard, the best speaker NEPA had. A Boston Southie, his prominent occipital bump always attracted attention, and his wit and mouth held it (Scollard 1975). This is the discourse he gave when NEPA was founded (and when it ended). It is the discourse I wish he could have provided the Italian critics. As a piece of persuasive rhetoric it is classic.

First, Bobby would set the scene and define his terms, and he would do this conversationally. "I'd like to go back to Soledad Prison, say in the early '60s." He has gently tapped your arm. "You could have anywhere from 4,000 to 10,000 prisoners. These consist of Chicano, Blacks, Paddy-dudes, and Indians. Paddies are Whites. I want to talk about a very heavy racial thing. And you got to remember, in Soledad, which was called the Gladiator School, your life ain't worth a pack of cigarettes at any given time" (1975). Nobody could talk the tough talk better than Bobby; in addition, that final phrase—"at any given time"—was pure bureaucratese. By the end of the introduction, our attention was riveted.

Second, Bobby would lay out the problem as it *appeared*. "The race problem was always generated by the administration, and different guards. Not all guards, but some." Bobby always seemed to speak to the most skeptical in his audience, and the skeptics know that there are guards and there are guards. He would continue, casually, slipping in a clue. "The thing was they used to have a thing called riot season. Every year just around the end of October, first part of November, you ran into this race riot. Automatically it popped up some place and the whole place was locked up. Guards were working overtime, blah, blah, blah." The blah-blah tells you Bobby has no patience for the guard's excuses; we have heard them all, he implies. "Guys would get wiped out with double-ought buckshot, and numerous amount[s] of killings, stabbing, shootings. Lots of guys got wasted. No guards got wasted. No administration got wasted. But a lot of cons got wasted." He has so vividly—his hands were jabbing the air—described the carnage, only the cool and alert remember when it transpired.

Having described the *appearance* of the problem, Bobby then moved into the third part of his discourse, the *reality* of the problem. "What was taking place was this: As soon as the riot was quelled and everything was down, just automatically that check for overtime happened to come about a week before Christmas. So all the guards could get their goodies for the kiddos." His sarcasm and mock sentimentality emphasized that his analytical tool was historical materialism. "So, now groups within the prison, the Black community, the Chicano, the Indian, the Paddy-dude, decided to put two and three guys together, see if we could get our heads together. We figured out, baby, we're wasting us and not them. As one Black dude said to me, 'Hey, lookit, we've got to have respect for each other, but that doesn't mean you have to kiss me and I have to kiss you.' " Ethnic divisions are not overcome: They are accepted as a starting point. Regardless of sexual orientation, the word "kiss" has made the speaker's point. Everyone is thinking now. Bobby continues with his signature phrase, "We just got to make it. Beautiful. It got going. We set up a thing. It took a lot of work, without getting bagged."

The oration moves into its fourth part, the solution, and by now Bobby is fully in his stride—confident, humorous, and eloquent. He savors every syllable. "And what happened was, we had what we called a lay-in. Nobody, and I mean nobody, from the nicest fink down to the biggest swish, nobody but nobody moved out of their cell. That bell rang that morning, everybody laid dead. Nobody went to work, nobody wanted to work, nobody did nothing. Therefore no violence. Therefore no overtime. And we laid there." He pauses, a long pause. He waits. He smiles. "So the first move we had already anticipated, was that the administration come down and say, 'Hey, we want to talk to the Chicano community.' 'Hey, baby, let's talk to the White community over here.' " How he enjoys, how every con and ex-con enjoys this part, the prison administration pleading, entreating, sweet, useless supplications! "Ain't nothing happening. Either you talk to all of us at once, or you ain't talking.' " Bobby is shouting away, now one voice, now another. You feel you are on the tier. You feel you too could deal with the most powerful prison system in the world, the system that formed Eldridge Cleaver and George Jackson.

He comes to the fifth part of his discourse. Bobby has saved the best for last—victory. "We laid there eleven days. Warden got us a 10¢ raise in industry, a right to sit anywhere we wanted in the mess hall, and a lot of other good little things that they told us wouldn't work, but still are working today." The prisoners triumphed over the administration and the guards; Bobby has triumphed over cynicism and despair. He is satisfied. History and its lessons have been passed on.

Classic oratory such as this learned in the forum of the prison yard, would have been appreciated in the land of Cicero, Aesop, and Machiavelli, not that Aesop was Italian. Bobby knew effective teaching was done by stories, and this was as true today as ever, Gramsci notwithstanding. Otherwise, as a result of the Walpole experience, I was learning the reciprocal nature of learning, and that you get out as much as you put in. My own research work was beginning to gain confidence as a result.

CHARLIE MARKS IN MARION (1972–1974)

Marion had replaced Alcatraz as the most secure prison in the federal system. Its cornerstone was placed by Robert F. Kennedy. It was located in Carbondale, Illinois. It had an antiseptic feel in its external appearance. It was surrounded by very nice green grass, no trees or bushes, just green grass. One of the new Kodak plants had the same outside landscaping, but at Kodak the cameras were more discreetly placed. It looked a little bit like a golf course. It provided a panorama of unobstructed surveillance. You could easily see a golf ball coming, or anything else.

Twice I visited Carbondale, Illinois, to visit with Joseph Harry Brown, my student. Teaching older students is a satisfying experience. Joe was as sweet a bank robber as you could hope to find. His occupation had affected his thinking which was methodical and bold. Joe would ask questions I could not answer at the time but which I would remember long afterward. "How do you control the thoughts in your head?" I did not know at all.

We believed that we had to start all over again. The old Marxism did not work any more; the Stalinists had made a wreck of things, and the Trotsky-ists were not much better. Many of the radicals and militants did not think that prisoners were members of the working class. They thought they were all lumpen. This was the image I tried to erase; it was an obstacle to clear thinking. The *Oxford English Dictionary* quotes the *Black Panther* newspaper (27 April 1974), "The outlaw and the lumpen will make the revolution. The people, the workers, will adopt it." What did they mean by worker? They meant someone in a factory. If that definition was accepted, it did not leave you much identity in the Marxist tradition. It was therefore with a certain sectarian pleasure that we discovered that Bobby Seale had worked in a steel plant, and Malcolm X had worked for Chevy. There was an absence of self-esteem or self-respect to the term "lumpenproletariat." It reminded one of Stagolee, but now with menacing overtones. I tended to take the attribu-tion, lumpenproletariat, personally, as a direct insult. I was not alone in this. Frances Fox Piven and Richard A. Cloward found the term "not only offensive for its denigrating implications but also an abuse of Marx," as they wrote in a book that I later used at Attica (Cloward and Piven 1977, xxiv). Lumpen is a nasty image, and despite constant rubbing much erasing remains to be done.

It was around this time that I began to call Karl Marx, Charles Marks, as the English census taker spelled his name when the great revolutionary was exiled in London. Also it was worth pointing out that the most frequently cited chapter of *Das Kapital* (pronounced with a mock German accent) was the tenth chapter on "The Working Day" which was first translated into

English, not by professors in England, but by Saint Louis railroad workers at the beginning of the strike of 1876. It seemed a way to remember that the point was not that we were on his side, but that he was on ours!

I taught political economy to Joseph Harry Brown, Marxism to be exact, and I had an exacting method of teaching. We read *Das Kapital* chapter by chapter, and, when necessary, paragraph by paragraph. "Many have spoken of it, but few have really studied it. The legacy of the marxist tradition has served to all but remove the book from the battlefields of class struggle" (Cleaver 1979, 3). I taught by catechism, or by question and answer. This was partly required by the correspondence method of teaching. It was partly pleasure in the transmission of systematic thought, and it was certainly a method of exacting comprehension and avoiding ambiguity. Since there are thirty-three chapters in the first volume alone and I would write nine or ten questions per chapter, with review questions at the conclusion of each of the eight parts of *Das Kapital*, this made for quite a number of questions.

Some questions were designed to teach the fundamentals of the labor theory of value, such as the following. "Use-values must therefore never be looked upon as the real aim of the capitalist; neither must the profit on any single transaction. The restless never-ending process of profit making alone is what he aims at." Who strives for use-values? Who for surplus-value? Why does Marx in the chapter on the labor process refer to products and not to commodities? What is the difference between the exchange-value and the use-value of the commodity labor-power? "A single violin player is his own conductor; an orchestra requires a separate one." Even so, the capitalist conductor does more than mark time. What is his two-fold role? Does surplus-value originate in cheating?

Some questions were fundamental but without the particular terminology of political economy, such as: What determines the length of the working day? or with a terminology all their own, such as: What is "devil's dust"?

Many questions were designed to explain the origins of profit, or surplus-value: How does the capitalist conceal the difference between the necessary part of the working day and the surplus part of the working day? Why is it necessary to do this? Marx writes of the "decisive importance of the transformation of value and price of labor-power into the form of wages." Why is this so important to the capitalist mode of production? Are wages a means of purchase or a means of payment?

Questions that tended to call attention to prisons were naturally especially important. What conditions must precede the appearance of labor-power on the market? What is the relation between wages and the industrial reserve army? What forms does the relative surplus-population take? "From a social point of view the working class, even when not directly engaged in the labor process, is just as much an appendage of capital as the ordinary instruments of labor." What is Marx's reasoning? What consequences does it have for our analysis?

Nor were the questions always easy, and they might contain traps, such as: If the exchange-value of a raw material (say, cotton) alters in value (owing to overproduction or to shortages, for example), how is the value of the yarn into which it is made affected? If a textile manufacturer uses gold spindles (when under prevailing productive conditions steel would do just as well), how is the value of his product, yarn, affected?

Only rarely did our method of catechizing take us outside of the text itself. "To accumulate is to conquer the world of social wealth, to increase the mass of human beings exploited by him, and thus to extend both the direct and the indirect sway of the capitalist." What light does this throw on the problem of imperialism?

We drove to Illinois to award Joseph a bachelor of arts degree from Franconia College. This was done in a ceremony at which several other prisoners were also receiving degrees from other universities or colleges. There was a lot of ceremony at the occasion—flags, printed programs, speeches, and heartfelt pride of relatives; only the stale Wonder Bread sandwiches of cheap bologna reminded one of the location. I was beginning to feel some pride too. Later I learned that the print shop at Marion, Illinois, had printed up the questions I had been sending in the form of a pamphlet. Prison education, more so than college education, was an exchange. Coming back from a conference which had blown our minds, or approaching received wisdom in light of a prison experience, we had reason to quote Marx's Third Thesis on Feuerbach: "The materialist doctrine that men are products of circumstances and upbringing, and that, therefore, changed men are products of other circumstances and changed upbringing, forgets that it is men that change circumstances, and that the educator himself needs educating" (Marx 1959, 244).

Some prisoner movement people used to display a poster with Gene Debs saying something to the effect that, "While there is a soul in prison I am not free." We understood the sentiment, but strictly speaking we were happily driving on the highway while Joseph Harry Brown returned to his cell. Later Joe wrote an open letter to the prisoners of Brazil and he characterized the free enterprise system, as one

whereby the lives and labors are wrung from the ignorant and uneducated by the greedy and rapacious. Where, after a lifetime of work, one's meagre savings are wiped out by inflation or a spell of unemployment, where one's home is taken because mortgage payments cannot be met, where machinery is left idle and the workers turned away because a profit cannot be made, where men turn to crimes, sisters and daughters turn in despair to drugs or prostitution.[4]

The winds of repression were gathering force. Leaving Franconia to take employment at the University of Rochester initiated a hiatus in my prison teaching. Marxism was becoming imprisoned. Developments in the academic world and the prison world were changing. The introduction of chemotherapy and the development of special control units within prisons and of some prisons as special control units unto themselves were undermining the conditions of the prisoner movement. The atmosphere was no longer conducive to prison teaching. Chemotherapy turns people into zombies, incompatible with learning. Thought was not going to take wing while students shuffled along on thorazine.

Meanwhile, the changes in academia were many and manifold. Here I want to mention two intellectual developments. In one of these, *Crime and Social Justice*, the journal from Berkeley, California, had issued its editorial challenging street crime, and restoring, it seemed to me, the old moralizing notion of lumpenproletariat, a turn that left me dismayed.

Crime and Social Justice has been quick to support the defense committees of the San Quentin Six and Joan Little, to name two of the more recent celebrated political trials, while consistently refusing to join the conservative call for law and order in response to crime in the streets. Does this mean that we hold some twisted notions about right and wrong, that we uncritically view people ripping off citizens on the street as modern Robin Hoods or as individuals attempting to survive in the sense of Victor Hugo's Jean Valjean? Our response is an emphatic "NO!" Recent studies in criminology tend to either gloss over the issue of street crime or to portray it in romantic terms. Crime is often characterized as a form of primitive political rebellion or a rational attempt to survive under oppressive conditions. For some activities in specific historical periods, such as the spontaneous urban rebellions of the 1960s, this is certainly correct. But for most street crime, this Fanonist imagery serves to distort and glorify acts of reactionary individualism. (Editors 1976, 2)

The passage does not bear examination. Fanon does not offer images; he describes an experience. Of course, the experience differs in Africa and America, in the National Liberation Front and the Black Panther Party. Did the collective suggest that the spontaneous urban rebellions of the 1960s were activities of Robin Hoods? Robin Hood belonged to a period in the transition to capitalism in Europe, about five centuries ago. Not even the government inquiries suggested this. The concept of "street crime" is an unclear idea and hence repugnant to reasoning. I tried to understand the situation. The California comrades were facing especially severe repression in COINTELPRO. Ronald Reagan was elected governor, and he brought along his advisor, Edwin Meese, a half-baked criminology professor. Despite my efforts to understand, on the other side of the continent I felt abandoned by this tergiversation.

I wanted to remind them of Sam Melville, a founder of the Attica Anti-Depression League and a member of the Attica Liberation Front, who had handwritten a clandestine newsletter, called *The Iced Pig*, in the summer before George Jackson was killed and before the Attica holocaust. Even now, more than twenty years later, the urgency comes through in the abbreviations (t = the, u = you); speed was everything. In July 1971 he wrote the following:

Of primary importance is t coming awareness of ourselves as *political prisoners*. No matter how heinous t "crime" u have been convicted of, no matter how many people u offed, drugs u pushed, whores u ran, places u robbed, u are a political prisoner just as much as Angela. *Every act has a cause & effect*. T *cause* of your "crime" is that u found yourself in a society that offered no prospects for a life of fulfillment & sharing with your brothers & sisters. A society where u were taught to compete & beat t guy next to u because if u didn't, he'd beat u. A society whose every facet and angle is thoroughly controlled by t Pigdogs of t corporation giants of Amerika. T apparent *effect* of your "crime" is that now u find yourself locked behind tons of steel & concrete, completely brutalized, cut off from any warmth & affection. But t *real effect* is that u have become waste material to Amerika's ruling class. (Melville 1972, 161–62)

We can look at his argument juridically and we can look at it philosophically. Juridically, Sam says that no matter what your crime was, you are a political prisoner. The Crime and Social Justice Collective shows us an inert idea: What crime you committed is everything. Sam Melville shows us an idea in motion. The contrast, philosophically, is between Being and Becoming, between a dead idea and a live idea. The idea was in motion, and so was the situation. At one moment, August 1971, racism and division were rampant in the prison; at the next moment, September 1971, unity and solidarity among ethnic groups seized the world's attention. Action changes ideas: Right action precedes right ideas: the owl of Minerva flies at dusk when the day is done. Seize the Time, was a Panther slogan. Objectively, the situation had changed by the mid-1970s: The trend now was an absolute growth of the prison population. Time serving replaced time seizing.

I was closer to the other academic development. In 1975 we graduate students at the University of Warwick published *Albion's Fatal Tree: Crime and Society in Eighteenth Century England*. In this we resolutely argued against that division between lumpenproletariat and well-dressed proletariat (in German *lumpen* means "ragged"), but its companion volume, *Whigs and Hunters*, written by our guide, E. P. Thompson, concluded with an unqualified hymn of praise to the rule of law, worthy in my rebellious opinion to Nebuchadnezzar himself. Thompson was seriously distancing himself from the antinomian generosity. In the spring of 1980 the Critical Legal Studies conference was held in Buffalo, New York, opening on the birthday of Walt Whitman, who gave us an American expression of antinomian generosity:

Let me have my own way,
Let others promulge the laws, I will make no account of
the laws,

> Let others praise eminent men and hold up peace, I hold up agitation and
>   conflict.[5]

> You felons on trial in courts,
> You convicts in prison-cells, you sentenced assassins chain'd and
>   handcuff'd with iron,
> Who am I too that I am not on trial or in prison?
> Me ruthless and devilish as any, that my wrists are not chain'd with iron,
>   or my ankles with iron?[6]

Later E. P. Thompson wrote, echoing conversations we had had, "People starve: their survivors think in new ways about the market. People are imprisoned: in prison they meditate in new ways about the law. In the face of such general experiences old conceptual systems may crumble and new problematics insist upon their presence" (1978, 201). It should be noted that he does not say that "the lumpenproletariat is imprisoned." He does not say that "criminals are imprisoned." He writes about people. Old conceptual systems were crumbling, new problematics were knocking at the door. People *were* imprisoned, and they *did* meditate. However, our experience was that they meditated less upon the law than upon freedom. At Walpole, they said "the guns and the keys."

"He is great, powerful, formidable, the man with the white hair, for he has in his pocket the mighty talisman which makes one man cry, and one man pray, and one laugh, and one cough, and one walk, and all keep awake and listen and think the same maddening thought," says "The Walker" in Arturo Gionvannitti's poem composed in Salem Jail after the 1912 Lawrence Textile Strike (Kornbluh 1972, 186). There were, and there are, other ways of getting out than by meditating upon the law. The prison can be attacked from the outside, and this has happened—from the Peasant's Revolt of 1381 to the Gordon Riots of 1780, and in our time in Port-au-Prince (1991). Individuals can escape. Amnesty can be declared, as medieval kings used to do on their coronation. Leadbelly sang his way out. Laws that are made can be unmade.

What was missing from this is the "history from below" of the Warren Court. Each of the decisions granting more room to the prisoner, acknowledging some human rights to the defendant, was brought about by a prisoner. Lawyers like to take the credit. Two exceptions have been published: the right to counsel and the right to remain silent—Anthony Lewis, *Gideon's Trumpet* (1967) and Liva Baker, *Miranda: Crime, Law and Politics* (1983). There are powerful historical forces behind particular petitioners. In Gideon's case, this determination was of a southwestern Depression worker; in *Miranda*, it was of the Chicano struggle. But a true history from below approach to the Supreme Court remains to be written. There was no doubt where our legal rights originated: They arose at the base, down on the ground, among the grass roots, down to earth. Of course, lawyers helped. A superstructure was needed. We had a living example of the relationship in jury work.

A lasting achievement of the Attica defense was the National Jury Project, which put nonlawyers back in the courtroom and which renewed an old, old debate. In 1649, the year of the beheading of King Charles I during the English Revolution, it was said, "Take a cobbler from his seat, or a butcher from his shop, or any other tradesman that is an honest and just man, and let him hear the case and determine the same, and then betake himself to his work again." We liked the attitude. This was the maturity of people who scorned professional writ writers. We learned of the legal struggle in Vietnam to open up the juries on courts-martial, especially in mutiny and disobedience charges, to enlisted men, where formerly only officers had served. Although I had left my direct association with prison teaching, I by no means had left behind what I had learned, which came in handy when the 1,199-member Hospital and Health Care Workers Union went on strike at the University of Rochester. Four organizers were put on trial for arson. We organized a jury project. I thought back to the feminist criticism I had heard in London: By defense work we were going to clean up our own messes, and, indirectly, we had the Attica brothers to thank for it.

ATTICA AND THE BURNT-OUT DISTRICT (1979–1981)

It took an hour to drive from Rochester to Attica, through country that became increasingly desolate: potato farming, hidden factories, a salt mine. The prison was mammoth, yet it had these itty-bitty towers. Visitors were advised to lock their cars which did not inspire confidence in the maximum security. The screening and searching was not very good—no fault of the guards of course, who were friendly enough once they understood you were part of the routine. The metal detector was defective—a friend once walked in with a Swiss army knife.

"This is the end of the line. The next step is the death house." That is how Attica was introduced to me by one of my students. By the time I started teaching in Attica I knew one or two things that were owed to Attica. We knew that the teaching itself was a result of the holocaust, as the massacre of September 1971 was termed. Holocaust refers to sacrifice by fire. As a sacrifice, something is lost and something is gained. Education was one of the concessions that had been made. The library was another. So we came to a place with a tradition, and with pride in that history. This made history teaching easier. Forty-four men had died for these advantages.

"Attica, formerly the hunting grounds of the Seneca tribe of the Iroquois nation," began Sam Melville's first letter from Attica. Not far away in Cattaraugus, in the lands of the Seneca Reservation, my own parents lay buried. Indian ways surrounded us, as ghosts. These were the people whom Lewis Henry Morgan had studied and whose matriarchal communism influenced Friedrich Engels and through him became widely known throughout the world, perhaps the most well-known primary communists. The whole area was known historically as the Burnt-Out District. In class, Tom Skye, an Indian, said of the guards, "It beats working. Being a hack, all you need to know in order to qualify is how to count to 40 and swing a club." Then he asked, "What shall I do with this education? I could go out and invent pet rocks, or go to the reservation, make beads, mumble mumbo-jumbo and collect money."

We teachers had a specific role within the total institution. We were like the laundry room, or the kitchen, or the yard. We provided a place, a situation, where people could get together and talk among themselves. Otherwise, there was no such occasion. We were like the barber shop of old. In the few minutes before class, in the break during the middle of our two-hour meeting, and at the end of class, when books were being gathered up, papers were being put in order, and the students were returning to the hallway for the march back to their cells, people could have private discussions with whom they chose. I had much respect for the Genesee Community College which had already established its traditions, one of which was the prohibition of firearms in the classroom. Guards were welcome in the classroom, but not with their firearms. If they attended armed, we greeted their presence with silence. Once we had to explain this informal rule to the warden who favored us with a visit accompanied by an armed guard. The atmosphere of learning must be an atmosphere without fear or danger. Otherwise, how can the lamps burn?

On August 23, 1979, Lt. Donohue gave me an hour's lecture on "orientation" to the Attica Correctional Facility. This consisted of an opening statement, the reading aloud of the rules, the reading of the rules in silence, and the signing of a statement saying that the rules had been read. I then was taken to a display case containing makeshift knives, pipes, and other weapons, a case meant I suppose to provide physical evidence of the dangers awaiting. He introduced me to the guards' culture, with its icons and magic. He knew the whereabouts of the New York State death stick. Did I? Did I even know what it was? Donohue withdrew an old photograph from his desk drawer and showed me "Death Stick" Morris, the last man the condemned of New York State would have any contact with on earth. Morris escorted the condemned to the electric chair. He carried a thick, steel-weighted stick, about four feet in length, which he used to make sure that the condemned prisoner kept his distance. Following electrocution Morris carved the name of the unfortunate on the stick. A few years ago, an old woman died near Auburn where Donohue had spent most of his years. From her he learned that the stick was in her nephew's possession. He knows the location of his house and in which room the death stick may be found. That is all that Donohue would tell.

Donohue possessed a complete set of every postcard ever printed in New York State of the electric chair. He wished to frame and display these treasures at some appropriate place within the prison, such as the visitor's area or reception and administration area. His reason for not doing this struck an unexpectedly familiar chord with me. He would not mount an exhibit of the postcards because he believed the other guards would steal them. I had a similar lament about putting papers, booklets, or pamphlets of mine in the Reserve Reading Room at the University of Rochester. Lt. Donohue and I both believed our colleagues were thieves!

I was to teach "The History of Mankind, Including Women, from the Beginning to the Present." There would be fourteen classes. Assigned reading consisted of Kenneth Neill Cameron's *Humanity and Society: A World History*. At the beginning of my notebook, I had transcribed several quotations from Leo Huberman's essay called "How to Spread the Word." The good teacher never teaches a lesson without using the blackboard, and he should insist that the basic points he writes on the blackboard should be recorded by the students in a notebook, along with other notes they choose to take themselves. There is a sound reason for the blackboard and the notebook: some people learn by hearing; some people learn by seeing; some people learn only by combination of all these. I also transcribed, "The lecturer teaches subject matter; the teacher teaches people. The difference is crucial." I believed that I was a lecturer.

Malcolm X had said,

Of all our studies, history is best qualified to reward our research. And when you see that you've got problems, all you have to do is examine the historic method used all over the world by others who have problems similar to yours. Once you see how they got theirs straight, then you know how you can get yours straight.

Willy Sutton wrote in *Where The Money Is*,

I had made myself a vow in Dannemora that I would never allow them to imprison my mind. . . . I studied the religions of the world, went on crusades to search for the Lost Grail, smelled the foul air of the Spanish dungeons under Torquemada (that was easy), and attended the witch trials at Salem. I was spectator at the amphitheatre at Rome, and listened to the dying groans of the fallen gladiators.

On the first day, I began to lecture on the history of the world from the beginning. Having quoted Malcolm X and Willy Sutton, I proceeded to the Archbishop of Armagh who, in 1650, had set the origin of mankind at 9:00 A.M., October 23, 4004 B.C. I hoped that making fun of the Christians would get the attention of the students. But what does make us human? What gives us a history? Bipedal motion was my answer at the time—endurance and ability to carry loads over long distances. We could amble, stride, jog, sprint, walk, and saunter. A primate specialist might say, Without split-second timing man would fall flat on his face; in fact with each step he takes, he teeters on the edge of catastrophe. We are human too because of characteristics of our vision—we have a high point of view, commanding a greater field of vision; we can see more. We have depth perception and color vision. Our forward limbs are liberated. We can grab, carry, manipulate, or caress with fifty-eight distinctly different motions. With power grip and precision grip, we can play the violin, wring a towel, flip the bird, pull a trigger. We have been on earth for two million years, 99 percent of that time as hunters and gatherers. That experience determined our nature, I was trying to teach. Our earliest weapons were spheroids, the bolas that brought down Goliath. We learned cooperative activity with young, old, male, and female. Analysis of the distribution of ashes, bone, and tools at Ambrona, Spain, indicated the egalitarian distribution of food. I quoted Smohalla of the Nez Perce Indians: "My young men shall never work. Men who work cannot dream; and wisdom comes to us in dreams." I quoted Chief Luther Standing Bear: "The man who sat on the ground in his tipi meditating on life and its meaning, accepting the kinship of all creatures and acknowledging unity with the universe of things was infusing into his being the true essence of civilization."

After the first day teaching I wrote, "I spoke without stopping for 2½ hours, with the result of learning little about my students." I changed my teaching goals and methods. I had a new method: I was no longer going to lecture, others were. I had two goals: to bring insiders together and to bring outsiders in.

The students expressed their educational philosophy. "I want to know where my culture fits into the history of humanity," said one. "Wind, rain, and the elements can knock you down. Education is a stalk. History provides roots," said another. On a quiz I had asked, "Would you rather live in Paleolithic times or now and why?" Elijah Watson, who was in the box, or solitary confinement, wrote back, "I want to create history, not be history." "As Salaam Alaikum!" his letter began. He explained what Islam meant to him. First, he pointed out, "The Man don't control Islam," but he also made it clear, second, that "if the Imam bull shit, I'll call it to his attention." Later, he'd pass on to me his wisdom, "You grow from the head down, not from the feet up." "Once a man can make you shut up, you might as well be a rock or a tree."

"Everybody in the world knows about Attica, the guy here from Italy proved that." Our first guest lecturer was Professor Bruno Cartosio, the editor of *Primo Maggio*, a student of American labor history who had written about the Johnson-Forest tendency in the late 1940s, and a professor at the University of Milan. He brought the news from the factories in Italy, and from its prisons, now multiplied, as a result of the militarization of the struggle by the Red Brigades which he opposed unequivocally. Carl Sandburg had written about a similar dilemma in U.S. history:

> I sat with a dynamiter at supper in a German saloon
> eating steak and onions.
> And he laughed and told stories of his wife and children
> and the cause of labor and the working class.
> It was laughter of an unshakable man knowing life to be
> a rich and red-blooded thing.
> Yes, his laugh rang like the call of grey birds filled with
> a glory of joy ramming their winged flight through a
> rain storm.
> His name was in many newspapers as an enemy of the
> nation and few keepers of churches or schools
> open their doors to him.
> Over the steak and onions not a word was said of his
> deep days and nights as a dynamiter.
> Only I always remember him as a lover of life, a lover
> of children, a lover of all free, reckless laughter
> everywhere—lover of red hearts and red blood the
> world over.[7]

Our second guest lecturer was the distinguished Buddhist scholar, Dr. Neil McMullin, a former Jesuit who had given away the parish treasury to the parishioners in Tokyo. He had been a professional hockey player. He gave a lecture on Islam and Eastern religions. Talik, a prisoner whose spiritual exercises were deeply respected, honored our class with a visit to explain the Muslim call to prayer. One winter night he faced Mecca and sang the call in his beautiful voice. He explained that the first muezzin was an Ethiopian slave and companion to Mohammad.

Cardell Shaird, or "Blood," his prison moniker, was the librarian. He honored book learning. He studied Bakunin and Kropotkin. I was interested in dogmatic exchanges, but he brushed these aside with amused recognition but respect for sectarian argument. He understood while I was still learning that we had better things to do with our time. He was president of the Afro-American Cultural Studies Group (Linebaugh 1982). He organized the meeting in Attica honoring Martin Luther King Jr. Day, and he asked me to invite my boss at the University of Rochester, the historian Eugene Genovese, who peremptorily declined. On M. L. King Day the Afro-American Cultural Studies Group put on a program which included outside speakers. I was honored to be among them. All of us spoke our minds, and I can assure you that the guards did not like it one bit. It was widely believed that the Ku Klux Klan had a strong presence among them at Attica. It is a known fact that they are strong elsewhere in the state system, at Elmyra Reformatory for example.

Cynicism was widespread. Some of it was wide awake, such as, "Rockefeller hires a cotton picker to keep a potato picker down" or "To kill the Indians they hire Irish who're starving because of the potato famine. They're just blue-eyed niggers." And some of it was somnolent: "The World

Continues to rotate and Contradiction is the very basis for this Consistent rotation and so life goes on and the Courts uphold the laws of the Very rich, protecting the property and values of the Very fortunate . . ." ZZZzzzzzzzzzzzzz.

We read Rousseau. "The savage . . . breathes only peace and liberty; he desires only to live and be free from labor." And I think we all were ready to be savages. "I see him," wrote Rousseau, "satisfying his hunger at the first oak, and slaking his thirst at the first brook; finding his bed at the foot of the tree which afforded him a repast; and, with that, all his wants supplied." This was not the human nature known at Attica. People also desired to be useful to one another, as well as to love and to be loved. The students pointed out to me what their experience made it second nature to recognize: Rousseau, like Robinson Crusoe, was motivated by fear.

On Europe in the Renaissance we read Fernand Braudel, *Capitalism and Material Life, 1400–1800*. It was not a popular book. Its margins were narrow and the print was small, and he writes about the dust of history. Rockne Duncan, another student, summed up Renaissance dust:

Because I drive a Mercedes-Benz, because I wear Gucci loafers, because Vidal Sasoon is my hair stylist, I am a superior person. This is perhaps the hardest transition for a man who's been in prison to make. Because in prison a man is what he is. In society, however, a man is what he has in his pockets. Not helping the situation is the constant bombardment of bullshit by the men on Madison Avenue.[8]

The next course I taught at Attica was called "The American Worker." I had asked the distinguished historian George Rawick for advice. He warned against workers' control ideology which was, at the time, the practice of self-policing. I asked Marty Glaberman, the eminent sociologist, for his help as well. Both agreed that Cloward and Piven's *Poor People's Movements* would make a good text. From their account of the unemployment movement of the 1930s, the sections on "electricity squads" and "gas squads" easily evoked the widest response. Everyone had a story to tell about how he had outwitted the gas and electric company or had obtained free power by tapping into municipal sources. The stories ranged from Atlanta ("keeping two mean dogs in the basement") to Buffalo where employees of Niagara-Mohawk dispensed their skills to neighbors. In New York City, lines were simply run across the sidewalk to the city power lines on telephone poles. This free energy required an annual change of habitation, at least, to stay one step ahead of the authorities. Literally, these students knew how to keep the lamps burning even in desperate circumstances.

A third outside lecturer was Earl Smith, who lectured on the 1939 Mombasa General Strike in Kenya. He quoted Pliny the Elder: *Ex Africa semper aliquid novi*, "Africa always has something new." Then he quoted Eugene Debs, "The capitalists own the tools they do not use, and the workers use the tools they do not own." We had learned about Africa before;

one of the students was a learned nationalist who introduced me to J. A. Rogers, and openly wondered, since I had never read Rogers, what my qualifications to teach history could possibly be. It is true that I knew little African history, so my ears were wide open when Earl Smith explained how Chinese and Indian workers had built the railways from the interior to the coast, by forced labor, or slavery. That was in 1905. He explained how the English and Australian settlers organized large-scale enterprises, agricultural plantations of tea, coffee, cotton, and ground nuts. The agricultural laborers formerly had owned the land, communally. He showed how the railway and dock workers were the most militant, even though the grievance committees were divided by ethnicity, even though they worked a seven-day week and a twelve-hour day. He explained how the missionaries were used by the workers and how Christianity could become dangerous.

David Hardisky, formerly a brakeman on the New York Central, a worker in Southern California too at Douglas Aircraft, had come back east to become a Ph.D. candidate at the University of Rochester. He spoke about the Rochester General Strike of 1946, against the prevailing view that there was no working class in Rochester. He told us about the strikes of that year; 6 million workers walked out in America. In Rochester it was led by the ash can collectors and the garbage workers. They made 50¢ an hour, working twelve hours a day. Thirty thousand struck. The Department of Public Works was Italian, foremen were Irish; Bausch and Lomb hired Germans. This kind of analysis was music to the ears of students at Attica. The Italians had been disenfranchised in the 1920s. He gave background to the strike. It was after 1877 that armories were constructed in American industrial cities, generally along the railway tracks. He quoted the preamble of the IWW. Students wanted to know about the history of the Teamsters and the meaning of the "Internationale." Asked about the role of the church, he quoted a prayer,

> I pray dear Lord for Jesus' sake,
> Give us this day a T-Bone steak,
> Hallowed be thy Holy name,
> But don't forget to send the same.

Gary Gorton, the economist and our fourth lecturer, had worked with the wildcat strike of the 1973 Independent Truckers' strike. He was an economist. He gave a lecture whose title he wrote on the board, "Their Economy and Ours: What Is Money and How to Get It." There are six ways of getting money—to make it, to sell something for it, to work for it, to borrow it, to steal it, or to get it from the government. They organize us by dividing us, and they use money to accomplish this. We can change the power relations, he instructed, like the Wobblies did, or the unemployed of the 1930s, or the Black Power movement. "Communism is what we want," said Kenneth Smalls. "Well, how do you get that?" Gary Gorton replied and said encouragingly, "You've probably got ideas." Smalls replied, "Yeh, I had an idea and that's why I'm here."

Rockne Duncan wrote how he saw the economy working:

Everyone gets caught in the lame's role. The honest, law abiding citizen engages a prostitute. The prostitute turns over the proceeds to her pimp. The pimp is cheated out of the money in some crap hole. The gambler splurges it all on cocaine. In turn, the Cocaine Man makes a Bee line to the local Cadillac dealer, with his accumulated profits. The Cadillac dealer isn't above sporting with girls. The cycle is renewed. Of course there are several variations as to how this farce can be carried out.[9]

Carl Estabrook, a fifth lecturer, came to teach about Aristotle and Plato. He defined dialectics as mutually influential interaction in which both parties are changed. The Romans jailed the Christians because, by believing in only one god, they were atheists vis-à-vis all the other gods. "It doesn't matter what you believe, as long as you are on your knees." Why did the Roman patricians want the Christians on their knees? It was simple, but none of us had thought of it. The Christians were the urban proletariat. The word "pagan," he elaborated, originally meant a countryman. He explained how Roman civilization was defeated by technology based on the stirrup. In the discussion; one student commented, "There can be no boss without people giving their authority to him." And another contributed, "The only way to change this class society is to understand it." It was clear to all of us that Carl's lamp had been burning for a long time.

Lee Smith, our sixth lecturer, when confronted with his first shut gate in the labyrinth from the intake center to the classroom, did not wait for a guard to open it; he pushed it open himself, reminding me of *The Can Opener*, the Wobbly newspaper in the Cook County Jail. Lee was an organizer with the Western New York Committee on Occupational Safety and Health. He said that 2.2 million people get hurt on the job every year. Each year 100,000 die from work-related causes. He got people talking about their injuries on the job—Tom Skye had lost a thumb on a ninety-ton press; Ed Laraby had his foot crushed at a Schenectady steel plant. He reminded us that the substances causing such a toxic stink in Love Canal were once in the workplace. Chevy Buffalo removed safety regulations to speed up production. Today's employer wants the worker's time and health. Why are plastic garbage bags considered progress? They are not biodegradable. They cause cancer to those who make them. Companies reduce the cab size, and truckers lose their hearing. He explained to us that our first line of defense comprises the five senses. He concluded with an organizer's tribute to Saul Alinsky, who said that as long as you can supply people with action they will be with you. Even as he admired him, he questioned. Alinsky taught that arrests demobilize an organization. Lee noted that, "Jail, No Bail," the slogan in the Civil Rights Movement, disproved him. He provided a magnificent conclusion to the course.

At Attica, after ten years of learning, I felt I had learned how to teach. The students there told me that if I had something to say, then I should say it, and to listen while someone else is speaking. These were lasting gifts. It was at this moment that I was let go from the University of Rochester. I shall not say that certain chickens had come home to roost; instead, I would like to tell a Creek fable.

The Terrapin proposed to the Wolf a race, and he scornfully accepted. The race was to begin at the top of one hill and to extend to a fourth hill. That night the Terrapin summoned all his kinsfolk to help him and they were to take their stations all along the route, each to wear a white feather on his head. The time came, the word was given, and when the Wolf reached the top of the second hill he saw a Terrapin ahead of him running down the hill; the white feather waving in the grass. He soon passed him, but, on reaching the third hill, there was the Terrapin still crawling ahead. He ran himself out of breath, but, on reaching the last hilltop, to his mortification there sat a Terrapin at the stake, his plume waving in triumph. (Nabokov and MacLean 1980, 5)

NOTES

1. The IWW poem was reproduced in *The Literary Digest* (1919, April 19), p. 72. It is also one of several appearing in *Rebel Voices: An IWW Anthology* (Kornbluh 1972), p. 61.

2. "Stackolee" appears in Bruce Jackson's *"Get Your Ass in the Water and Swim Like Me": Narrative Poetry from Black Oral Tradition*, by Bruce Jackson, 1974. Reprinted by permission of Harvard University Press, Cambridge, MA. Copyright © 1974 by the President and Fellows of Harvard College.

3. See "New Song," in Jim Fleming and Peter Lamborn Wilson's (eds.), *U.S.A.* (New York: Semiotext(e), 1987), pp. 240–48.

4. Letter from Joseph Harry Brown is from the author's files.

5. From "My self and Mine," in Walt Whitman's *Leaves of Grass* (London: Cassell and Company, 1909), p. 231.

6. From "You Felons on Trial in Courts," in Walt Whitman's *Leaves of Grass* (London: Cassell and Company, 1909), p. 360.

7. From the "Dynamiter," in Carl Sandburg's *Chicago Poems* (New York: Henry Holt and Company, 1916), p. 44.

8. Rockne Duncan's comments and those of other students are from the author's files.

9. See note 8.

6

Teaching "Criminology" to "Criminals"

Edward Sbarbaro

This chapter examines how teaching critical criminology, using pedagogical methods influenced by the work of Paulo Freire, affects prisoners-students' understanding of the criminal justice system. It is based on my experiences teaching critical criminology during a five-year period in Colorado state prisons.

Critical criminology means breaking through the myths that legitimate the criminal justice system in order to expose the political and economic roots of crime and punishment in society.[1] Courses have included criminological theory, deviance, punishment and corrections, juvenile delinquency, and crimes of the powerful.[2] Although I taught critical criminology content during the entire period, Freirian methods were adopted gradually. Freire's methods as described in *Pedagogy of the Oppressed* (1970) were particularly relevant because the situation of prisoners in the United States is similar to that of Third World people, who are oppressed by ideologies and institutions that dominate through violent forms of social control. Critical pedagogy begins with a rejection of conventional methods of teaching—what Freire calls the "banking" concept.

Education thus becomes an act of depositing, in which the students are the depositories and the teacher is the depositor. Instead of communicating, the teacher issues communiques and makes deposits which the students patiently receive, memorize, and repeat. This is the "banking" concept of education, in which the scope of action allowed to the students extends only as far as receiving, filing, and storing the deposits. . . . In the banking concept of education, knowledge is a gift bestowed by those who consider themselves knowledgeable upon those whom they consider to know nothing. (1970, 58)

In critical education, dialogue replaces depositing. This necessitates student/teacher partnership in which the views and experiences of the student are expressed and respected. Paulo Freire equates critical educators with the genuine revolutionary leaders who

do not go to the people in order to bring them a message of "salvation," but in order to come to know through dialogue with them their *objective situation* and their *awareness* of the situation, . . . the various levels of perception of themselves and of the world in which and with which they exist. (p. 84)

In the criminology courses I taught using Freirian methods, I began each topic with students working independently, at first reading critical criminology materials and preparing essays that encouraged reflection and analysis. Then, the students met with me in small groups to discuss the readings and relate them to their experiences. During the period of study, specific issues emerged repeatedly in the discussions and student essays. These I call *resonating issues*, which can be grouped into three topics: the social construction of crime and punishment, crime and social structure, and alienation. In order to re-present here the exchange that took place on these topics, I first outline the theoretical information presented to the students for each topic. Then I reproduce a selection of comments drawn from students' essays that demonstrate how the topics illuminated their experiences and analysis of crime and punishment. I conclude each topic with a brief observation on this exchange on critical criminology.

ON THE SOCIAL CONSTRUCTION OF CRIME AND PUNISHMENT

The core texts read by the students who participated in the criminology courses discussed in this chapter were *Exploring Criminology* (1988) and *On the Take* (1978) by William Chambliss, *The Criminal Elite* (1989) by James Coleman, and *The Rich Get Richer and the Poor Get Prison* (1990) by Jeffery Reiman. Most students in the courses simultaneously enrolled in a class called "Mass Media and Alienation," for which they read Richard Schmitt's *Alienation and Class* (1983), Michael Parenti's *Inventing Reality: The Politics of the Mass Media* (1986), and Erving Goffman's *Asylums* (1961).

At the beginning of these criminology courses, prison students have been well aware that the size of the incarcerated population of the United States has exploded and that the poor, the uneducated, and minorities are overly represented in prisons and jails. They were also cognizant of the criminal justice system information that insists that crime is on the rise and that the poor and minorities are the criminal element. Students begin their study of criminology by reading parts of Reiman's and Chambliss's books which analyze how the production and dissemination of official crime statistics construct a particular image of crime and criminals. This image emphasizes street crime by excluding from the definition of criminal activity harm caused by corporate activity and government policy. The Unified Crime Report (UCR), compiled and published by the Federal Bureau of Investigation (FBI), justifies this ideology in a cloak of scientism.

UCR information is considered to be the most authoritative source of criminal justice statistics. The statistics are used by the media, government departments, politicians, and all research centers. However, the UCR is not an independent audit of the criminal justice system. Those agencies that stand to gain most from statistical evidence showing either a rise or fall in the crime rate are the same agencies that collect and interpret the data. Since the UCR is based on crimes reported to the police and the police are not required to verify the actual occurrence of the crimes they in turn report, the police can manipulate the data in a number of ways. For example, if a politician who ran a "tough on crime" campaign seeks reelection, with sufficient influence she or he can arrange to adjust the number of crimes reported to suit her or his purposes, a strategy actually used by Richard Nixon when he sought a second term as president (Milakovich and Weiss 1975).

Students learn that the main focus of the UCR is street crime, specifically, assault, murder, rape, robbery, larceny, and car theft—crimes within the enforcement scope of local police. However, this list does not include all serious forms of crime. In fact, state and corporate crimes (suite crimes) typically involve more money and harm than street crimes. But, street crimes are reported to and acted upon by police, who in turn report them to the FBI. From reading Coleman's book, students learn that suite crimes are reported to and acted upon by regulatory agencies (if reported at all) and thereby escape being recorded in the UCR. Following the media, which support their own corporate interests and political campaigns, the public has come to equate crime with street crime, which it fears as the most serious threat to its well-being. Meanwhile, corporate and state crime is kept out of the picture.

The following student's comment shows how the foregoing analysis of the social construction of crime is a resonate issue that needs to be discussed early on in making sense of crime and punishment:

There was, however, one issue that captured my attention in this . . . course, that being the so called "ideological message" of the American criminal justice system. This subject hit home with me in a big way because like most people in this country, I was raised to believe that our government and its representatives (the state), would always act on my/our behalf and for the common good. In this course I have learned that this is an ideological message which the ruling class, and the established institutions in this country use to eliminate any threat to power. This subtle, yet powerful message, combined with the "false image" of crime that the criminal justice system conveys to the public, ensures the continued existence of the status quo, by providing a smoke screen that allows the rich and powerful to conduct business as usual without fear of the law. (Marcus Huber)

The media's role in reproducing criminal justice system ideology is an issue which resonates strongly among prison students, as demonstrated by Donald Clay's remarks:

In the media, a certain image of crime and the typical criminal responsible for same is fabricated and polished. Crime, it should be noted, is a serious social problem— all crime. However, the media does not focus on all crimes. Instead, crime is portrayed through the media as one-on-one street crime, committed by youthful thugs of color and questionable moral character. This image represents a half truth and is therefore an abject lie, since the crimes of corporations are omitted. Thus the prevailing image of crime—young, black, urban male—is formed and perpetrated through propagandistic news coverage and vivid portrayal of street crime in prime TV programming.

Discussions regarding the social construction of crime require students to assess their assumptions critically. I have observed in the classroom that prisoners, like all newcomers to the study of criminology, tacitly assume there is consensus about deviance, that people agree on what is right and wrong, that this agreement is embodied in the law, and that this consensus legitimates the criminal justice system. The preceding comments suggest that students can successfully break through this myth. This breakthrough parallels the Freirian conception of transcending magic and naive consciousness as a transitional stage toward a more critical consciousness (Freire 1981, 41–58). Initially, students come to realize that deviance is really a matter of "who can pin a label on whom." The next stage is to move beyond this critique of the consensus myth in order to consider the political economy of crime. At this point, the concepts of ideology and class are introduced and students come to see that labeling is usually in the interest of the ruling class.

STRUCTURAL ANALYSIS OF CRIME AND PUNISHMENT

Early in these discussions, students favor a conspiratorial conception of crime and punishment. This perspective is challenged by asking them to consider Parenti's argument that while the ruling class is not above conspiracy, a more accurate understanding sees its power as the result of a shared interest in maintaining existing economic interests (1986, 224). To approach this understanding, students are asked to consider structures of power and wealth from the perspective of the structural contradictions theory of law and crime.

Students read Chambliss's *Exploring Criminology* in order to examine a comprehensive theory of crime that goes beyond the social construction of crime statistics and recognizes that crime is ubiquitous and is committed by all people, but enforcement is reserved for the working class. Chambliss explains that the central structural contradiction of capitalism is between private ownership and public production. This results in two classes: a ruling class which privately controls the economic resources and an exploited working class which publicly produces goods and services. The quest for cheap labor necessitates a surplus labor force and "run-a-way" shops resulting in unemployment and low wages. In pursuing their respective interests, the working class will endeavor to increase its income while the ruling class will pursue greater profits. Members of both groups may be tempted by illegal activity; for example, pilfering by workers and price fixing by industrialists. The state, according to Chambliss, must appear to control this illegal activity; that is, it must seem to be relatively autonomous of the interests of either class in order to appear as sustaining the rule of law. Thus, within limits a government will pass laws that criminalize the predatory behavior of both classes and thereby ameliorate the class struggle and preserve state legitimacy. But on balance, when it comes to enforcement and punishment, the full force of the state is directed at the crimes of the working class while the crimes of the ruling class are sanctioned by inaction. While the latter may actually do greater damage to a greater number of people, students learn from reading Reiman's *The Rich Get Richer and the Poor Get Prison* that the degree of harm does not determine the state's response.

The criminal justice system does not protect us against the gravest threats to life, limb, or possessions. Its definitions of crime are not simply a reflection of the objective dangers that threaten us. The workplace, the medical profession, the air we breathe, and poverty we refuse to rectify lead to far more human suffering, far more death and disability, and take far more dollars from our pockets than the murders, aggravated assaults, and thefts reported annually by the FBI. What is more this is human suffering that is preventable. (1990, 78)

Thus, corporations face the soft glove of regulatory agencies and fines while the poor face the iron hand of the police and prisons. A facade of equality (i.e., the rule of law) legitimizes the state, but the reality is the disproportionate incarceration of the working class (Keller and Sbarbaro 1995). Conventional criminology has ignored class conflict. It has explained the high incidence of poor people and people of color in prisons as indicative of some pathology, individual or cultural. Critical criminology rejects pathology theories, which blame the victims of social and legal injustice for their situation, and examines instead structural contradictions responsible for the disproportionate representation of the poor and minority groups among prison populations.

Structural analysis of crime and punishment resonates strongly among prison students. For David Jensen an accurate appraisal of the harm of crime is illuminating:

Our politicians emphasize street crime as the major threat to our society. Most street crimes are committed by the less fortunate. With the emphasis on street crime being the most dangerous to society, the rich and powerful gain control of the less fortunate by prosecuting them to prison for their crimes. The rich and powerful are able to draw attention away from crimes they commit, white collar crime, with the emphasis being on street crime. Statistically though, white collar crime is usually more damaging to society. When someone commits fraud, for instance, the amount of money involved is much greater than the man committing robbery. . . . The person committing murder will not kill as many people as a company which pollutes the environment.

This student describes her personal experience with the structural inequities of punishment:

One of the first things that angered me as I read *The Criminal Elite* was the story about the children's clothing that was supposed to be fire retardant but proved to be very flammable. This hit a nerve with me because I am currently serving an eight year sentence for an accidental fire. I was in a bar on December 27, 1986, and accidentally started a Christmas tree on fire. . . . The entire bar burned. Two men died in the fire and two women were injured.

Originally, a man was arrested for the crime with three witnesses saying he did it. I could not live with what I had done so I turned myself in and took responsibility for the tragedy. While reading *The Criminal Elite*, I was struck by the feeling that I was the only one who took responsibility for this crime. The bar was made of wood and had no fire extinguisher or sprinkler system. They found the two men close to the rear fire exit that had been chained and locked to prevent people from sneaking in without paying the cover charge. I am in no way blaming others or denying my responsibility. I just feel now that others shared in the responsibility. No one from the children's clothing company spent a day in jail for their crime. I am angered still as I write this. (Tina Gellner)

A structural analysis which connects power, law, and ideology to crime resonates in the comments of these students:

I believe that there is a major problem in the ideology and the structure of government in America. Most people point fingers of blame toward the social-psychological make-up of individuals in society and to street crime as the cause for deviance in America; however, the ideology of this capitalistic society and the inherent structural defects in politics, and the judicial, legislative, and executive systems of government on both the federal and state levels not only seem to initiate the deviant behavior in this society, but moreover these systems push to sustain this behavior in the white collar sector. Deviant behavior in the white collar sector enhances the achievement of the established social goals of capitalism: wealth and power for the elite and the maintenance of the separation in a two class system. (Michael Marant)

Wealth and high income permit the affluent a means to avoid the process of [prison] degradation reserved for the underclass. Our criminal justice system is a two tier system of injustice. Crimes by the affluent are either ignored totally or treated lightly vis-à-vis the treatment of individuals relegated to lower class status. The relationship between those with economic clout and the criminal justice system protecting their economic interest is appallingly clear when legal representation is required. In the courtroom . . . the wealthy have access to the finest attorneys . . . and the poor are assigned to counsel of questionable ability. . . . This fraudulent disparity is the norm, not an aberration. (Donald Clay)

Like most people in our society, I was raised to believe that the law represented what was good and right. I naively believed that those who wrote the laws and enforced the laws were the good guys. I never dreamed they were capable of bringing harm to those they served. I know how naive this sounds, but keep in mind that I come from an upper-middle class background, from a law abiding, Christian household. In other words, I bought the American apple pie ideology, hook, line, and sinker. (Marcus Huber)

What can be done? Can students in prison transform the world? The question of change is as central to the work of critical criminologists and Freire's pedagogy as it is to the students in the prison classroom. Organized political action is prohibited in prison, punishable by solitary confinement or forced transfer to Security Housing Units (e.g., the infamous Marion prison in Illinois). Thus, the politics of change is an ever-present part of the criminology dialogue. In these excerpts, two students attempt to move from a critique of current prison practices to proposing change:

It is my opinion that major reforms are required in the criminal justice system before a workable solution can be implemented. The state legislatures around the country continuously make changes in the laws concerning the punishment of criminals and the power of the policing agencies and court systems. One cannot continue to paint over a rusty surface and expect the root of the problem to be solved. The damaged foundation must be repaired before the new paint is applied. This analogy holds true for the criminal justice system. The lawmakers cannot continue to shuffle new and old laws to run a system that is faulty. The system must first be reconstructed. Where we must begin is with a new ideology, an ideology that supports a society that offers truly equal opportunities to all its citizens. (Michael Marant)

Ultimately the real issue of crime and punishment begins with a political ideology and ends with the public misconception of who is responsible for crime. Crime is certainly cause for alarm; however, even street crime should be dealt with in a reasoned way, far removed from the revenge motive.

Our legislators, self-absorbed and riding the crest of public sentiment, are passing laws with vindictive intent, rather than addressing the real problems of poverty, unemployment, and bigotry which contribute to criminal behavior. Additionally, law makers are guilty of creating long-term problems with their short-sighted solutions to a growing problem. So far, overcrowding is the only result of passing tougher, longer sentencing bills. (Donald Clay)

The value of the Freirian approach of proceeding in stages is confirmed by these comments. Students have shifted their search for the causes of crime from a narrow focus on the individual to the social structure. They discuss crime in terms of class and relate this to contradictions inherent in capitalist economic structure. Students need not utilize the most sophisticated and abstract aspects of Chambliss's structural contradictions theory nor accept it without criticism. The concept of a relatively autonomous state, for example, is difficult to corroborate when they see that the vast majority of laws serve the interest of the ruling class. What is significant here is that students suggest the need for a new ideology and for attacking the root causes of crime in poverty, inequality, and racism. These proposals temper radical transformation with the reforms of social democracy.

ALIENATION

Critical criminology links the subjective experience of oppressed people who are victims of a criminal justice system with social structure. In *Alienation and Class*, Richard Schmitt develops the Marxian concept of alienation rooted in the class structure of capitalism to include the subjective experiences of the individual.

In our society, it is the pervasive alienation that shapes and interprets the source of pain. Alienation is, to that extent, a societal problem. It is the structure of our society, with its division into classes that produces alienation and thereby sets the context in which love and death, strength and weakness, meaning and despair acquire the precise significance that they have for us. In speaking of alienation, we speak of the very particular ways in which unhappiness is experienced in our society. (1983, 3)

This analysis allows students and teacher to rename our individual malaise as alienation and to recognize that it is rooted in a common social condition. Prison intensifies alienation. Whole dimensions of the person are denied, family and culture are marginalized, and interests and skills become irrelevant. Everything is dichotomized. When students read Goffman, they find this dichotomy registered in his analysis of "total institutions" wherein "there is a basic split between a large managed group, conveniently called inmates, and a small supervisory staff." Under these conditions, each "grouping tends to conceive the other in terms of narrow hostile stereotypes, staff often seeing inmates as bitter, secretive, and untrustworthy, while inmates often see staff as condescending, highhanded, and mean" (1961, 7).

Reading Schmitt and Goffman encourages students and teacher to reconsider the forms alienation takes in prison. This is clearly the case in Marcus Huber's observations:

Instead of being used as a tool for reducing crime, prisons are being used as a factory that produces crime. . . . What can we expect? When you deprive a man of his dignity, and take away all hope for a life of freedom and liberty, you injure that man in ways you cannot even begin to imagine. When you keep a man in prison for years, controlling every aspect of his life—the hour he wakes, the number of minutes he washes, the color and style of his clothes, the people he is allowed to interact with, the hour which the lights go out—you are preventing him from ever becoming a responsible individual. You are taking away his self-worth, and you are denying him his humanity.

Huber also responds to Christina Jose-Kamfner's article (1990) by comparing prison to existential death:

It is not hard for me to accept the comparison of a lengthy prison sentence to existential death. In order to cope with the pain one feels at being separated from family and friends and a meaningful life, it becomes necessary to block out the pain and in effect go numb. The senses, the emotions, everything goes numb, and is replaced by a cloud of indifference, despair, and finally hopelessness. At this point, for all intents and purposes you are dead, and many prisoners attempt suicide. But, for those who get past this period of depression, a wondrous thing happens . . . hope. . . . Because of this, most people survive their incarceration.

Donald Clay holds a different view:

It is an undeniable fact that one experiences a loss of personal identity, as is generally the case being incarcerated. In addition the prevailing alienation, loneliness, and stark inconvenience to regular routine once enjoyed while free, does impact on one's struggle for significance. However, I think it should be referred to as existential estrangement perhaps, but definitely not existential death.

The topic of prison alienation brings about a dialogue rich with personal insight into prison conditions. It illustrates what Giroux and Freire describe as the "opportunity to give subjectivity a central place in developing critical pedagogy" (1987, xiv). Prisoners discuss the source of alienation which lies in domination and control, and they explain how this leads to a loss of dignity and humanity. They are empowered by the opportunities to make problematic their experience of alienation within the context of larger social problems of society. In this light, it can be seen how prisons are not places of rehabilitation but rather "crime factories."

CLOSING REMARKS

Has the study of critical criminology transformed students' reality? From their comments, it is clear that there is a substantial fit between their experiences and the image of crime and punishment that emerges when viewed from these theoretical perspectives. But does this qualify as critical pedagogy in the spirit of Paulo Freire's *Pedagogy of the Oppressed*? I would answer yes, to the extent that the critique of the criminal justice system and its ideology, which is present in the selected commentaries of the students, identifies "discrepancies between dominant versions of reality promulgated in formal institutions and the lived experience of subordinate groups to such institutions" (Livingstone 1987, 10). Although my visits to prisons are brief and my role is dangerously close to that of prison staff, the dynamics of prison classroom dialogue have served to help me "to remain engaged in collective dialogue with people more fully immersed in oppressive social relationships" (p. 10). The dialogue has not been "restricted to narrow educational concerns" but has been expanded to include the capitalist social structure in the search for a more genuine representation of crime and punishment. While the harsh direct control of prison restricts prisoner-initiated change, the transformations in their consciousness and the desire to facilitate change demonstrate that "sooner or later . . . formerly passive students turn against their domestication and the attempt to domesticate reality" (Freire 1970, 61).

Razor wire separates prisons from the rest of society, but the contradictions that created the prisons exist throughout society. The fear of crime which justifies prisons that take away all freedom also justifies the laws which erode everyone's freedom. Critical criminology and the pedagogy of the oppressed form a powerful partnership in the struggle for liberation.

NOTES

I would like to thank all the students in the Regis University PATH program for their involvement in this project. They have been part of a continuing and expanding dialogue concerning crime, punishment, and society. I also want to note that the title of this article became a matter of discussion in a prison criminology class. When it was suggested without quotes, prisoners found it offensive not because they denied having committed crime, but because they had come to understand the forces that contributed to their incarceration and label as criminals. A more accurate title might be "Teaching Critical Criminology to Victims of Injustice Who Are Labeled Criminal and Incarcerated."

1. This definition of critical criminology is deliberately vague. It encompasses a group of theories critical of the conservative view which sees the etiology of crime in the individual and asserts that law represents a societal consensus (MacLean and Milovanovic 1991). Further, critical criminology argues that crime must be understood in terms of the political and economic conflicts of capitalism. While I

consider structural contradictions theory to be on the cutting edge of critical criminology, I realize that not all students will integrate this theory into their critical consciousness.

2. I have occasionally been asked if any attempt has ever been made to censor the content of college courses in critical criminology. In a dialogue about this issue, students noted that it would be a bigger problem for me to bring donuts into prison than it would be to bring in Marxist ideas. We theorized that in the prison atmosphere direct social control is primary and ideological control is secondary, while in open society the situation may be reversed.

7

Prison Education: A Contextual Analysis

Dante Germanotta

The contradictions of Western capitalist culture are nowhere more apparent than in modern penal institutions. The stream of critical literature coming out of the 1970s, which addressed itself to the history and practice of imprisonment, contributed significantly to a proper analysis of the role of prisons in capitalist society. The journal *Crime and Social Justice* and the publication of essays on the prison and the prisoners' movements entitled *Punishment and Penal Discipline*, edited by Tony Platt and Paul Takagi (1980), are examples of this literature. Basic class analysis unmasked the pretense of the medical model of "corrections" and was accompanied by social movements inside and outside of the prison walls. At the same time, contemporary capitalist society, driven by the logic of its own development, moved into another cycle of imposing harsher regimens in prison settings, taking comfort in a particular set of research findings which centered on the work of Robert Martinson (1974), who, after defining the limitations of his own study, found no credible evidence that rehabilitation had ever worked (Michalowski 1985, 234). State authorities used the occasion of this research to promote the idea of punishment as "just desserts" for the crime committed rather than as an avenue for individualized rehabilitation. Raymond Michalowski holds that even the promise of individualized rehabilitation might have "represented an attempt to legitimize an essentially repressive system of social control aimed at restraining working class and non-white lawbreakers while permitting extensive social harm by the owners and representatives of capital" (p. 234). This "discovery" that rehabilitation was not working (although it is more likely that it was never seriously attempted) became the convenient ideological cover to usher in the current public policies of imprisonment, which today provide the backdrop for any consideration of prison education and its relationship to critical pedagogy.

Critical analysis of institutions, or activities within these institutions, bounded by capitalist economic and juridico-political structures, must begin with certain basic assumptions. The current constellations of power continue to perpetuate themselves in a way that is plagued by certain inherent and inevitable contradictions. The survival of the market system requires some measure of freedom and equivalence between individuals so that a certain level of rationalized exchange can take place. On the other hand, this "measure of freedom and equivalence" prevails by coercively maintaining unequal relations at the level of production. Penal institutions are the ultimate vehicle used to police the borderlines of these unequal relations. Living and working within prison settings will make this abundantly clear, if you choose to apply this analysis.

For developing theoretical perspectives on contemporary issues such as prison education, we may rely on basic class analysis to provide a useful conceptual framework which will assist in avoiding the pitfalls concomitant with traditional liberal views which tend to overindividualize definitions of both the problem and the solution. Still, it may be useful here to note the prefatory comments of Henry Giroux and Paulo Freire in their "Series Introduction," which appears in *Critical Pedagogy and Cultural Power* (1987). They suggest that among the important themes that run through this series is the notion that the usual language of critique, depicting class oppression as the fundamental explanatory variable, needs to extend itself and provide an adequate theory on behalf of those "social movements that did not reduce their political projects and historical understanding to the imperative of class analysis" (p. xiii). Giroux and Freire speak of the "production of subjectivities" and "the reconstruction of a political and pedagogical discourse" within domains that traditionally have been called mere ideology. Such theoretical discourse drives a wedge between the polemical positions that view education as mere ideology and education as political training for immediate revolution.

This is not a discourse about the binary coding of reproduction vs. resistance. Instead, it is an attempt to understand how forms of subjectivity are regulated and transformed through the structured character of such social forms as language, ideologies, myths, significations, and narratives. (pp. xiv-xv)

The task of bringing education into prison settings should be one of the proving grounds for the reconstruction of education, where education, liberal arts or otherwise, is seen as having an impact on the "production of subjectivities" and highlights "the significance of a critical pedagogy that gives primary importance to forms of teaching and understanding that begin with the social and historical particularities of peoples' lives" (p. xv).

I have chosen to develop an analysis of prison education and its relationship to critical pedagogy in the context of current penal practices as they are reflected in the concrete experiences of those whose life struggles are being forged by the impact of these practices. Insight into these life struggles may provide a useful point of reference to practitioners who need to develop realistic strategies during times of social regression. If we begin with prison education as it is played out in the public sphere, it becomes clear that it is full of contradictions. For example, I have been working in the state of Massachusetts where the recognition of the value of an educated citizenry has one of the longest histories in the United States. Etched in stone, at the top of the north exterior side of the Boston Public Library are these words: "The Commonwealth requires the education of the people for the safeguard of order and liberty." Usually, the relation of public education to "order" is not lost on public officials, but the calculus of contemporary state officials finds discipline and punishment more effective than education in controlling those citizens who have been criminalized. Even education as ideology appears threatening to current controllers, who seem to need more coercive strategies given the continuing economic deprivations of the lower classes. Thus, anyone who moves educational activities in the direction of critical pedagogy would likely face severe reaction.

Recently, one of Boston's more notable practitioners in the field of prison education, Elizabeth Barker of Boston University, was featured in a segment of the national television program "Sixty Minutes." That same segment included an interview with William Weld, the governor of Massachusetts, in which he was asked his opinion of prison education. Weld was particularly adamant in his opposition to any higher education entering prison settings and indicated that "these professors" could find better ways to utilize their talents and their time. Not long thereafter, reflecting the influence of central state policy on local practice, Professor Barker was banned from entering almost all of Massachusetts' prisons after having spent the last twenty years coordinating Boston University's prison education program and even establishing one of the only master's degree programs in the country. Ironically, the Massachusetts Correctional Association, whose membership consists of the state's correctional professionals, including the commissioner of correction, honored Barker as their 1993 person of the year for her legendary work. But they did nothing to lift the ban that continues to keep her from that very work.

Such contradictions are hardly rare for those attempting to teach or learn within the various educational settings of our current social and cultural institutions, particularly in prisons. It might prove instructive, in this regard, to review the experience of Malcolm X as he negotiated his own development in the same recalcitrant prison environment, the Norfolk

Prison in Massachusetts, from which Barker has been recently banned. The educational development of Malcolm X within Massachusetts prison settings is one of the more significant and least appreciated episodes in the chronicles of prison education. It is a prototype of the relationship between critical pedagogy and prison settings.

Before considering the case of Malcolm X, some comment here concerning a possible distinction between *prison education* and *prisoner education*, or self-initiated learning, may be useful. This is particularly important to develop in the context of a discussion on critical pedagogy. Are prison education and prisoner education two sides of the same coin, or do they need to be seen in dialectical perspective? Is one the thesis and the other the antithesis? As will be made clear in the material here, the education of Malcolm X was a case of prisoner education. He basically educated himself while in prison with some assistance from friends and brothers in the Muslim community. He only minimally participated in the formal educational activities that were offered by the prison education staff. I would argue that prisoner education can and should occur anytime a prisoner becomes engaged in educational activity, formal or informal. The question of genuine legitimacy for any educational enterprise rests upon some measure of self-transformation occurring—the issue of formal accrediting or licensing aside. Prisoner education can take place within general prison education programs, sponsored by an outside agency or by the prison itself. It can take place through self-initiated learning or through experiencing the graphic contradictions of prison life itself.

The relationship of all of this to critical pedagogy raises the analysis of education to another level. It can be argued that education, at any level or of whatever formal or informal definition, is not genuine education unless it is a transaction that includes elements of critical reflection, defined by educational theorists such as Paulo Freire (1970). At the least, to open up discussion of prison education as critical pedagogy contributes to the attempt at broadening our understanding of the educative process as it occurs both within traditional liberal programs, which are nurtured and defined by colleges and universities, and within those many settings where education occurs outside of formal academic settings. Promoting the assumption that all pedagogy is political effectively blurs the lines between all varieties of educational experience and raises pertinent questions for all educational activities. The question is whether it is at all possible to sustain general prison education programming if one allows critical pedagogy a more conscious and deliberate place. Prisoner education occurs whether or not prison education exists in any particular prison setting. The larger question is whether prison education itself can be one of the spheres that can be included in the broader reaches of education which Giroux and Freire define as almost any place where "the production of subjectivities" is taking place. The education of Malcolm X within a prison setting provides a model of self-transformation which did not take place within traditional prison education programming. The case of Richard Cepulonis, which will also be reviewed here, is a case where self-transformation took place, at least in some important ways, in the context of involvement in formalized prison education activities. What do these case studies suggest regarding the possible relation of prison education to critical pedagogy? A review of them may suggest some of the major issues to be addressed in answering this question.

THE CASE OF MALCOLM X

The transformation of Malcolm Little to Malcolm X was described in a recent article in the *Boston Globe* as follows:

Nearly four decades ago, behind the concrete walls of Norfolk prison, a troubled young brother named Malcolm Little came to learn. . . . He studied by moon-light. . . . He studied every word in the dictionary . . . and he studied so much he needed glasses. . . . He had fire and thirst, entering prison as a nickel-and-dime street hustler and leaving as one of the world's most articulate spokesman on one of the world's more enduring problems—racism. (Manly 1993, 31)

The prison files of Malcolm X recently have been opened by the Massachusetts Department of Correction and are now available for research purposes. I obtained access to these files with the collaboration of Robert Hayden, a historian of African-American history in Boston. They contain letters written by Malcolm to prison officials as well as departmental documents and records relating to various aspects of his imprisonment. They are particularly revealing as commentary on the pursuit of genuine educational development in prison settings. Ultimately, Malcolm educated himself through remarkable self-discipline responding to his growing intellectual curiosity, his spiritual awakening, and his intense search for his identity, now intimately linked to his first consciousness of black history. He initially assumed that educating oneself and one's fellow prisoners through an intellectual search for identity, possibly leading to a remarkable self-development, would be a social good. He soon encountered the inevitable reaction from contemporary Western society, magnified exponentially in prison settings.

His letters to the prison administrators are telling as he defines the contradictions he was beginning to experience. In a letter sent to the commissioner of correction on June 6, 1950, he indicates that the Muslim prisoners had no record of disciplinary infractions and that they spent most of their time keeping to themselves and studying. He then writes: "One of the Muslims is illiterate; his flesh-and-blood brother requested of the deputy that they be placed in work-shops together so that he could teach and assist him in acquiring an education during their spare moments between tasks." He tells the commissioner that the deputy turned down the request "without hesitation." "He actually refused to allow two Brothers to *rehabili-tate themselves.*" He then proceeds to recount another request.

Also, in our earnest attempt to learn something about our own people we set out to purchase some books on Black History. The books were authored by L. A. Rogers (historian, anthropologist, Egyptologist, etc.), a noted member of the *Pittsburg Courier*'s editorial staff. We were also refused this request and were informed that it was against the law for us to have them or to delve into "things of that nature" (the speaker evidently forgot himself). Is it actually against the "law" for a Black man to read about himself? (Let me laugh!).[1]

Malcolm finally points out that Muslims in prison have not been allowed to write to Muslims in Detroit on the pretext that "inmates cannot write to relatives of other inmates." Prison officials chose to ignore the distinction between religious brothers and brothers connected by blood. He asserts: "I am certain that you have acquired enough degrees to know that all Muslims are *Brothers in Truth.*" Malcolm finally indicates his frustration with a system that officially opposes the gathering of true knowledge by its charges:

Allah will forgive a man who robs another man of his money, because the robbed-man can always get more money. But, when you deprive and rob a man of knowledge, there is no forgiveness, because that robbed-man is completely helpless and at the mercy of anyone who wishes to use him as a "tool."[2]

What prison authorities made of Malcolm X is best summarized in a report issued by a prison psychiatrist on May 4, 1951, one year after Malcolm had written the letters quoted above.

This twenty-six year old colored man from the British West Indies has a most peculiar appearance, with his bald head, carefully trimmed beard, and general air of importance. He reached the eighth grade in school and has average adult intelligence.

He complains of frequent severe headaches. His pupils react normally. He has no knee-jerks, although ankle jerks are normal. His history says he took drugs for a number of years. He claims to be a Mohammedan, but his conversation expresses a confused jumble of ideas which make little sense.

He is a responsible offender, although a peculiar personality characterized by disordered, incoherent thinking. However, he is in touch with surroundings and has no delusions or hallucinations.[3]

Prior to his imprisonment, the only focused learning Malcolm did, after completing the eighth grade in Detroit, related to various hustling activities (Malcolm X 1966, 154). During his early days of imprisonment, in 1947, at the Charlestown Prison in Boston, Malcolm met a fellow prisoner he called

"Bimbi." Bimbi was apparently the prison library's best customer and held ongoing informal discussions with small groups of prisoners.

He liked to talk about historical events and figures. When he talked about the history of Concord [Massachusetts], where I was to be transferred later, you would have thought he was hired by the Chamber of Commerce, and I wasn't the first inmate who had never heard of Thoreau until Bimbi expounded upon him. (p. 154)

Bimbi recognized Malcolm's potential and encouraged him to pursue more education. This opportunity came when he was transferred to Norfolk Prison in 1948. Much later, when he became internationally known, an English writer called Malcolm X from London and asked, among other things, the name of his alma mater. His answer was "books."

I have often reflected upon the new vistas that reading opened to me. I knew right there in prison that reading had changed forever the course of my life. As I see it today, the ability to read awoke inside me some long dormant craving to be mentally alive. I certainly wasn't seeking any degree the way a college confers a status symbol upon its students. My homemade education gave me, with every additional book that I read, a little bit more sensitivity to the deafness, dumbness and blindness that was afflicting the black race in America. (p. 179)

Malcolm's reading list began with a dictionary and eventually included Schopenhauer, Kant, and Nietzsche, among others. This extraordinary self-education emanated from a strong religious and political motivation. He realized through extended and intensive discussions with members of his family and brothers from the Muslim faith that the development of his new identity was inexorably linked to his growing knowledge of black history, black religion, and the political experience of the American black community. Before embarking upon his compelling educational venture, he had attempted to write letters to religious and political figures. For example, "I did write to Elijah Muhammad. . . . At least 25 times I must have written that first one-page letter to him, over and over. I was trying to make it both legible and understandable. I practically couldn't read my handwriting myself. . . . My spelling and my grammar were as bad" (p. 169).

This remarkable motivation impelled him to start with a simple dictionary and read the entire volume, word by word. "With every succeeding page, I also learned of people and places and events from history. Actually, the dictionary is like a miniature encyclopedia" (p. 172). Malcolm estimates that he wrote one million words of notes. Thus began his reading, accompanied by his self-transformation, that probably, before he was through, could have earned him a degree from St. John's University in New York, where the whole curriculum is made up of book lists.[4] While his range of readings included Will Durant's *Story of Civilization*, H. G. Wells's *Outline of History*, W.E.B. Du Bois's *Souls of Black Folks*, and Carter G. Woodson's

Negro History, he found J. A. Rogers's three-volume work, *Sex and Race* (1967–1972), most intriguing.

Sex and Race told about race-mixing before Christ's time; about Aesop being a black man who told fables; about Egypt's Pharaohs; about the great Coptic Christian Empires; about Ethiopia, the earth's oldest continuous black civilization. (p. 175)

The sections of Malcolm's autobiography that chronicle his literary development attest to his familiarity with classical literature, his emerging *Weltanschauung* regarding the history of the black race, and an intellectual range of interest beyond the average college undergraduate of today. Like Jean Harris, the upper-middle-class white woman who was convicted of killing Herman Tarnower and spent years in prison, Malcolm was "rehabilitated"— not by the system but in opposition to it. Ellen Goodman, a columnist for the *Boston Globe*, in reviewing the years that Jean Harris spent behind the walls, concluded that "the self-esteem that eroded in long years of her destructive relationship with Tarnower was, remarkably, rebuilt in resistance to prison's attempt to destroy her" (Goodman 1992). In cases like these, critical pedagogy defines the processes of self-education/prison-education that can come out of the caged womb of prison settings. When the engagement with education comes through more formal structures of prison education, association with critical pedagogy becomes more complex.

THE DIALECTICS OF PRISON EDUCATION

I would propose that given the inevitable clash between critical pedagogy and contemporary prison culture any prisoner who begins to explore the possibilities of educational advancement will move through three phases of development. During the first phase, the prisoner may make some connection with whatever prison education program is available and treat it as he or she would any other prison program. The basic assumption is that the program has nothing really to offer that coincides with the real interest of the prisoner. The rewards are much more indirect and unrelated to education. They consist of some temporary relief from the stressful, often life-threatening confines of the cell block. They might add to the accumulation of "good time" and take days and sometimes months off time served. They might allow for another entry in the portfolio for parole hearings, or another source of a letter of reference on college stationary. All of these rewards are purely practical and arguably have no bearing on the central function or purpose of education.

The next phase for the prisoner engaged in prison education is one characterized by fleeting glimpses of the intrinsic value of education. It is one described by Ivan Illich when he speaks about the stage of enlightenment coming to the Brazilian peasant under the tutelage of Paulo Freire's

Pedagogy of the Oppressed. In a taped lecture, Illich quotes one of the peasants as saying, "Yesterday I could not sleep because yesterday I wrote my name."[5] It is a realization that one can objectify oneself in the positive sense of that term. Forces that surround us turn us into victims until we place them in a larger, more conscious, context which explains their origins and their temporariness, as well as their amenability to our actions. When they read literary accounts of human experience, prisoner-students get a glimpse of the commonness of all human struggle, which disabuses them of their sense of isolation and terrible uniqueness. They experience this when they read sociological literature and discover that social and individual reality intersect, that social formations are often the creations of the human mind and ultimately of human labor, and that, as Karl Marx reminds us, we make our own history if not always as we please.

It is a Malcolm X gaining a profound understanding of how alternative interpretations of history create a fulcrum for leveraging white man's dominance or black pride, whichever one chooses to establish. Once Western intellectual development became influenced by the work of the French *Philosophes*, who ushered in what we have come to designate as the Enlightenment, pedagogy as critique was given major credence.

Thus, the *Philosophes* investigated all aspects of social life; they studied and analyzed political, religious, social and moral institutions, subjected them to merciless criticism from the standpoint of reason, and demanded to change the unreasonable ones. More often than not, traditional values and institutions were found to be irrational. That was another way of saying that the prevailing institutions were contrary to man's nature and were thus inhibitive of his growth and development; unreasonable institutions prevented men from realizing their potential. (Zeitlin 1968, 3–4)

Although higher education in its early beginnings in France reflected less critique and more concern for establishing social order, gathering knowledge for its own sake led inevitably to recognizing the value of critical reflection. This recognition, along with the growth of revolutionary movements, eventually joined theory with practice, and challenged by ongoing social and political struggle, more intense at some times than others, higher education faced the task of defining the relationship of learning to praxis. The possibility of transforming oneself as well as the world through critical reflection and subsequent praxis gradually came into larger relief, and the debate over "objectivity" and "pedagogy as political" was set in motion. This history of liberal arts education is played out in particularly salient ways in the educational cycle of prisoner-students. Once critical reflection begins, in the context of formal education being pursued in a prison setting, prisoner-students find their own life history placed in a new perspective, and they begin to see the possibilities of genuine personal transformation and eventually of transformation of the world. They look to higher education to deliver on these possibilities. Instead, a tragedy unfolds, and the second phase of the prisoner's educational journey comes to an abrupt end.

Anyone teaching college courses in a prison setting will recognize this juncture. It is marked by such comments of prison administrators as, "You are educating the wrong prisoners." The most promising students are suddenly transferred without regard for educational interests. Prisoners who end up in isolation units are punished by being deprived of educational programming. Prisoners who somehow persevere and end up with degrees are often transferred to sites where advanced educational services are not available.

Thus, the third phase in a prisoner's educational cycle is marked by a mixture of newly acquired self-esteem and a keen sense of frustration. Prisoners now find themselves with a whole new set of creative energies and a genuine set of new commitments, but they are still in an environment where new reputations are more easily acquired by becoming an informer than by demonstrating educational enlightenment. Prisoners are again forced to make their own opportunities. They may initiate a prisoner-run AIDS education program, they may organize a youth outreach effort, they may mobilize a project of typing braille books for the blind, or they may set up a computer laboratory. Almost always such projects are established through contacts between prisoners and outside groups and resources. Their life span is relatively short because, as soon as program success leads to some higher status for the prisoners and logically calls for more privileges, the programs are cut short.

Unfortunately, such program possibilities, limited as they are, become available for only a few of the educated prisoners. Most languish in their cell blocks aware that they will merely be marking time again, but now with knowledge and a set of skills that will be vastly underutilized. Some few find it possible when they are finally released to make appropriate use of their prison education, however acquired. Malcolm X, whom the prison psychiatrist defined as "confused" and "incoherent," rose to great heights as an articulate leader in the modern transformation of the black community. Others become counselors, assisting youth and ex-prisoners with finely honed insights born of their own struggles and imprisonments. Most face the hard dilemmas of ex-prisoners and devise survival strategies, hoping to put their prison experience behind them forever. The fact that few return to prison underscores the irony in the fate that prison education has endured. Rather than encouraging further exploration concerning the impact of education on prisoners, the prison system continues to resist and destroy the very element that has demonstrably made a significant difference in turning human lives in new and constructive directions. The case of Richard Cepulonis will bear this out in rather remarkable ways.[6] It chronicles significant educational development, with elements of critical pedagogy interlaced, in certain instances dialectically, with more formal structures of prison education. It also exemplifies the stages of prison education discussed here.

THE CASE OF RICHARD CEPULONIS

Richard grew up in one of the larger cities in Massachusetts where, according to him, "Some people found the only job they could get was menial labor and crime was more lucrative." Richard's life of crime included the offenses of assault, armed robbery, and possession of a machine gun. He entered prison at the age of twenty-four in 1972 and ultimately received an aggregate sentence of from fifty-eight to eighty-two years. This included both state and federal sentencing, running concurrently. The extraordinary length of his sentences results from the harsh penalties imposed for the possession of a machine gun (forty to fifty years) and the fact that he was given the maximum permissible sentence of from eighteen to twenty years for the assault charges. He had two periods of incarceration, serving most of his time in the maximum security prison at Walpole, Massachusetts. In 1986, although Richard had used his fourteen years of prison experience to change his life radically and to establish the remarkable personal history described below, the Advisory Board of Pardons turned down his request for a commutation. In her letter to Richard, dated March 27, 1986, Joyce Hurley, the pardon coordinator, wrote:

Please be advised that under recent date the advisory Board of Pardons voted not to grant a hearing on your petition for commutation. . . . The full membership denies this petition due to the long and troublesome history of armed robberies and assaults. In addition, the members indicate that this petition presnets [*sic*] no merit at this time. . . . A copy of this report has been forwarded to His Excellency, the Governor for review.

In 1987 Richard chose to make an escape from prison and has not been heard from since.

Two newspaper items set the context in connecting this case to issues in prison education. In June 1990, *The Tab*, a newspaper in the western suburbs of Boston, printed an article featuring the updated list of the "Most Wanted Criminals" as issued by the Massachusetts State Police. Among the profiles could be found that of Richard Cepulonis. In June 1985, *The Patriot Ledger*, a suburban newspaper from the Boston South Shore, featured a front-page article with the headline, "College Degree 'Opens World' for Prisoner." Accompanying the article was a large picture of Richard, wearing a cap and gown, standing at an open prison gate. Richard had just received a baccalaureate degree from Curry College, having graduated with honors from the Justice Education Program, the first prisoner in the history of the Walpole Prison to earn such a degree. The saga of Richard's achievement is the story of contemporary prison education.

Richard, in one of his interviews with the press, unwittingly acknowledged what I have defined as the first phase of the educational pilgrimage of prisoner-students. "By 1981, I had reached my bottom," he said, holding the degree and a gold tassel signifying he graduated with honors. "My experience in the prison was counterproductive. I thought it would be a nice idea to go to school if for nothing but diversion" (*Boston Globe* 1984). With no greater motivation than that, he began to attend whatever few classes were being offered at the prison.

Even before his perfunctory interest in the college courses began, he had developed some serious interest in the application of the law to prison settings. Richard had entered prison in 1972, and soon thereafter he had become aware of the growing amount of prisoner litigation that was taking place. In 1980, while confined to the infamous segregation unit known as "Block 10," he filed a suit in the United States District Court alleging that prisoners in this block were denied access to the law library and thereby to their constitutional rights. He won his case, and the prison was ordered to establish an adequate law library in this segregation unit. His second noteworthy suit occurred in 1982 when he filed a class action suit, declaring unconstitutional a state law that prohibited city and town clerks from mailing absentee ballots to prisoners. This case was eventually heard by the United States Supreme Court and it was remanded back to the Supreme Judicial Court of Massachusetts, saying that the right of prisoners to vote should be resolved at the state level. The Supreme Judicial Court, in 1983, ruled that prisoners had a right to vote, and by 1984 prisoners were voting in the presidential election.

Richard, initially, did not connect his rather heady legal work to his interest in school, but the connection soon was made. He then entered into his second phase of the prison education cycle, and his expectations had been bolstered by a growing sophistication in his understanding of the legal process, particularly as it related to the rights of prisoners. The bank robber was testing the notion as to whether law was ultimately a social good. At the least, he was finding in the law a means to advocate and advance the civil rights of prisoner-citizens. He quickly became aware of the importance of education and searched for the legal mandates that might extend such opportunities beyond what was then available. He found such a mandate in Massachusetts General Law which outlined the duties of the commissioner of correction, including the following:

(e) Establish, maintain and administer programs of rehabilitation, including but not limited to education, training and employment, of persons committed to the custody of the department, designed as far as practicable to prepare and assist each such person to assume the responsibilities and exercise the rights of a citizen of the Commonwealth. (Chapter 124, Section 1)

The most pertinent words here were "as far as practicable" since the University of Massachusetts, Amherst, had just given the prison system a proposal for a baccalaureate program whose cost would be borne by federal scholarships (Pell Grants) and the university itself. It should be quite "practicable" for the commissioner. The prison system, of course, turned the proposal down.

Higher education programs at any level, offered in the prisons, are difficult for the Department of Correction to explain to the public. . . . The Department of Correction is uneasy offering matriculating higher education programs within the prisons. It would be difficult to have the inmates graduate only to return to the usual prison routine.[7]

Richard then set in motion a piece of litigation that was to make both legal and education history. On June 24, 1982, he filed a Complaint for Relief in the nature of Mandamus in the Norfolk County Superior Court seeking a court order directing the commissioner of correction to perform his statutory duty, particularly in regard to educational programming. At that time, prisoners had been filing such a volume of civil complaints against the Department of Correction that the court had decided to establish a courthouse annex at the prison to hear these complaints. This particular case was the first in Massachusetts' history to be heard in a state superior court holding sessions at a state prison. The national news journalist Morton Dean, of CBS News, was on hand to tape Richard's arguments before the court. It was a remarkable scene as a prisoner became the prosecuting attorney in a court held in the prison setting where he was being held, examining the commissioner and the associate commissioner of correction, who were being defended by an assistant attorney general of Massachusetts!

Although the court ruled that the commissioner had greater discretion under the law than Richard allowed, the court also advised the commissioner that it would be well to review the educational programming as it then existed at this prison, since many of Richard's arguments could easily lead to further litigation. The court was not pleased with the many gaps in the knowledge of the commissioner regarding what was actually being done at the prison regarding education. As a result of this trial, the prison system soon accepted a proposal from Curry College to establish a baccalaureate program at Walpole State Prison. Richard not only became a Curry College student, but he became the first student to graduate from this program and the first prisoner ever to earn a B.A. degree within the Walpole Prison walls. After all of this, Richard was still refused transfer requests to prison sites where he might have been able to continue his educational journey—he was transferred to other sites—and he was refused parole hearings when he became eligible to request them. As quoted earlier, the Advisory Board of Pardons in March 1986 denied the petition "due to the long and troublesome history of armed robberies and assaults" and concluded that his petition presented "no merit at this time."[8] The "long and troublesome history" had happened at least thirteen years previous to this denial and well before Richard had turned himself into a responsible and educated civil rights' advocate. Richard again wrote to the governor in April 1986 and received a reply including the following observation: "Many factors go into assessing a petitioner's level of rehabilitation. While your educational achievements are exceptional, a petitioner's criminal record, institutional history, and ability to interact with other inmates and officials are important."[9]

Richard's prison behavior, in fact, had been quite exemplary; his interaction with his fellow prisoners was very positive. His only problem was his criminal record, and he had tried, with reasonable success, to put that behind him. In desperation, he resorted to escape, apparently hoping against hope that the survival skills learned through negotiating an experience of imprisonment would be adequate for any stress concomitant with "life on the run." He might have remembered his reading of Dostoevsky which he had referenced in one of his papers written for a sociology of law class in 1983.

After he had spent four years in a Siberian prison, the great Russian novelist, Dostoevsky, commented surprisingly that his time in prison had created in him a deep optimism about the ultimate future of mankind because, as he put it, if man could survive the horrors of prison life he must surely be a "creature who could withstand anything."[10]

I think it reasonable to assume that Richard finally decided that the life stresses concomitant with escape were worth enduring if it meant the possibility of finding some way to make appropriate use of his newly acquired knowledge and skills. Clearly, he found the prison environment unresponsive to the newly hopeful dimensions of his life.

It is an indictment of the prison system when prison officials, faced with the promise of prison education illustrated in cases like that of Richard Cepulonis, remain cynically shortsighted in their assessment of the role of higher education in prison settings. In spite of the fact that the promise of earning a college degree is likely to provide more positive incentive than merely attending isolated and periodic classes, prison officials ignore the implied possibilities here with the comforting thought that expecting prisoners to earn college degrees while in prison is inconsistent with the current philosophy of correction. They define goals that are more compatible with concerns of control and security than with the responsibility to facilitate the genuine transformation of prisoners' lives. They propose the offering of college courses "to reduce idleness."

Philosophically, the Department's interest in offering a college program to inmates is not to assure the attainment of an associate's or bachelor's degree, but rather to reduce idleness in the population while simultaneously providing a means for rehabilitation.[11]

The Department of Correction has consistently taken this position, and in the state of Massachusetts there would be no degree programs in the prison settings were it not for prisoner litigation, as noted here, or bold initiatives by outside educators. In the last two decades, educators outside the ranks of Department of Correction staff were the initiators of a rather significant surge in prison education programming in Massachusetts. It started with Elizabeth Barker, a Phi Beta Kappa graduate of Stanford University (1933) and a member of the Boston University English faculty since 1964. A lifelong social activist, it was hardly surprising that, during the summer of 1969, she would decide to bring her university debating team to a prison setting for a practice scrimmage in preparation for an appearance on the television program "The GE College Bowl." Beyond her own expectations, the prisoner team bested the university crew and, learning that she was an English professor, proceeded to deluge her with their poetry. This experience changed her perception of prisoners, and by 1972 she was coordinating a series of college courses at Norfolk Prison. It was only her tenacity and single-mindedness that enabled a few of these prisoner-students to earn degrees from the university in 1977, since the Department of Correction's education policy discouraged such granting of degrees.

In the late 1970s and the early 1980s, with the encouragement and cooperation of activist prisoners, a number of colleges and universities devised various strategies to bring college programs into prison settings. All of these initiatives faced strong resistance from the Department of Correction. The ongoing practice of the department had been to discourage such developments, and this attitude was increasingly reflected in policy documents. By 1985 a commissioner's report included language that put the department on report as opposing college degree programs in prison settings. This report recommended that "all [educational] programs focus on the needs of the individual with an emphasis on competency development, rather than completion of degree requirements or attainment of certificates."[12] This policy statement reflected the growing struggle over prison higher education that marked the beginning of the 1980s. It finally prompted prison educators in the state of Massachusetts to seek some joint strategies. In the spring of 1983, some of them came together at the invitation of the Justice Project of the American Friends Service Committee in Cambridge, Massachusetts, the first time they had gathered in one place for a common assessment of their work. By September 1983, the Massachusetts Council on Prison Education had been established.[13] Because, from the beginning, the council recognized the dilemmas facing prison educators, and that the source of these dilemmas was most often a prison system mired in a recalcitrant punitive philosophy, reflecting the society at large, it established a tenuous modus *vivendi* with the Department of Correction. At times, the Department issued internal directives to its school principals that they were not to attend meetings of the council, and at other times the prison education officials would join council members at regional conferences and share panel membership discussing issues of prison education. The council was instrumental in finally establishing a baccalaureate degree program from the University of Massachusetts, Amherst, in the prison system. After four years of agonizing negotiations with the Department of Correction on the need for such a program in the western regions of the state to complement the programs of Boston University and Curry College in the east, the program was finally established at Gardner Prison and has enjoyed impressive support from the university.

Although outside educators continue to engage in prison education activities, they do so in struggle and under the constant tensions coincident with bringing the possibility of genuine education to prisoners who currently face what I have chosen to define as a three-phase experience in their encounters with the educational process in a prison setting. Under current political, social, and economic arrangements it will not change. The current attempt by federal legislators to deny all incarcerated citizens access to Pell Grants, the federal scholarships for all citizens of documented financial need, is only the latest evidence of the constraints exercised by current power holders.[14] Recently (1993), Walpole Prison, where Richard Cepulonis earned his college degree, has introduced a much harsher regimen, modeled on a most repressive federal prison in Marion, Illinois, and under a new classification system is denying almost all programming, including education, to a large proportion of its population. Whatever limited education staffing had been provided in prison settings has been decreased by at least one-third as new funds are earmarked for new prisons and increased security measures.

CONCLUSION

Having reviewed the cases of Malcolm X and Richard Cepulonis, what tentative insights might I propose regarding the relation of prison education to critical pedagogy? After experiencing ten years of struggle in attempting to bring higher education into prison settings, both as the director of the Justice Education Program of Curry College and as the president of the Massachusetts Council on Prison Education, I have been forced to conclude that any education that includes elements of critical pedagogy—and the genuine tradition of liberal education always contains such elements—is destined for salient and ongoing struggle when practiced in prison settings. It produces persistent dilemmas for the educator and presents the students with glimpses of new possibilities that are, nevertheless, ringed about with new and more and more irrational punishments. It compels the develop-

ment of strategies in both teaching and learning that bring unique challenges to the formal educational enterprise. It is clear that critical pedagogy
is facilitated by the prison settings themselves, sometimes in overt and
direct ways, when prison officials see educated and enlightened prisoners
as a threat to their harsh but fragile regimens, prompting them to irrational
reprisals at the slightest provocation. On the other hand, in a more indirect
or general sense, coercive institutions deny the aspirations of the human
spirit by definition. They impose goals and directives upon their charges
that originate outside of their own consciousness and which therefore
become artificial and unrelated to actual human growth. Both prisoners and
prison educators must find ways to define education dialectically. There are
times when prison education cannot or does not rise above the level of
serving the purposes of the controllers. At these times, prisoners are compelled to give the appearance of adopting formalized educational goals and
then devising strategies to utilize the privileges such appearances provide
to advance a real attempt at development. At these times, prison educators,
while not denying generally the efficacy of conventional modes of liberal
arts learning, are compelled to recognize that the prison setting itself has as
much to do with the true enlightenment of prisoner-students as does the
prison college classroom. One would not suggest that anyone go to prison
purposely, but once you are there it can become a politicizing and educational force in your life, and if you are ready for the real world lessons it is
teaching you, you can turn a life catastrophe into a life transformation.

When Malcolm X came to himself, his thirst for knowledge drove him to
read every book he could find. His experience of the prison along with his
growing realization of the extraordinary impact of white domination on the
mental productions of humankind, led him to a self-initiated critical pedagogy with which he educated himself with only a minimum of formal
prison education.

Richard Cepulonis, on the other hand, found the possibilities of his own
transformation enhanced by his participation in a regular prison education
program, which had enough elements of critical pedagogy to reinforce the
process of change he had begun in his own life, again spurred by his
experience of incarceration. "Prison education opened up a new world for
me," he said. "It caused me to take a look at myself and the world around
me. I can honestly say that going to prison has been more of an asset than
a liability" ("Bank Robber" 1985).

He would not recommend prison to anyone, but once there he found
ways to turn it into an "asset" in his own life, giving credit for many of his
newly emerging critical insights to prison education. Whether or not Richard or Malcolm traveled a full enough journey through critical pedagogy
to become radical critical theorists in the complete sense of that term, their
incisive critique of their own lives and of the larger world, which had
previously made them victims of undefined forces, was fueled by some

decisive elements of critical pedagogy, both in conjunction with and independent of regular programming in prison education.

Educational development within the world of the prison is a dialectical process. The attempt to bring education to prison settings can be in itself a political education for prison educators just as enduring the humiliations of imprisonment, particularly the added and clearly unjustified layers of humiliation, can educate the prisoner. Formal education can be a tool of humiliation or a fulcrum for transformation. The degree to which formalized education coincides with human transformation, especially in prison settings, is dependent on the strategies of prison educators and on social and historical factors—that is, the degree to which any one society has truly committed itself to the full development of *all* of its citizens. This, of course, would involve a major restructuring and a new design in the allocation of resources. Prison educators, in developing realistic strategies, must take the measure of the coincidence of formal education and human transformation allowed in prison settings within the current social and political constellations of power. They must distinguish between the activities that support this coincidence and those that impede it and make ongoing decisions around these judgments. Such decisions create the tensions necessary for prison education to assume the forms that define its relation to critical pedagogy.

NOTES

1. June 6, 1950, letter of Malcolm X to Commissioner Mcdonald, Massachusetts Department of Correction.

2. Ibid.

3. Psychiatric Report on Malcolm Little, May 4, 1951, Massachusetts Department of Correction files.

4. While all of this was happening, he did attend some formal educational activities, some of which were being brought in by Harvard and Boston universities and others offered by the prison educational staff. Evaluation of his schoolwork documented in his prison education records refer to him as "average," "average student dropped for being disturbing influence," "average, ranging from 60 to 95, attitude poor, dropped at own request." In Latin, he was rated "average to excellent" and for his Great Books Discussion Group the instructor wrote "quite active discussion, had his own ideas but was OK." The records appear in file documents of Malcolm X at Department of Correction, Boston, Massachusetts.

5. Ivan Illich, "Yesterday I Could Not Sleep because Yesterday I Wrote My Name," tape no. 299, the Center for the Study of Democratic Institutions, Santa Barbara, California.

6. Information and material related to this case were made available to me by Richard Cepulonis over the period of his incarceration. I was both his teacher and academic advisor and followed closely the significant events of his life in prison.

7. Letter of January 28, 1982, from Dennis A. Humphrey, associate commissioner of correction, sent to Professor Walter Silva of the University of Massachusetts, Amherst.

8. Letter of March 27, 1986, from Joyce Hooley, Massachusetts Advisory Board of Pardons coordinator, sent to Richard Cepulonis.

9. Letter of May 19, 1986, from Dianne Wilkerson, assistant legal counsel to Governor Dukakis, to Richard Cepulonis.

10. Excerpt from paper written for sociology of law class in 1983.

11. Letter of September 17, 1982, from the associate commissioner of correction to the assistant attorney general of Massachusetts.

12. Preliminary report from the [Massachusetts] commissioner of correction for proposed program expansion, 1985, p. 10.

13. Recorded in an announcement letter of November 2, 1983, from David Collins, coordinator of the Justice Support Project of the American Friends Service Committee, Cambridge, Massachusetts: "On the 13th of September 1983, Professor Dante Germanotta of Curry College became the sole incorporator of the Massachusetts Council on Prison Education. At that meeting, members were appointed and a Board of Directors was created."

The first official meeting was held on November 9, 1983, at the same locale, and representatives from the following schools were either present or had expressed serious interest: Boston University, Bridgewater State College, Bunker Hill Community College, Curry College, Harvard University, Massasoit Community College, Middlesex Community College, Mt. Wachusetts Community College, New Hampshire College, Roxbury Community College, University of Massachusetts (Amherst), and University of Massachusetts (Boston). The adopted purposes were to advocate for (1) a coherent, integrated course of study throughout the prison system; (2) an alternative social and intellectual environment within the dominant prison society wherein prisoners can cultivate the characteristics of creativity, reflective analysis, social responsibility, and a sense of self-worth; and (3) a right based not only on society's interest in the reformation of prisoner citizens but also on a social commitment to the principle of educational fairness in a just society.

14. When Senator Jesse Helms of North Carolina heard complaints from some of his constituents concerning college programming in prison settings being supported by federal funds, he introduced a bill that, if passed by the U.S. Senate, would deny all prisoners access to such funding. Most of the prison education programs in the United States depended on this funding. The U.S. Congress finally passed a compromise bill which, while granting continuing funding to prisoner-students, nevertheless denied access to this funding to prisoners with life sentences without parole and to all prisoners in any state that spent less on higher education in 1993 than they had spent in 1988. These provisos effectively blocked hundreds of former prisoner-students from continuing their education while withholding such opportunity from hundreds of newly incarcerated prisoners.

8

Prisoner Higher Education and the American Dream: The Case of INSIGHT, INC.

Robert P. Weiss

> There's things we can do with those who have fallen from grace, and I think INSIGHT stands as a symbol for that. (J. P. Morgan, June 16, 1985)[1]

Established in 1975, INSIGHT, INCORPORATED, is a nationally prominent college program at the eighty-year-old maximum security prison at Stillwater, Minnesota, near Minneapolis. INSIGHT, which offers a B.A. degree from the University of Minnesota, has three unique characteristics that make it an important subject of study for those interested in prisons and pedagogy. First, INSIGHT did not originate with the efforts of reformers from the outside. It was initiated by prisoners, and a prisoner administrative staff is responsible for its operation. Second, the program is financially self-sufficient, providing tuition-free education for its several dozen members. INSIGHT's operating budget, which originally came from foundation and corporate charitable contributions, now comes from the profits of a prisoner-run business enterprise. INSIGHT's independence from direct state and federal tax money has given its directors considerable administrative latitude. The third unusual characteristic, and one of central theoretical importance to this volume, is the extent to which INSIGHT members embrace capitalist ideology as a foundation for their program. INSIGHT is a strong, independent program which embraces dominant conservative ideology and conventional values and which presents a contradiction to critical criminologists. What are radical educators to make of this?

INSIGHT is administered by a staff of prisoners, who defer to a board of directors on major policy. Established by the prisoners to help alleviate initial concerns by prison officials, the board is composed of three members from the institution's staff, representatives of the legal and business community, two university faculty members, and one prisoner who serves as president. Prisoners are responsible for all of the administrative details and daily program oversight. This staff provides students with educational support services, such as tutoring, academic planning, encouragement, and help in finding project resources. INSIGHT also provides postrelease advisors who help students near release with housing, job arrangements, and assistance in registering at a local college.

In an extraordinary example of prisoner self-government, INSIGHT members have created a separate community in which its student-workers conduct the major spheres of their lives—work, study, and sleep—in a single area, separate from the general population. Cell Hall D provides freedom and comfort unusual for a maximum security prison. Prisoners have little external supervision. In Auburn-style Stillwater prison, the corridor between the four-tiered steel cell block D and the cathedral-windowed cell house wall facing it has been made into a student lounge. Freshly painted and carpeted, the lounge contains tables, plants, a magazine carousel, study lamps, typewriters, and a small library. Students move with freedom and ease from their unlocked cells to quiet yet convivial work and study areas in the cell block. While minimally policed by guards, this self-contained environment facilitates formal and informal control by fellow prisoners. INSIGHT's advisors work closely with students, monitoring their academic progress. And the office of J. P. Morgan, the program's principal founder and decade-long director, keeps a paternalistic eye on operations.

Executives of several large corporations and a number of smaller companies in the Minneapolis area help INSIGHT operate as a nonprofit corporation. In the early years, most of its budget came from contributions and grants.[2] INSIGHT now manages its own telemarketing business for large and small Minnesota firms. By June 1985, Telemarketing Services earned INSIGHT just above $150,000, enough to provide all tuition and administrative support services free for the forty-four full-time students for that year. Since then, INSIGHT has been able to decline further benevolent help, an independence prisoners believe crucial to INSIGHT's success.

INSIGHT's business ventures and its supporting capitalist ideology are keystones of the program because economic enterprise provides an opportunity to demonstrate personal responsibility. Their organization is not a "rehabilitation" program in the meaning of that concept as it developed after World War II (Hawkins 1983). INSIGHT's leadership explicitly rejects the "treatment ethic" of the 1950s and 1960s, which viewed convicts as patients and coerced their therapy. In contrast, INSIGHT is a voluntary program. More than that, it is an elite program with strong competition for membership based on "merit." Its self-reliance demonstrates the virtues of competitiveness and the work ethic, qualities associated with another remarkable Minnesota treatment program, the Free Venture industries program (Auerbach et al. 1969). Part of a federal government initiative, Free Venture is a free enterprise prison industrial program based on the notion that penal industries should simulate normal (i.e., free world) working conditions, especially in worker incentives and production expectations. Free Venture proponents stress responsibility and volition, key concepts of the justice model of correctional management (e.g., Fogel and Hudson 1981). This approach is influential with Minnesota business and political leaders (Weiss 1987).

INSIGHT, INC., weds capitalism and education in a remarkable embodiment of the achievement tenet of American Dream ideology. For motivation, inspiration, and symbolic rewards, INSIGHT draws on the values and beliefs associated with the American Dream, and the behavior of INSIGHT participants is rich in symbolism and ritual that dramatizes achievement against great odds. For their part, state authorities, the business sector, and the media bestow honors and other symbolic rewards on the INSIGHT organization and its membership. Disciplined and self-sufficient, its members confidently act out liberal corporate values intended to impress its audience of Minnesota business leaders. This appeal to these outsiders is crucial to its success. INSIGHT is elite reformation, and its association with corporate leaders outside of prison gives their organization unusual leverage with prison authorities and the state's politicians.

At the same time, however, appeal to business elites also influences cleavages within the prison among fellow prisoners, and it aggravates tensions with guards. As members of the class closest to prisoners, guards are the ones most fearful of prisoner status transformation and therefore the greatest champions of the principle of "least eligibility" (Rutherford 1986, 93).[3] Thus, appeal for INSIGHT's reforms must be made over the heads of the guards and, to some extent, beyond prison administrators as well, although Minnesota has a penal tradition of free enterprise, rehabilitation, and liberal governance and has a prison population that favors prisoners with middle-class backgrounds.

INSIGHT's image is carefully managed, and its rituals and discourse are central to the program's success in selling itself to skeptical prisoners, penal officials, and audiences external to the prison. This process of image management will be a focus of this chapter. I begin with the prevalence of the American Dream in INSIGHT ideology. Then I examine how INSIGHT reconstructs the American Dream for its members and how it uses symbols and rituals to assert its authority. Finally, I provide an analysis of INSIGHT as normative control, but a control with constraints and contradictions imposed by social and organizational structures. Alienation on the inside and unfulfilled promises on the outside could gather momentum with continued recession and fiscal crisis. Even with these weaknesses, however, INSIGHT confronts radical educators with serious theoretical questions. Although popular and empowering, is the INSIGHT program merely a substitution of ideological control for more repressive means? Should INSIGHT be condemned on the basis that it helps to reproduce the class structure and legitimate the relations of domination?

Data for this chapter come from the author's experience teaching for INSIGHT as a University of Minnesota criminology professor in the spring quarter of 1985. The author also spent several hours in interviews with INSIGHT staff for his nomination to the INSIGHT board of directors. These encounters revealed much about the philosophy of the program and the motivation of its founders. In addition, I examine local and national news media accounts of INSIGHT's activities and of INSIGHT's advertising and promotional materials as examples of its skill at image creation, particularly its manipulation of American cultural success symbols.

INSIGHT AND THE AMERICAN DREAM OF SUCCESS

For this discussion of the American Dream, I shall borrow a useful working definition from a 1986 national opinion survey conducted by the Roper Organization for the *Wall Street Journal* (1987, 3). The American Dream is the "promise of a society in which individuals have the opportunity to improve their relative position, regardless of their race, creed or class." In common language, anyone with talent and ambition can "get ahead in life." The Dream as metaphor exists within a cluster of associated beliefs (with differential allegiance based on class strata position) that deal with initiative and class mobility, human nature, education and achievement, luck, and fate. These beliefs help to rationalize the prevailing distribution of wealth and income by deflecting criticism from the social structure and its top occupants onto the economic victims at the bottom.

The *Wall Street Journal* survey found that the American Dream is still a powerful ideological force. Two decades of media attention to the counter-reality of economic stagnation, income polarization, and news accounts of Wall Street shenanigans have not soured the public on the dream of success nor led them to question the basic power arrangements. Belief in egalitarianism, progress, materialism, and individualism remains strong, according to the survey (p. 8). Showing realism, however, the poll takers observe that Americans define their dream less as "getting rich" than in terms of such specifics as home ownership, educational achievement, and the nebulous "freedom of choice in how they live" (p. 9). With their dreams thus qualified, economic security was reported to be of principal concern. But nearly half of the respondents believe that it is not important for them to exceed their parents' living standard.

Respondents report that the "biggest threat to the Dream" comes not from the machinations of the rich, but from illegal drugs, crime, and declining educational quality, in that order. Respondents see failure as a personal problem, generally the result of moral deficiency, inability, or lack of achievement. Sixty-six percent of survey respondents said that they felt they have control over their lives (p. 21), with less well-off respondents expressing a greater belief in luck or fate.

While it is not surprising that the middle class still retains a high valuation of individualism and possesses a strong belief in the American Dream, however qualified, what about prisoners? Robert K. Merton (1957) and the subcultural theorists who worked in his theoretical tradition (Cloward and Ohlin 1960; Cohen 1955) predicted that, faced with structural barriers, those near the bottom of the social structure would be more likely to react against middle-class values of success, resort to crime, or retreat or withdraw from competition, that is, reject the American Dream. Merton also suggested the possibility of rebellion: a public rejection of conventional means and goals and advocacy for new values and standards of success that have a "closer correspondence between merit, effort and reward" (1957, 155).[4] Radical theorists might reasonably expect that these social pariahs would be fertile ground for critical insight and rebellion (e.g., Sbarbaro, chapter 6 of this volume). As double failures—failing at both the legitimate and the illegitimate worlds—and in a desperately powerless and mortifying position, convicts should be better able to understand the distinction between "the personal troubles of milieu" and "the public issues of social structure," in C. Wright Mills's terms (1970, 7).

New Left versions of radical theory would predict that, with political education and outside support organizations, convicts would readily attribute their predicament to the capitalist system (Atkins and Glick 1972; Pallas and Barber 1980). But this romanticizes prisoners, who rarely become revolutionaries. Confronted by their professor with data on economic inequality, they commonly respond with an attitude of "hip-cynicism." Karl Marx was wrong. Humans are greedy and competitive by nature. "Even if we had revolutionary change, inequality would only reassert itself," they argue. "Greed is human nature," and students just want their share. After all, "Isn't that why we're in college?" What is most remarkable is that, in accepting this ideology, prisoners must find some way to rationalize their failure to gain from within that system, if only to protect their own self-esteem. The following section attempts to locate INSIGHT in the failure construct; that is, it considers how prisoners cope with the contradiction between their personal failure and their embrace of the American Dream.

FOUR STRATEGIES

Prisoners pay a high price in lost self-esteem for their belief in the dream of opportunity. The knowledge that they blew their opportunity to "get ahead" leads many to one conclusion: "There must be something wrong with me, so what's the use in trying." This self-defeating attitude is central to the psychology of their powerlessness. Yet, in other contexts, prisoners express a strong belief in complete personal freedom. The pain of guilt, however, is the burden for the existential view. For many, the psychic toll becomes intolerable, and they fall into psychopathology. But most resolve this tension in some rationalization that denies their responsibility.

First of these is to attribute their failure to luck or fate; however, continued frustration can turn into a more extreme form of determinism, *fatalism*. Those who explain away their past by arguing that they had no control over their actions deny their power over the future. Fatalism is common among "state-raised" youths and those from struggling neighborhoods bereft of good jobs, decent schools, and hope, who have no stake in society or nothing to lose by going to prison (Terry 1992). Seeing little difference between the worlds of the streets and prison, fatalists fail to enroll in rehabilitation programs and leave prison without attempting to acquire any skills for legitimate (or sophisticated illegitimate) life. Soon returned to prison, fatalists orient to the inside, focusing on making out in the prison's subterranean economy of force and fraud as hustlers.

Not all prisoners resort to extreme resignation and defeatism. *Cynicism* is a common alternative attitude. Cynics attribute their failure to "the system": to not knowing the "right" people, to not being able to pull strings. Others attribute their failure specifically to racism. The cynic is commonly the type of deviant Merton (1957) identified as the "innovator," the person who, out of frustration, pursues cultural goals of pecuniary success employing illegitimate means, most commonly in the form of crime.[5] In prison, many cynics direct their energies toward self-improvement, however, taking advantage of programs that promise to enhance their prospects for a fair share, perhaps sharpening their criminal skills while increasing parole prospects. Prison is experienced as a special deprivation, and in the 1960s and 1970s these "illegitimate capitalists," as Huey Newton (1973, 52) contemptuously called them, often agitated for prison reform as "political prisoners." In his study of Stateville Prison in the mid-1970s, Jacobs (1976, 481) identified Chicago street gang leaders as innovators, who advocated the use of institutional programs to educate and train their members.

A third reaction can be found among prisoners who reject cynicism and fatalism and who instead accept responsibility for their misdeeds; many of them attempt to atone for them by *turning to religion* to unburden themselves of guilt. Some become what Merton termed "ritualists," who scale down pecuniary success goals while compulsively participating in staff-sponsored programs. This career appeals to lower-middle-class whites, and finds expression in many conventional religious prison groups (including evangelical and Colson-type ministries), whose members' obedience and discipline claim little earthly reward save enhanced parole prospects. But religious conversion serves the important psychological function of allowing convicts to create a "new self," renounce their past deeds without denying them, and so retain the values of individualism they grew up with.

Few prisoners, however, have strong religious convictions or possess a radical political commitment that could serve to "insulate the true believer against the assaults of a total institution" (Goffman 1961, 66).[6] Some try to immunize themselves from the "pains of imprisonment" by seeking special compensations on the inside for helping custodians maintain informal controls. The most common of these *conformists* are "rats," in prison argot (Sykes 1958, 90). Those who occupy this role betray their fellow prisoners for personal advantage, as does the "center man," the one who is willing to get along with institutional officials. These are the lowest and most despised adjustments. Closely behind them are the character roles modeled after Asklepieion-type Transactional Analysis groups, whose members get special luxuries and privileges in exchange for cooperation and because they share some of the basic ideals of the administration. They accept the oppressor's norms and identify with them. Unlike center men, however, members of these psycho-drama groups are basically outside oriented, "training" to become "therapists" in the national organization after parole (Griffin 1993).

Employing a mixture of therapies, including attack therapy, marathons, and primal therapy, Asklepieion (whose members other prisoners call "groders") fosters child-like dependence. Prisoners take on the role of "child" in relation to the "parent" role of prison officials. Griffin observes,

Consequently, intercommunication becomes artificial, stilted, and utterly meaningless in its content. Everyone sounds like a pseudo-intellectual. . . . Although some "groders" pretend that this practice is a fakeout on the "man," it is still a real social practice. Changing the words to describe it does not change reality. (p. 24)

Groders are alienative because they are contemptuous of other cons, who view them as "mental enemies."

While there are several strategies to deal with personal failure and hold fast to the American Dream (i.e., fatalism, cynicism, religion, and conformity), INSIGHT provides a rationalization or conformity with a difference, conformity without slavish submissiveness, a kind of radical embrace of failure in order to move beyond it and at once embrace success.

CONFORMITY WITH A DIFFERENCE

INSIGHT men are incorruptible but not slavishly submissive. Nor are they alienated or outright contemptuous of other convicts, like the brainwashed Asklepieion elite group. Unlike groders, INSIGHT men have a way to actualize their power—to act on their imaginings. They do not just talk about success. The light has not gone out in their eyes, as Griffin describes the humiliated groders at Marion Federal Penitentiary. The men of IN-SIGHT admit their guilt, but they do not dwell on their past misdeeds. This is a main tenet of INSIGHT philosophy, according to J. P. Morgan (Benidt 1985): The past is the past. Brad Vogelpohl, an INSIGHT advisor serving a life sentence for the hammer bludgeoning of his girlfriend, concurs: "What we were is not as important as what we are and what we're going to be." And therein lies a big problem for many staff members.

INSIGHT's unusual attitude creates tension with many guards. To achieve their independence from official pressures and sanctions, INSIGHT enforces a conformity based on sanctions more severe than those imposed by the official regime. But some custodians view INSIGHT discipline as a mixed blessing. Unlike center men (Sykes 1958, 89), who might embarrass staff by taking "on the opinions, attitudes, and beliefs of the custodians," INSIGHT men threaten the self-esteem of guards in several ways. First, INSIGHT men have an extraordinary amount of countervailing power and influence, which puts into question the "meaning of punishment" in the view of the guards. Second, conflict arises from their perceived incorrupti-bility, which contradicts the received wisdom of the staff concerning the character of prisoners.

Third, and perhaps most important, INSIGHT members threaten guards' self-esteem by promoting a version of the American Dream that is out of the normal reach of their keepers.[7] As college students with promis-ing careers upon release, INSIGHT threatens the self-esteem of the poorly educated, low-paid, low-status guard. INSIGHT prisoners must continu-ally resist attempts by resentful staff to reassert a more familiar reality, one more in conformity to their stereotypes of convicts. Thus, from the view of many guards, INSIGHT men conform too well; their success, ironically, is viewed as an insubordination of sorts.

THE SYMBOLIC DIMENSION OF INSIGHT

INSIGHT is a cleverly crafted cultural construction by which its mem-bers manage to alter their subjective reality and sustain a new identity transformed by rituals and the use of material symbols, involving textual discourses, the interior design of a cell block, ceremonies for admission and graduation, and role models. All of this is referenced to American Dream symbolism. This analysis will show how, by deftly "manipulating a set of socially given symbols" (Mills 1963, 434) of the American Dream, INSIGHT has formed a countercommunity with counterdefinitions of prison reality and prisoner identity (Berger and Luckmann 1967, 165–67). These potent symbols are able to call out a response in important others, including some of the state's most powerful political and corporate leaders. And, most important, they influence convict behavior. INSIGHT regulates conduct by shaping meaning; it is a signifying practice which, along with its own socialization rituals, is a mechanism for social control.[8]

We will begin with INSIGHT's Telemarketing Services brochure, a very important piece of symbolic material because INSIGHT's telemarketing business—along with computer programming and home computer instruction service—generated 70 percent of INSIGHT's six-figure profit report for 1984 (Benidt 1985). The brochure speaks to business managers, including chief executive officers of 3M, Control Data, and other major corporations, who must be convinced of convict trustworthiness to represent their business image. Thus, the brochure announces INSIGHT's philosophy of punishment as well as its business services. In communicating with the business sector, important analytic themes concerning subjectivity involve status consistency, social perception and moral judgment, and the psychology of success.[9] Prisoners are socially invisible; they come to the attention of the public generally as the result of violent protest. To gain power otherwise—to replace force with communication—prisoners must become visible to power-holders as subjects who have qualities other than their master-status as criminals. This reality extends to their business promotion—that INSIGHT prisoners are worthy people who will also make money for their clients. But business opportunities available to convicts are limited, and telemarketing is a problematic choice.

Successful telemarketing requires a higher degree of trust than does face-to-face sales, especially product sales to new customers. The brochure is not just a sales pitch on the merits of their service, but must speak to the legitimacy of the entire enterprise. In attempting to convince potential customers that Telemarketing Services will appeal in turn to their customers, INSIGHT's brochure must deal with a disturbing subtext—the concern of what the client's customer would think if the criminal status of its sales force were revealed.

Since telemarketing is often a suspect business anyway, INSIGHT makes a special effort to demonstrate that its members have not only the intelligence, but also the moral character to do business with them. They do this by acting out the "norms of success," especially those related to ethics. INSIGHT must show potential customers that they can distinguish between the norms of success—"the type of personal characteristics and the types of behavior which 'ought' to be successful" (Ichheiser 1970, 180)—and the "conditions of success," or only what is instrumentally necessary. Their brochure says (between the lines) that they will follow the rules, they will employ legitimate means. Hence, INSIGHT warns of "the common mistake" of unrealistic expectations and exaggerated claims, where "companies become willing victims to overzealous telephone sales representatives with slick promotional gimmicks." This is a sort of insider's advice.

Yet there still is the danger that INSIGHT men will be perceived as psychopaths. To get everything out in the open, INSIGHT men readily reveal the nature of their crimes. This is intended to reduce the nagging subtext of distrust by a display of responsibility. INSIGHT men are willing to be held accountable; they take full responsibility for their past actions— no sad story line, no self-pity. The brochure says: "Insight changes attitudes and values. Once self-conceptions improve, students no longer view themselves as victims of circumstance, but as commanders of their destinies." As penal discourse, the brochure underscores the capitalist values of activism, achievement, and freedom espoused by nineteenth century bankers, industrialists, and railroad magnates.[10]

The image reconstructed in the brochure's philosophical statements aligns with the correctional rationale called the "justice-as-fairness" model (Fogel and Hudson 1981). This correctional ideology is prominent in the higher circles of Minnesota state government, and strongly advocated by then state commissioner of corrections, Kenneth Schoen. Its penal discourse depicts individual subjects as "responsible, volitional, and aspiring human beings, and does not conceive of them as patients" (Schaller quoted in Fogel and Hudson 1981, viii). It is pragmatic, utilitarian, and rationalistic, viewing action as the result of free moral agency. Assumptions about persons shape its assumptions about social policy, and the "justice" conception of social authority contrasts with the discourse of liberal penal welfare correctionalism. The "justice perspective" at Minnesota weds neoconservative notions of privatization of penal industry with the neoliberal values of humanitarianism and civil libertarianism (Weiss 1987).

On the business side of image making, Telemarketing Services' large, glossy, three-page foldout brochure is professional in appearance, appealing to both business motives and concern for rehabilitation. The opening two pages address the business advantages to their services, "providing a 'human response' " and "an exchange *you* can control." From the front cover photo of a fashionably groomed telemarketer presented in film strip repetition, the emphasis in the text is on uniformity, measurement, and monitoring for quality control. For customers who know that INSIGHT offers a reliable, inexpensive service, the rehabilitation angle provides a moral rationale for a cost that could be viewed by competitors and labor groups as exploitative. Finally, the brochure invites potential customers to come in and look around for themselves, to look behind the images. This can be done on an individual appointment basis, or at the annual open house.

OTHER SIGNIFYING PRACTICES

A visit to Cell Hall D leads to a consideration of the symbolic import of INSIGHT's physical environment, its interior design. Garland (1991, 201) points to institutional architecture as another method by which penal practices signify meaning. Architecture is "the external imagery of the prison," its iconography, and is what is most visible to the public eye. INSIGHT was limited, of course, by the basic structure of the Auburn-style prison, but within this constraint they have created a corporate environment. If Stillwater is in the "architecture terrible" tradition, INSIGHT men have—through furnishings and decoration—made Cell Hall D into "architecture corporate." It announces that social authority is not absolutist or authoritarian, nor is it welfarist or rehabilitative in the medical-model tradition of the 1950s and 1960s.

Cell Hall D is not just a classroom, then. It is also a business—a location to act out the norms of success, demonstrating the efficacy of the "normalization" school of penology (Schaller 1981; Hawkins 1983). The "realistic" work environment includes commercial business furniture (not state issue) and the latest computers. In INSIGHT's "offices," converted D Block cells, men are busy working on computers and phones. On their off-hours, they can be found studying in their carpeted lounge—while their cells are left open and unguarded. In replicating as closely as possible conditions in the nonpenal world—in rewards as well as expectations—the work ethic is best promoted, according to justice theory. INSIGHT businesses stand in sharp contrast to make-work industries producing state-use goods (e.g., license plates) characteristic of penal industry nationwide. "Strict concern for custody or a view of work as part of the criminal's punishment can destroy a program of efficient production," Sykes (1958, 16) observed long ago. INSIGHT stands for the way in which individuals ought to relate in a just society; ideal social relations are depicted as market relations, not as punitive or therapeutic ones.

An annual Christmas open house is another occasion for the public to mix with INSIGHT students. The open house is a familiar institutional ceremony, but INSIGHT's is distinguished from the typical "institutional display" (Goffman 1961, 101)—variety shows and mess hall dinners—by its sophistication. The INSIGHT open house is a banquet catered from outside, typically roast turkey or prime rib, with floral arrangements and linen tablecloths. The 1984 dinner was attended by 150 guests, including business, political, and academic dignitaries.

Rituals are central to social structure. Rituals symbolically mark interaction: They announce the beginning, sequencing, and termination of interaction. INSIGHT's two most important rituals are the "entering," or conversion, ritual and the college graduation ceremony. They are richly symbolic. The screening and acceptance process, in which prospective INSIGHT students undergo a three-step initiation, is the beginning of the resocialization process, the first stage in the process of conversion. Prisoners, who have at least a year left on their sentences, first take a battery of major inventories and examinations. As a second stage, those who achieve minimum scores on the aptitude tests undergo an extensive interview by the INSIGHT executive committee, which is concerned with such intangible qualities as sincerity, desire, and commitment to study and self-improvement. Third, those accepted by the committee are admitted on a ninety-day probationary period. Then, prospective students must sign a contract that requires full-time student status, a minimum grade-point average, and a pledge to be quiet and harmonious and not to discredit themselves, the program, or the prison administration. They also must agree to undergo a urinalysis at any time and to work full-time for INSIGHT or Minnesota Correctional Industries (MCI). Any violation of these rules can result in immediate expulsion from the program.

The program is policed by advisors, a cross between spiritual advisors and cops. Violators of INSIGHT norms who are expelled suffer a mode of "social death," to borrow a concept from Orlando Patterson (1982, 40–41) used in another context. If prisoners in general can be described as "the domestic enemy" within free society, a "product of a hostile, alien culture," and therefore excommunicated by imprisonment, the INSIGHT norm violator suffers further "extrusive" social death, an "insider who has fallen, one who has ceased to belong and had been expelled from normal participation in the community [of outsiders] because of a failure to meet certain legal or socioeconomic norms of behavior" (p. 41).

Various activities help solidify INSIGHT members' consciousness against counterreality. Most important are testimonials repudiating alternative realities. Such testimonials mark the new from the old reality in one's biographical history. The old reality becomes totally negative. "Switching worlds" of subjective reality, or "alternation" according to Berger and Luckmann (1967, 160), requires "a radical reinterpretation of the meaning of these past events or persons in one's biography." Thus, much is said about how the INSIGHT experience has transformed them. J. P. Morgan, the program's most significant member, sets the tone with this repudiation of (pre)alternation life: "Shortly after the start of my sentence (life imprisonment for a double murder, jail escape, and kidnapping a farm family), I had 'hit bottom.' I found myself in isolation and hoping that someone would kill me. I had gone as low as you can in life." In creating INSIGHT, "I decided to pick myself up and do something positive while in prison" ("McNeil/Lehrer News Hour," 1985, June 16). In terms of his dedication to INSIGHT goals and converts, he told a reporter: "I like to see people change. It just gives me good feelings to see them turn their life around, especially guys who have been stuck in the mud for so many years, in and out, in and out" (Benidt 1985).

INSIGHT graduation ceremonies are occasions for poignant testimonials: "The biggest thing they give you is a chance to be a man again," said graduate Larry Keithahn as he received his diploma in business, marketing, and communications at the 1984 ceremony. And graduations are quite impressive symbols in themselves. The 1984 graduation commencement address was given by the president of the University of Minnesota; and former chief justice of the U.S. Supreme Court, Warren Burger, attended the 1983 commencement and reception (Norton 1984).

A final level of signification are *atonement practices* that "suggest the (social) relations that hold *between offenders and victims* [italics added]," in Garland's (1991, 214) words. These are perhaps the most powerful methods by which INSIGHT signifies meaning. They reaffirm the capitalist values of morality and philanthropic strategies to ameliorate problems. The most recent gesture has been to award annual college scholarships to needy area high school seniors. "Inside Insight," the organization's quarterly newsletter, notes in vol. 1, 18 that the INSIGHT Crime Victim Fund received letters of commendation from the lieutenant governor, the warden, and the president of the Citizens Council on Crime and Justice in honor of its first anniversary in 1983. The men of INSIGHT donated over $3,600 to the fund from their monthly earnings. Governor Al Quie declared July 22–28, 1979, "INSIGHT Week" in Minnesota, and J. P. Morgan was named "Good Neighbor of the Week" by the state's major radio station. The newsletter also noted that the INSIGHT Telemarketing Service received an award from United Way and Control Data for its HOMEWORK program, a Control Data service that provides computer instruction to the homebound. This program symbolizes INSIGHT solidarity with the physically disabled. In accepting the award, George Chamberlain said that his "personal reward comes each time a student receives their [*sic*] certification and joins the working community." He and Roy Wahlberg, another HOMEWORK instructor, told a reporter that "they're touched by communicating electronically with people imprisoned in handicapped bodies" (Benidt 1985).

INSIGHT AND ITS CONTRADICTIONS

INSIGHT is a vehicle for convict self-transformation, a means to renegotiate identities, and a way to acquire cultural capital so convicts can achieve status legitimately. It is a powerful mechanism by which convicts assimilate the dominant value system. The success of INSIGHT lends empirical support to the hypotheses advanced by Matsueda, Piliavin, Gartner, and Polakowski (1992) in their study of the prestige of criminal and conventional occupations among ex-offenders. The respondents in Matsueda's study "ranked conventional occupations uniformly higher in prestige than criminal occupations" (p. 752), suggesting that "the lower-class and other disenfranchised groups are not irretrievably immersed in a deviant subculture, helplessly following deviant values and norms. Rather, they have no legitimate opportunities and must develop and follow alternative norms" (p. 768). "Subcultures are intimately tied to structural opportunities," Matsueda et al. (p. 768) conclude from their study. Those who have access to conventional opportunities could be expected to pursue legitimate occupations, and thus be subject to conventional social controls. As we have seen, INSIGHT provides just such access. Legitimate capitalist values can penetrate prison walls.

The INSIGHT program is contrary to sociological prediction because studies of prison society (Clemmer 1958; Sykes and Messinger 1960) and deviance theories (Cloward and Ohlin 1960; Matza and Sykes 1961) suggest that prisons are the most unlikely environments for the adoption of conventional norms and values. The high degree of alienation produced by the coerciveness of the typical prison usually militates against the positive and moral feeling required by rehabilitation. Moreover, from a philosophical perspective, the powerlessness of prisoners as "outsiders" should make them very skeptical of the dominant class ideology. Yet, my colleagues in several different state prison systems have observed that in classroom discussions prisoners are on the average quite conservative politically. While most welcome "radical" critiques of the criminal justice system, when class discussion turns to the larger social structure, prisoner-students generally equal or exceed their middle-class counterparts on campus in enthusiastic acceptance of the American Dream. This is not what many radical (or conventional) deviancy theorists would expect (Pallas and Barber 1980; Cohen 1955).

While legitimated by the state's top penal officials and supported by Minnesota's corporate class, and promoting conventional capitalist ideology, the INSIGHT program comes from "below," so to speak, with a remarkable degree of prisoner allegiance. INSIGHT's claims are credible to a skeptical prisoner population because INSIGHT has demonstrated its effectiveness in empowering prisoners and improving their treatment. Unlike most rehabilitation programs, it delivers for both convicts—providing a liberal arts education with some employment potential—and the state, which gets model behavior. INSIGHT illustrates that conventional values can be embraced by members of the lowest stratum of the class structure. The success of this program has special implications for subcultural theory, which theorizes "the lower class" as irretrievably immersed in a dysfunctional subculture (see Inniss and Feagin 1989). INSIGHT as an alternative form of conformity reconstructs the American Dream which enables prisoner-members to rationalize the assault of the failure construct on their psyches. Thus they reconstruct their identities within the dominant ideology. But, just how far reaching or enduring the INSIGHT program will be has yet to be determined. Overall, Minnesota's prison population is mostly white, and the state's sentencing practices historically have diverted property offenders from maximum security prisons. We can assume that many prisoners sentenced for crimes of violence, including sex crimes, were oriented to conventional success values anyway. Some were business owners or professionals before incarceration. So, through system selection and self-selection, the men of INSIGHT are the crème de la crème of prisoners. And this breeds resentment among other convicts.

INSIGHT clearly contributes to the stratification of Stillwater prison society. So does its ideological twin, the Control Data Corporation–Minnesota Free Venture industrial program, whose workers received the highest prison wages in 1984 in exchange for abiding by work rules that would have made old Henry Ford blush (Weiss 1987, 279). The exalted status of these two elite programs antagonizes many prisoners, especially those who were not admitted or were expelled from the programs. A measure of INSIGHT's status with the general prisoner population can be implied from reading a decade of *The Prison Mirror*, Stillwater's award-winning paper. There are numerous stories celebrating the achievements of students in the various programs of the Education Department, but one searches in vain for an article on INSIGHT (including a period when the *Mirror*'s editor was an INSIGHT student).

As for MCI, disgruntled workers have joined in a class action lawsuit (Walker 1992) challenging the state's practice of paying less than the minimum wage for goods and services produced by prisoners and used in interstate commerce. The suit also alleges that convicts are being forced to work under threat of losing good time or serving lengthier sentences. While many consider working for INSIGHT and Free Venture a privilege, a lumpenproletariat or "stagnant surplus population" is made of those who refuse to participate in private industrial initiatives. They enter a new category of deviance, doubly stigmatized. As in the operation of the labor market in the free world, those who refuse to work must clearly be "less eligible" than those occupying the lowest stratum of the working class. In a world as spare as prison, that condition might mean longer sentences.

Historically, Minnesota prisons are not as stratified as other state institutions, and this accounts in part for their largely nonviolent and democratic character. But INSIGHT and Free Venture reproduce within prison the class structure. They create class cleavages that administrative tradition and the state's demographics have blunted. INSIGHT men occupy the top stratum, with the best-paying jobs and matriculation with the University of Minnesota (for the general population, the Education Department contracted with the less prestigious Metropolitan State). And, for the most part, these elites are from the cultural majority, from whom historically the top occupants of the social structure have been drawn. So, we must look with great skepticism on J. P. Morgan's aspiration to see the INSIGHT program adopted by "every prison." The prison world outside of Minnesota is not predominantly white. The history of "black capitalism" promoted by the Black Muslims is revealing. This "legitimate" capitalist program receives little or no outside financial support. And the practice of their religion, Islam, is still repressed in many prisons, or certainly is not viewed as favorably by prison officials as the "gospel of success" preached by INSIGHT.

Furthermore, in this economy, it is not at all certain how much longer INSIGHT can claim postrelease employment success. The American Dream will convey legitimacy to the INSIGHT regime only so long as there is some correspondence in postrelease employment reality. Since opportunity for upward mobility underpins the American Dream, chronic recession is likely to bring on a "crisis of belief," breaking down the viability of symbols manipulated as rewards. And, in regard to employment and recidivism, insofar as the two are correlated, INSIGHT may actually be setting its graduates up for a very hard disappointment, and may sharpen the frustration of failure. Warden Erickson observed:

A college degree helps inmates look differently at life. They set their goals a little higher in terms of how they want to live. I don't mean just money, but in the kind of job they look for, the kind of neighbourhood they want to live in, what they want to do with their families. (Quoted in Benidt 1985, 10)

How are they going to live up to their lofty expectations of success? Will the threat of defeat turn them cynical? Will they be motivated to use "those tactics, beyond the law or the mores, which promise 'success' " (Merton 1957, 169) where they would otherwise have been satisfied with their accomplishments? After all of the praise and attention the men of INSIGHT receive in prison, how will they deal with postrelease anonymity?

NOTES

1. Comment made by J. P. Morgan on "McNeil/Lehrer News Hour." (June 16, 1985).

2. For instance, Control Data Corporation contributed a $60,000 computer-operated training program.

3. "Least eligibility" refers to the principle of nineteenth-century English poor-relief, intended to discourage relief of the able-bodied, which held that the living conditions of workhouse relief (and by implication, prisons also) should never be more "eligible" (i.e., comfortable) than the standard of living of the lowest paid, free worker. Rusche and Kirchheimer (1968, 94) observe: "This principle, incorporated in the Poor Law of 1834, is the leitmotiv of all prison administration down to the present time."

4. Reference should be made to critiques of the functionalism in Merton's theory. One of the earliest but still cogent critiques of the value consensus assumption appears in Taylor, Walton, and Young (1973, 102): "There are no good reasons for assuming . . . that men born into different social positions and in widely different relationships to the structure of opportunity, will want or be able to internalize the dominant social goals." For a partial rejoinder, see Messner and Rosenfeld (1994, 60–61).

5. In his classic essay, Merton (1957) situated much of the motivation for crime and deviance squarely within the American Dream. Structurally blocked from legitimate means, "innovators" identify with criminal subcultures that pro-

vide an illegitimate opportunity structure (Cloward and Ohlin 1960). Values are the link between social structure and individual action (Gerth and Mills 1964), and the development of subcultural theory has stressed the centrality of values. Criminal subcultures promote a distinct value system and an alternative status hierarchy that work against internalization of the dominant norms governing legitimate means.

6. Although there are socialists and clandestine groups in prisons today, most of those who question basic power arrangements have been repressed by officials or co-opted or modified into conformity (Gilbert 1991, 77–81). Even during the height of prisoner political consciousness, rebelliousness was rare. In "An Attica Graduate Tells His Story," William R. Coons observes: "The average reader would be surprised how conservative the average con is, and in many instances, how patriotic his sentiments. The only time cons begin to get radical is when they feel their backs are against the wall. The long termer's dream is to get back into society as he knew it" (Atkins and Glick 1972, 117).

7. The guards, who are from the same social class, are extreme carriers of the principle of "least eligibility," and they are not enamored of the prospect that their subordinates are training for jobs that promise higher wages and prestige than those of their own occupation. But, because INSIGHT convicts are connected to powerful outside forces, staff must at least outwardly defer. In the liberal corporate capitalist milieu of the Minneapolis community, INSIGHT graduate parolees can have a realistic expectation of employment in the computer industry; some have gone directly to work at Control Data Corporation, 3M, local insurance companies, and other businesses.

8. On the function of language as a system of social control see Mills (1963, 433). Garland points to penal practice as "a locus of cultural production," and he outlines some of the methods, audiences, and types of meaning created by penal culture. According to Garland (1991, 197–98), there are several methods by which penal practices signify meaning. One area, penal discourse and knowledge, includes "speech acts, performances and publications," policy statements, and philosophical statements.

9. This discussion of the social psychology of social perception follows Ichheiser (1970).

10. According to Turner and Starnes (1976, 69), there are at least nine dominant values that help legitimate the structural arrangements that preserve the system of privilege and poverty: "(1) activism, (2) achievement, (3) progress, (4) materialism, (5) freedom, (6) individualism, (7) egalitarianism, (8) morality, and (9) humanitarianism." These are "criteria for assessing the desirability of others."

9

A Note on Prison Activism and Social Justice

Edward Sbarbaro

Official sanitized histories tend to disregard the struggles of oppressed people for social justice. Just as the sustained determination of the oppressed in the labor and civil rights movement is discounted if not erased, so prisoner political activism is not found in those texts that portray the history of the United States as a story of progress.[1] A comprehensive prison history would remind us of both prisoner struggles for improved prison conditions and the intimate relationships of these struggles with those of all oppressed people.

This note registers some thoughts on an aspect of these relationships that has received no attention in the literature of prison education: thoughts on prisons as places transformed by prisoners into schools of liberation, where prisoners educate themselves and each other for the purpose of furthering social justice. As teachers who locate ourselves on the side of political struggle for liberation, we should be documenting and investigating the social, political, and economic forces that shape the formation of these schools, and we should be considering their implications for our own practices.

POLITICAL ACTIVISM AND EDUCATION IN THE UNITED STATES

An early example of prisoners transforming incarceration into an educational experience comes from the history of the Industrial Workers of the

World. IWW leaders imprisoned in the Cook County Jail (Chicago) in 1917 held "educational meetings" consisting "of a series of talks on each of the various industries represented by the IWW members present. These 'One Big Union' talks covered not only the history of the industry but also its technological and functional integration with the industries of the nation and the world" (Chaplin 1948, 233).

The Black Power movement also has an extensive history of teacher-prisoners who furthered the struggle by educating and organizing other prisoners. In his autobiography, Malcolm X describes the political significance of his self-study, of studying with other Black Muslims while in prison, and of his "first experiences in opening the eyes of my brainwashed black brethren to some truths about the black race" (Malcolm X 1966, 182). Malcolm X regarded his prison education as essential to the development of his historical consciousness (p. 179). He describes the prison environment as generally ripe ground for radical teaching and recruitment:

This is probably as big a single worry as the American prison system has today—the way the Muslim teachings, circulated among all Negroes in the country, are converting new Muslims among black men in prison, and black men are in prison in far greater numbers than their proportion in the population. (p. 183)

Malcolm X's experience illustrates an important dilemma confronting the U.S. criminal justice system. When large numbers of an oppressed group are incarcerated together, they are positioned to raise their consciousness and to challenge their conditions of confinement.[2] Today, in the United States, it is estimated that there are well over 100 prisoners incarcerated for their political activities (Deutsch and Susler 1991, 93). These political prisoners, and those who are politicized by their prison experience, continue to transform the prison into schools teaching radical historical consciousness that will support struggles for social justice. Rita "Bo" Brown, a former political prisoner, describes how "revolutionaries" continue organizing even when they are on the inside: "For many this has meant organizing resistance to oppressive prison policies, publishing prison news letters, providing legal help and assistance, facilitating courses, work stoppages and hunger strikes. For others it has meant becoming AIDS activists" (Brown 1993, 17).

This level of political activism does not go unnoticed by prison authorities. Its influence can be gagged by the repression with which prison activism is met. At present, in the United States, politicized prisoners who are outspoken and make efforts to politicize others have been transferred to the federal penitentiary at Marion, Illinois, where sensory deprivation combined with solitary confinement is used to break their spirits (Amnesty International 1987; Dowker and Good 1993).

THE INTIFADA

While the United States has a history of prisons as sites of political education and activism, the most stark example of prisons transformed into schools for radical pedagogy are found in South Africa, Ireland, and Palestine. In this brief note, it is sufficient to provide a schematic description of one of these examples.

The Palestinian uprising, known as the *intifada*, began in December 1987. Jonathan Kuttab states that "what has occurred in the communities living under Israeli occupation has been nothing short of revolutionary. The revolt has so transformed and radicalized the way people act and interact that it produced a new consciousness in Palestinian thinking and relationships" (1988, 26). Central to the *intifada* is an identity which emerged among a generation of Palestinians who were born and socialized in the West Bank and Gaza under Israeli occupation. Particularly important among the formative experiences which contributed to their consciousness is serving time in Israeli jails. Moughrabi estimates that from 1967 to the present at least one-third of a population of 1.5 million have been imprisoned, and those who entered prison with limited political awareness emerged as "committed and politically sophisticated cadres" (Moughrabi 1992, 55). In 1985 over 1,000 Palestinian activists were released from prison as part of a prisoner exchange. The Israeli Defense Ministry estimates that approximately 80 percent of this group joined the *intifada* when it began in 1987, and two-thirds of these former prisoners were rearrested in its first year (Ya'ari 1989, 27–30). In the first twenty-one months of the *intifada*, over 50,000 Palestinians were incarcerated in Israeli prisons and detention camps. This has resulted in close ties between prison activists and Palestinians involved in the struggle on the streets.

The Palestinian prison movement actually began in 1970, three years after the Israeli occupation of the West Bank and Gaza Strip. Rights won by the Palestinian prisoners increased their relative autonomy within the prisons. These rights were the basis for transforming the prisons into "academies," which became instrumental in organizing a struggle that extended beyond the prison walls. According to Ehud Ya'ari, the Israelis, who were adept at foiling external threats to their security, failed to observe the internal threat organized by Palestinians within their prisons.

Three of Israel's maximum-security facilities, where men are under constant supervision, were the forge in which the machinery of and tactics of the "intifada" were wrought. Over the years, in full view of the Israeli jailers, Palestinian security prisoners [who are held separate from "common criminals"] built an independent network whose cohesion, intellectual verve, and rich store of experience would manifest themselves in all their power during the Palestinian uprising. (Ya'ari 1989, 22)

Several new methods of organization and struggle which developed in the prisons later became part of the *intifada*. For example, in prison, as in the *intifada*'s United National Command, decisions were made by unanimous agreement rather than majority rule, and all factions had equal representation regardless of their size or standing. In both situations, political decisions emerged from wide-ranging popular discourse at the local level and were distributed by pamphlets or hand bills called *nida'*, which translates as "call to" rather than "order" (Moughrabi 1992, 56). Their leaders arose out of this early prison experience. In the occupied territories, a prison record is a mark of distinction, not a stigma, and almost a necessity to speak on behalf of the Palestinian cause. Of the approximately twenty people who have served its high command, all but two have prison experience.

POLITICALIZATION AND CONVENTIONAL PRISON EDUCATION

These histories show that prisons have been and continue to be transformed into schools of liberation where prisoners develop political consciousness. A multiplicity of factors influence the nature of this educational activity, including the intensity of the resistance to the hegemony of the dominant ideology and strength of support for prisoners' struggles by outside organizations.

As a teacher for a prison education program, administered by a college and operating with the approval of a department of corrections, I ask myself and others who identify with struggles for social justice to consider what, if any, part we may play in similar processes of politicalization? Can prison educators like ourselves ally with those prisoners who engage in this process? Does the formal organization of our programs provide sufficient autonomy from the dictates of penal authorities to permit us to engage and thereby supplement and complement prisoners' schools? The problematics raised by these questions are central concerns in this volume. Here, I will restrict myself to comment on the last one, the question of autonomy in relation to postsecondary education programs.

The 1980s brought a shift in prison ideology which made possible what Ray Jones calls an "accidental praxis" that gave postsecondary prison education increased autonomy relative to other prison programs (Jones 1992). At this time, the ideology shifted from a "rehabilitation model," which emphasized therapeutic programs, to a "justice model," which worked to protect society. Budgetary considerations followed, directing resources to prison security rather than programs. This created a program void that colleges were able to fill. Since these programs were administered from college campuses and prisoners received grants separate from prison resources, these prison higher education programs enjoyed some independence of prison control. Nonetheless, Ray Jones's concerns about prison college education in Massachusetts should be universally heeded.

The principal dilemmas higher learning must confront is its unintended collusion with the penal apparatus, which arises from the coincidence of interests it shares with the Massachusetts' Department of Corrections. Entry into the prison milieu transforms the fundamental character of education. Its basic premises and values are undermined by the coercive environment in which it operates. . . . As prison higher education programs become increasingly integrated with corrections, there is the danger that they will become complicit [sic] in the process that has historically done little but degrade and defile (1992, 17).

The pervasiveness of prison social control and its threat to educational autonomy are reflected in attempts to legitimate prison education as rehabilitation based on the moral development of prisoners. This legitimation tacitly accepts a main tenet of the criminal justice ideology—that the etiology of crime lies in the individual rather than in the social structure. MacLean finds that prisoner education poised as moral education is really social control, which will be evaluated in terms of reducing recidivism rather than on pedagogical merit (MacLean 1992, 27; also see Wotherspoon 1986).

It remains to be seen if the marginal independence available to college programs is sufficient to allow educators to support prisoners' educational activism. For reasons noted by Jones and MacLean, this is problematic. Nonetheless, those who would describe themselves as critical pedagogists must ask how their practices and theories engage this activism which is part of prisoners' culture and history. The examples of the IWW, the Black Power movement, and the *intifada* show that there is a history of political education in prison that has been an effective mechanism in the struggle for social justice. Educational programs seeking to be critical pedagogy must have a conscious relationship with these forms of education, which might begin by pursuing research that documents and analyzes this history. In doing so we may embrace this culture of resistance and thereby support the struggle.

NOTES

1. Historical accounts of people's struggles in the United States include H. Zinn, *A People's History of the United States* (1980) and R. O. Boyer and H. M. Morais, *Labor's Untold Story* (1955).

2. Also illustrative of political activism is the work of Sundiata Acoli, a member of the Black Panther Party and a leader of the Black Liberation movement. See his "A Brief History of the New Afrikan Prison Struggle" (1992). For a debate on the extent and nature of political activism by prisoners, see Ratner and Cartwright (1990, 75) and Gaucher's dispute with them (Gaucher 1991). On the penal press as a form of prison education which offers support and information to prisoners and their struggles for social justice, see Gaucher (1989).

10

Prison, Higher Education, and Reintegration: A Communitarian Critique

Peter Cordella

The argument in favor of prison higher education is predicated on its reintegrative potential. It is promoted as an investment in human capital because it enhances the prisoner's capacity to work and thereby gain access to the dominant culture (Becker 1964). To a lesser extent, it is seen to be a means to facilitate the moral development of the prisoner (Duguid 1981). In both perspectives, the potential for reintegration rests primarily with the individual rather than society, and both presume that the positive identity of student/graduate can replace the negative identity of criminal/prisoner.[1] Theories of social control have suggested, however, that reintegration is primarily determined by structural conditions rather than by an individual's will and personal accomplishments (Bayley 1976; Braithwaite 1994). Sanctions, whether they be punitive or therapeutic, can either stigmatize or be reintegrative depending on the extent to which individuals in a given society are integrated into networks of reciprocal social obligation. The general absence of such interdependency in contemporary capitalist society suggests that incarceration is by far more stigmatizing than reintegrative. Consequently, the stigma of being a prisoner constitutes a "master status" that negates whatever positive status may be achieved by earning a university degree.

Frank Tannenbaum, in his original formulation of labeling theory, suggested that "the person becomes the thing he is described as being. Nor does it seem to matter whether the valuation is made by those who would punish or those who would reform" (Tannenbaum 1938, 20). Rehabilitation as well as punishment contributes to the master status because "in either case the emphasis is upon the conduct that is disapproved of" (p. 20). Because rehabilitation is perceived to reinforce the deviant role rather than ameliorate it, labeling theorists would predict that the master status of prisoner conferred upon the deviant is irreversible. Kai Erikson has argued that "the ceremonies which accomplish this change of status . . . are almost always irreversible" (Erikson 1962, 311; also see Becker 1963).

John Braithwaite's communitarian critique developed in *Crime, Shame and Reintegration* argues that the permanence of the master status is dependent on the nature of the social setting from which the individual comes and will return. "Stigmatization is less likely in communitarian cultures because the complex experience that people have of each other makes it more difficult to squeeze the identities of offenders into crude master categories of deviance" (Braithwaite 1994, 97).

Braithwaite goes on to point out that in atomized societies the prisoner's label becomes a master status because "people are not interested enough in each other to engage in malicious gossip, and when forced to interact with offenders, they are not knowledgeable about them to respond to them other than according to the appropriate deviant stereotype" (p. 97). The irreversibility of the master status is not a given but a culturally determined phenomenon: "in anonymous [atomized] urban communities which rely heavily on punishment, exclusion and stigma for social control irreversibility is much more of a problem than in [communitarian] cultures characterized by reintegrative shaming" (p. 97).

Atomism and communitarianism are conditions of society. In order to give atomism and communitarianism precise meaning, it is necessary to formulate them as ideal types. As such, atomism and communitarianism do not describe actual societal conditions but the general rubric against which the process of becoming a student-prisoner may be understood. In atomized societies the *preponderance* of social relations are defined in contractual terms. Individuals are required to do nothing more than meet implicit or explicit contractual demands. Individual lives are structured according to the contractual obligations and guarantees one has accumulated over time. Externally imposed sanctions in the form of laws replace personal intentions as the dominant motive for individual action. In communitarian societies, individuals are enmeshed in interdependencies which are based on mutual help and trust. Culturally, group commitment takes precedence over individual interest. Communitarian culture "resists interpretations of dependency as weakness and emphasizes the need for mutuality of obligation in interdependency" (p. 100). Communitarianism is described by the social philosopher John Macmurray as a compatibility of ends: "Our intentions must not be merely possible, they must be compossible with those of all others" (Macmurray 1977, 32). Compossibility of intentions is what distinguishes reciprocal social obligation from utilitarian cooperation and community from society.

In predominantly atomistic social conditions, individuals come together and commit to goals out of common self-interest. As individuals, people perceive themselves to be acting rationally in pursuit of their own self-interest, and behaviors are defensible by claiming rationality. Prisoners are understood to be rational actors, albeit deficient in their abilities to make good decisions. The criminal *chooses* to commit a crime and he or she chooses to be rehabilitated. Thus the reformed prisoner exemplifies the power of enhanced reasoning and self-initiated change. Prison education is promoted by its advocates as the ideal reform mechanism because it increases the human capital of prisoners while enhancing their moral decision-making abilities. Increased human capital provides prisoners with greater access to legitimate opportunities while enhanced decision making makes them more cognizant of the costs and benefits of their actions. Prisoner-students experience within the prison education program a controlled atomistic environment in which the contractual arrangement is based on individual merit (i.e., a meritocracy).

They are likely to return, however, to social conditions where "much effort is directed toward labelling deviance while little attention is paid to de-labelling" (Braithwaite 1994, 55). Without the process of delabeling, the potential for reintegration is diminished. Delabeling signifies a forgiveness by the community that ensures that the "deviance label is applied to the behavior rather than to the person. This is done under the assumption that the disapproved behavior is transient, performed by an essentially good person" (p. 55). In order for reintegration to occur, expressions of disapproval must be followed by gestures of reacceptance contingent upon reciprocal gestures of remorse and reform on the part of transgressors. According to Braithwaite the deterrent effect of any sign of disapproval, including penal punishment, is determined more by its social context than its severity: "[The] nub of deterrence is its social embeddedness; shame is more deterring when administered by persons who continue to be important to us; when we become outcasts we can reject our rejectors and shame no longer matters to us" (p. 55). In an atomized setting, punishment is administered within a framework of disharmony and fundamentally irreconcilable interests, while in a communitarian setting it is administered within a framework of reconcilable and mutually supportive interests. Punishment, Braithwaite asserts, is

a denial of confidence in the morality of the offender by reducing norm compliance to a crude cost/benefit calculation, whereas, shaming can be a reaffirmation of the morality of the offender by expressing disappointment that the offender should do something so out of character and, if the shaming is reintegrative, by expressing personal satisfaction in seeing the character of the offender restored. (1994, 72–73)

The impact of prison education in the context of nonreintegrative punishment is limited to the calculation of the cost/benefit relationship. Theoretically, the added human capital of an education makes future crime less likely because the legitimate opportunities available to the returning prisoners are now at least comparable to the illegitimate opportunities available to them. Prison education assumes more symbolic content in a context of reintegrative shaming. Involvement in education represents an attempt to better understand and thereby fulfill one's reciprocal social obligations.

Effective reintegrative shaming is dependent upon interdependency and communitarianism. The aggregate of individual interdependency forms the foundation of communitarianism. However, relationships of interdependency alone do not constitute communitarianism. Braithwaite notes, "We can be in relationships of interdependency without sharing a community with those people in any genuine sense of mutual help and trust. The relationship between judge and convicted criminal, for example, is one of great potential for shaming but no sense of community" (p. 85). For a society to be communitarian, the network of interdependence must have a symbolic significance to the populace as a whole and invoke personal obligation based on compossibility.

There are three elements of communitarianism: (1) densely enmeshed interdependencies, where the interdependencies are characterized by (2) mutual obligation and trust, and (3) are interpreted as a matter of group loyalty rather than individual convenience. Communitarianism, therefore, is the antithesis of individualism." (p. 86)

Because capitalist, Western societies are increasingly characterized by individualism, the capacities of such social forms as families, churches, and residential communities to exert informal social control have declined, thereby reducing the capacity for reintegrative shaming. "The ideology of individualism dismantles the sanctioning capacities of those intermediate groups between the individual and the State" (p. 86).[2]

Therefore, the society to which the prisoner-student returns is on balance based on a rational integration of functions which ultimately concentrates power "in the hands of those persons or groups that exercise superior function" (Macmurray 1977, 33). When an incompatibility of intentions arises between those who are deemed to exercise superior function and those who do not, "those who have superior power will achieve freedom at the expense of their functional inferiors" (p. 33). An intuitive or learned recognition of this superiority drives the majority of prisoner-students to participate in prison education as a means of transforming themselves from functional inferiors to people who possess functional superiority. In this respect, prisoners are no different from their fellow students outside the prison. Their principal motive for participating in education is functional transformation. Their understanding of crime, punishment, and reintegration reflects the ideology of individualism.[3]

There is, however, a distinct minority of prisoner-students whose understanding of crime, punishment, and reintegration reflects a communitarian ideology. These prisoner-students utilize their educational experience as a way of furthering their analysis of the limitations of justice in an atomistic society. Their analysis suggests that justice in an atomistic society is both negative because it is primarily defined in terms of individual prohibitions rather than collective obligations and static because it is based on a unitary (i.e., fear-inspired) rather than a bipolar (i.e., fear-inspired *or* mutualist-inspired) assumption of social interaction. The functional and impersonal natures of social relations in an atomistic society require an increasing reliance on state sanction. Their analysis reflects Braithwaite's conclusion that the societies that

replace much of their punitive social control with shaming and reintegrative appeals to the better nature of people will be societies with less crime. These societies will do better at easing the crushing discontinuity between the shift away from punitive control in home life and the inevitable reversion to heavier reliance on punitive control in the wider society. (Braithwaite 1994, 80)

Like Braithwaite this minority of prisoner-students recognizes a dual nature in human beings, one motivated by fear and the other by mutuality. They believe that by appealing to mutuality rather than fear, the "ideology" of social relations can be transformed from individualism to communitarianism, and in turn the response to crime can be transformed from stigmatization to reintegration.

For most prisoner-students education represents the possibility of enhancement of their personal opportunities to reintegrate into the dominant culture of society: The potential of education is functional. For a much smaller group of individuals, education represents the possibility of enhancing their critical understanding of the dominant culture and its alternatives: The potential of education is political. For both groups, their perceptions of culture and society are profoundly affected by how they define the ideology of social relations.

PRISON EDUCATION: SENSATE VERSUS IDEATIONAL

For the majority, the ideology of social relations is located within that which can be directly sensed and experienced; what Pitirim Sorokin defined as the sensate culture.[4] Sensate culture with its emphasis on the experiential and its focus on the individual generates an ethical understanding that is concerned with moral conduct that promotes human happiness, comfort, and pleasure. Sensate ethics by their very nature are bounded by the individual life course of the rational actor. Consequently, society is defined as a vehicle, designed to maximize the individual happiness of the largest possible number of individuals. From a sensate perspective, the success of prison education in reintegrating the prisoner is dependent on two variables: the extent to which the prisoner-student first accepts the inevitable dominance of sensate culture and, second, the extent to which the prisoner-student embraces sensate cultural values as the most efficient means to reintegrate into the dominant culture.

Education as a rational-personal investment in oneself is in itself a powerful symbol of sensate cultural values. Completion of a higher education degree is evidence that the prisoner-student accepts sensate values. Prison higher education programs represent an exercise in sensate culture that provides the "successful" prisoner-student with enhanced potential for entry into the dominant sensate culture.[5] The realization of such potential is ultimately dependent upon the capacity of society (whether communitarian or atomized) to reintegrate prisoners generally. Under existing social relations, this is not probable for the immediate or foreseeable future. Thus, the contradiction of sensate culture for individuals on the periphery of capitalism's concentric zones is more directly experienced although not always recognized.

It is important to keep in mind that the power of the prison is based on a sensate understanding of the human experience. The pain of imprisonment is defined exclusively in terms of a sensate understanding of reality. Education is a natural extension of the sensate nature of prisons. In the eyes of the penal elite, prisoner-students, motivated by the pain of imprisonment, recognize the sensate nature of culture and accept the sensate cultural values *as their own*. As if to complete the process, the prisoner-student is then juxtaposed against other prisoners (who are portrayed as idle and without remorse) as proof of the societal benefits of imprisonment and the legitimacy of sensate culture. These prisoners *cum* students reinforce the three central assumptions of the classical perspective on crime and punishment which informs the neoclassical ideology so prevalent in criminological discourse today (Clark and Cornish 1987; Vold and Bernard 1986, 26–34): (1) crime is primarily the result of individual decision making, (2) punishment serves as an instrument for deterrence and, by extension, reformation, and (3) reformation is primarily a matter of individual initiative. Prison education fits neatly into the overall classical perspective because it exists as a passive instrument for social reintegration that accepts as a given the sensate nature of culture and the corresponding network of atomized relations. As with all reform initiatives that become legitimated, prison education reinforces the underlying premise of the particular institution in which it is located (i.e., the criminal justice system), as well as the ideology of the dominant culture.

Prison education can also be utilized to challenge these assumptions and with them the hegemony of the dominant culture. For a small but significant number of prisoner-students, education is a potential means to a more ideational understanding of culture which invariably places them in opposition to sensate culture. Sorokin defined the ideational understanding of culture as the subordination of individual desires and functions to some greater ends (Sorokin 1970). For the ideational prisoner-student, that end is not necessarily other worldly (as Sorokin suggested) but rather a social end beyond the sensate, namely, the realization of communitarianism. Through prison education, the ideational prisoner-student gains a fuller understanding of the two potentialities of human action: one active, one passive; one intentional, one determined; one politicized, one depoliticized; and one communitarian, and one atomized. For the ideational prisoner-student, it is a choice between two cultural possibilities, not between legal and illegal behavior based on a rational calculation of the odds for self-gratification. Unlike the majority of their fellow prisoner-students, they choose to understand and act in terms of the ideational.

Ideational prisoner-students critique the dominant sensate culture in terms remarkably similar to those of Sorokin. Relying on their personal experience of the economically and socially disadvantaged environments from which they arrived in prison (keeping in mind relative disadvantages *among* prisoners in terms of gender, race, and ethnicity), the ideational prisoner-student perceives, as Sorokin did, the transition from sensate to ideational culture. Ideational prisoner-students see within the context of their own social environment that persons are increasingly defined in material terms, force and fraud are increasingly required to maintain social order, freedom is constrained and used as a myth of control by the unbridled dominant minority, both primary and secondary institutions continue to atomize as the result of the decline of trust and mutuality, and contracts and covenants lose their binding power, cumulatively leading to the decline of networks of social obligation. Prisoners generally have most acutely experienced this decline because of their overwhelming representation in the lower social class. The ideational prisoner-student possesses the potential to understand the reality rather than the rhetoric of the atomized society because he or she personally experiences its contradictions. An ideational critique of prevailing social conditions/structure is by its nature political.

Ideational prisoner-students, although small in number, pose a significant challenge to the sensate understanding of social life. The ideational transformation of the prisoner-student is similar to what Robert Merton describes as the rebellion model of adaptation. The ideational student, like Merton's rebel, seeks to change both the goals and the means of the dominant culture and, as such, is identified and labeled as a deviant. As rebels, ideational prisoner-students believe that the sources of social problems (crime being one of many) are interrelated and lie within sensate culture and social order and not with the individual. These students often arrive at prison and ultimately the prison school with profound dissatisfaction with sensate culture. They typically begin their education as powerful critics of the dominant culture. The intellectual starting point is the nearly total rejection of the goals and means of the sensate culture. They do not for the most part, however, come to their prison educational experience with a clearly defined cultural alternative in mind. Prison education interests the individual as a potential avenue to discover and become committed to a more ideational conception of culture. The ideational transformation of prisoner-students demonstrates the potential for critical pedagogy in prison education.[6]

MOVING BEYOND LAW TO PERSONS IN COMMUNITY

A critical analysis of sensate culture typically utilizes the individual's experience with the law as a way of interrogating atomized society. This analysis may begin by recognizing what Donald Black (1976) describes as the *behavior of law*. The behavior of law, argues Black, is determined by three aspects of social life that characterize a given society: stratification, morphology, and bureaucracy. By analyzing the configuration of these aspects it is possible to predict both the quantity and quality of law in a society. For example, on stratification: "as long as the standard is the same (cattle, bushels of grain or dollars) it is possible to compare the quantity of stratification across space and time. Variation of this kind predicts and explains the quantity of law" (Black 1976, 13). Law varies directly with stratification: The more stratification a society has, the more law it has. Within a given society, "the seriousness of an offense by a lower against a higher rank . . . increases with the difference in wealth between parties, whereas the seriousness of an offense by a higher against a lower rank decreases as this difference increases" (p. 25). Stratification also predicts the style of law, whether it is penal, therapeutic, compensatory, or conciliatory. For example: "Where the offender's rank is below the victim's, his/her conduct is more likely to be punished as a crime than in a case where the direction is the opposite" (p. 29). Consequently, "an offender who ranks above his victim is more likely to be asked to pay for his damage than in a case in the opposite direction" (p. 29). The actual quantity and style of law in a particular society or social situation is determined by the cumulative quantity of these aspects of social life.

Ideational prisoner-students recognize the behavior of law because they have experienced firsthand its differential application. Ideational prisoner-students are acutely aware that their low-level position in the stratification hierarchy, their marginal position relative to morphological integration, and their lack of membership among corporate elites makes them very vulnerable to the law. More specifically, they recognize that the law applied to them is both qualitatively and quantitatively different than the law applied to those whose relative position within the three aspects of the sensate culture is superior; it is qualitatively more punitive (rather than compensatory, therapeutic, or conciliatory) and quantitatively greater (longer sentences). Ideational prisoner-students see their own experiences with the law as indicative of a larger cultural trend away from networks of reciprocal social obligations toward the increasing use of law. Unknowingly perhaps, they are in fundamental agreement with Black's assessment that law varies directly with stratification, morphology, and bureaucracy. Yet like Black, the ideational prisoner-students also believe that the evolution of law is not linear but rather curvilinear in nature.

[S]ocial life has been drifting in two great patterns. On the one hand, the life of earlier times has been coming apart. On the other hand, what was separate has been drawing together. Thus social life has been moving away from the extremes of communal and situational life, the conditions of anarchy. All this time law has been increasing. If these drifts continue, however, social life will evolve into something new, neither communal nor situational but a synthesis of the two. (p. 132)

Ideational prisoner-students have witnessed within their own social environments the decline of the sanctioning capacities of intermediate social forms such as families, churches, and residential communities and the subsequent inability of legal mechanisms of social control to guarantee social order. Indeed, they have witnessed the response of a sensate culture to impose more law, to enact harsher sentences, and to call for more severe forms of punishment as a response to increasing resistance to economic deprivation and consequent normative disorder. If sensate culture were to wane, law would begin to recede. The formal rational approach to social order would give way to a more substantive approach. For the ideational prisoner-student, the more substantive approach to social order is prefigured in what Black referred to as the return of anarchy.

It will be a society of equals, a society of nomads, at once close and distant, homogeneous and diverse, organized and autonomous, where reputations and other statuses fluctuate from one day to the next. The past will return to some degree, yet society will be different. It will be communal and situational at the same time, a unity of opposites. To some degree, moreover anarchy will return. It will be a new anarchy, neither communal nor situational yet both at once. If these trends continue then law will decrease. (p. 137)

In this visualization of ideational culture, law recedes as networks of reciprocal social obligation emerge thus giving rise to more reintegrative forms of social control. For ideational prisoner-students, realization of the new anarchy requires a return to the ideational foundation of communitarianism. The social, economic, and political vision of the ideational prisoner-student is predicated on the intention of community. They envision what Stanley Hauerwas described as a community of character in which the trust engendered by persons in relation will reduce the inordinate reliance on bureaucratic interaction and legal coercion that currently characterize atomistic society.

The more it becomes unthinkable to trust a stranger, the more we must depend on more exaggerated forms of protection. But the human costs of distrust are perhaps the most destructive. For we are increasingly forced to view one another as strangers rather than as friends, and as a result we become all the more lonely. We have learned to call our loneliness "autonomy" and/or freedom, but the freer we become the more desperate our search for forms of "community" or "interpersonal relationship" that offer some contact with our fellows. (Hauerwas 1981, 81)

Ideational prisoner-students seek to take their critical understanding of ideational culture back to the community from which they came in order to establish a new social order based not on individual contracts but on reciprocal social obligation (see chapter 11 in this volume). Ideational prisoner-students are united in their commitment to the shared responsibility that defines persons in community. This commitment can either be weakened or strengthened by their prison education experience. If the orientation of the prison education program and individual faculty is primarily sensate, the communitarian commitment of the ideational prisoner-students will be discouraged. Conversely, if the orientation of the program faculty is more ideational, these prisoner-students may be encouraged to further redefine themselves in terms of persons in community rather than as individual rational actors.

However, course readings and instructors' attitudes sympathetic to communitarianism are in themselves not enough. The educational experience must be grounded in a vision of reciprocal social obligations. In order to realize this vision, considerations of means and ends are developed in a discourse of trust and compossibility rather than a discourse of individual rights. In order to achieve ends, individuals consider means to expand interpersonal relations rather than to develop or refine impersonal structures. For ideational prisoner-students, the restoration of communitarianism begins with them. For community to be restored, education itself must not privilege functional individual advantage (i.e., meritocracy) but must evaluate an individual's actions according to responsibilities to community (Tifft 1979, 398).

Therefore, we may speak of prison education as having not one nature but two potential constructs: one sensate, one ideational. In reality, the distinction is not so neat, but that is not the point. This dyad is exaggerated here because it permits us to grasp the essential difference between a form of education that prevents confrontation with existing, atomized social conditions and a form of education, perhaps a critical pedagogy, that prefigures communitarianism. Education may produce not one but two modes of adaptation: one based on conformity and one based on rebellion.

As long as the sensate nature and conformist mode of adaptation remain dominant, prison higher education will probably continue as a limited reform movement within the correctional model. If, however, the ideational should become more dominant, prison higher education is most likely to lose its legitimacy within the context of reform movements and institutional corrections.

As Bob Martin pointed out some time ago in his analysis of treatment as an ideology of control, the access of reform groups to the prison is primarily determined by their acceptance of the dominant ideology: "The consequences of the control over who enters the prison is to isolate prisoners from those groups who might foster radical political thinking. Conversely prisoner dependence on those who counsel moderation, gradualism, individualism and accommodation with the Department is increased" (Martin 1982, 161).

Like all prison reform movements, the continued acceptance of prison higher education is dependent not on its contribution to crime reduction or even its capacity to reduce recidivism. Survival is influenced by a wider range of contingencies. But how we as educators perceive and utilize prison education is far from being inconsequential. If we assume that human nature is unitary and self-interested, that social relations are contractual and functional, and that social structure is mechanical and evolutionary, then our practice will be primarily concerned with the socialization (or resocialization) of the student. The prisoner-student will be defined in passive terms. We will assume that they have much to learn from us and we have little to learn from them. The aims of education will be the enhancement of human capital and improved decision-making abilities. The observations and critique of culture and society that students bring to the educational enterprise will be ignored or distrusted because, after all, they will be spoken by functional failures, the personally inadequate.

Conversely, if we as educators assume that human nature is bipolar rather than unitary, mutualist as well as self-interested, that social relations may be personal and compossible, and that social structure may be intentional and communitarian, then prison education becomes a potential catalyst for cultural and societal change, modest as our contribution may be. The prisoner-student is transformed from a passive to an active participant in the educational process. We as educators then assume that we have much to learn from prisoner-students because, unlike many of us, they have experienced most acutely the contradictions of sensate culture and atomized society, and consequently they have a unique potential to understand the ideational and communitarian alternatives.

We as prison educators have much to learn from the communitarian analysis of the ideational prisoner-student. Such a critical analysis provides us with insight into the nature of the reintegration process as a structural rather than an individual phenomenon. In order to foster a critical pedagogy it is incumbent upon us as prison educators to transmit the ideational understanding of crime, punishment, and reintegration beyond the prison walls and to translate it into social action that leads to the reestablishment of networks of reciprocal social obligation that make reintegration not only possible but necessary.

NOTES

1. Although it is necessary for the purposes of analysis to develop generalized ideal types of prisoner-students, it is important to note that there are considerable differences among prisoners based on gender, race, and ethnicity that affect the potential for reintegration. The gender, race, and ethnicity of prisoner-students are likely to affect their level of atomization and their willingness to explore communitarian alternatives. See Juan A. Rivera (chapter 11) for a comprehensive analysis of the effect of race and ethnicity on the reintegrative potential of prisoners and their need for community.

2. Recent empirical studies (Sherman and Smith 1992) have concluded that the effectiveness of state sanctions, such as arrest and prosecution, in deterring domestic violence is most strongly influenced by the transgressors' involvement in intermediate institutions. In cases where the transgressors had a clear commitment to such institutions as family, church, or community organizations state sanctions proved to be more effective in deterring future incidents of domestic violence.

3. This analysis of prison education is based on class discussions the author conducted during his participation in the Boston University Prison Education program from 1987 to 1991. The discussions were conducted as part of a series of sociology seminars (Political Sociology, Social Problems, and Sociology of Law) given at the Massachusetts Correction Institution at Norfolk.

4. See Pitirim Sorokin (1970) for a complete discussion of sensate and ideational culture.

5. Any success these prisoner-students may experience in reintegrating as compared with released prisoners in general may in large part be due to their relatively small numbers and their profound symbolic significance. The infusion of limited numbers of prisoners with university degrees earned in prison entering the dominant sensate culture serves as "proof" that membership and position within the cultural system is determined primarily on the basis of individual merit and personal motivation.

6. For a more complete discussion of the rebel as an adaptation to strain, see Merton (1938). For an extensive critique of this theory, see Nettler (1978, 224–260) and Thio (1975).

11

A Nontraditional Approach to Social and Criminal Justice

Juan A. Rivera

In February 1990, the Sentencing Project released a report, "Young Black Men and the Criminal Justice System: A Growing National Problem." It revealed that one out of every four black men between the ages of twenty and twenty-nine are in prison or under some form of custody (Maurer 1990). For Latinos, the numbers are one out of every ten. In New York State, blacks and Latinos constitute 83.2 percent of the state's prison population, 50.6 percent and 32.6 percent respectively, even though they represent less than 25 percent of the state's total population. Moreover, Latinos are forecasted to become the majority in the New York State prison system by the year 2000. This implies that seven years from now Latino youth, ages thirteen to nineteen, will actually supercede African Americans as the primary victims of that dangerous parameter described in the Sentencing Project's report. For Latinos, the future looks bleak.

The high rate of incarceration of minorities suggests that something is wrong with the way we address our social and criminal justice problems. The problems of crime are addressed as though they are individual problems solely. The criminal justice system fails to recognize that crime stems not only from individual failures, but also from social factors: a combination of poverty, economic underdevelopment, displaced unskilled workers, discrimination, and a host of other factors that cause despair and learned helplessness. The criminal justice system fails to recognize that members of these ethnic communities need to participate in resolving problems of crime, punishment, and rehabilitation and that community involvement is in the members' interest since these communities suffer from excessive crime rates and become the haven of released prisoners. It is in their interest to ensure that individuals who were incarcerated return to these communities with a progressive and law-abiding attitude. Individuals returning to their communities must become socially, politically, and economically conscious about the conditions that keep them struggling for survival. The ex-prisoner will no longer see the community as prey, but instead will strive to strengthen it. To accomplish this goal, we must implement a plan of action unlike those already tried.

Prisoners have created a nontraditional concept to reeducate themselves so that upon release they can take up their lives in a way that will benefit themselves and their communities. Among other things, they come to see that criminal behavior is *not* harmful to the power structure, but that it is destructive to their communities and the people who live in them, most of whom are Latino or black.

Inside prison, the program aims to generate and instill a genuine change in the prisoner's attitude (rather than an artificial one aimed at satisfying the parole board) whereby a sense of community is inculcated in the prisoner, prompting him or her to return to it as a creative and productive force. Outside prison, the Community Justice Center has been established to extend what we call the Nontraditional Approach out into the community. The aim is to have the ex-prisoner and the community reintegrated to the benefit of both and to prevent further destruction.

THE FAILURE OF CURRENT PROGRAMS

Nothing viable has been implemented by the state to address the pernicious effect of high incarceration of people of color. The present system of justice fails both prisoner and community. Its administrators seem to subscribe to a contradictory mixture of rehabilitation and punishment models that thwarts genuine attempts at rehabilitation. For instance, the commissioner of corrections espouses higher education and rehabilitation, while the chair of the Board of Parole states "that officials must heed the 'vibes of the community' in focusing more on the original crime than on a prisoner's progress in rehabilitation" (Cline 1992).

Rehabilitation and educational programs have largely become a means to satisfy parole boards and keep prisoners occupied rather than a way to help prisoners, who essentially become captive/resistant participants. Moreover, the lack of specific guidelines for the parole board to follow increases the capricious nature of the present system. Prisoners are caught between conflicting agendas: They know that their rehabilitative efforts are not considered seriously, but not participating in rehabilitation programs can result in denial of parole. Prisoners do not participate in programs because they want to change but because they want to get out of prison. In all likelihood, the prisoner leaves prison unchanged. In fact, programs that work to reduce recidivism and help prisoners change their attitudes lose support. For example, the Network Program (Department of Correctional Services, 1988), initiated by prisoners and utilizing a cognitive approach, was discontinued in 1992 and replaced by the Alcohol and Substance Abuse Treatment (ASAT) Program. Unlike the voluntary Network Program, ASAT is forced on the prisoners by correctional counselors, who promote the program by asserting that it is required by the Board of Parole.

Furthermore, prison programs ignore issues of race. This pertains particularly to educational programs, which are meant to address the 75 percent of New York State prisoners who have no high school diploma (Correctional Association of New York 1993). Traditional prison educational programs maintain a white, middle-class, Eurocentric interpretation of the world, one that does not address the cultures of the majority of prisoners. Standard curricula require that prisoners relinquish their old customs and incorporate the so-called American value system in order to assimilate. Instead, prison schools, like schools outside prisons, need a curriculum that is culturally specific to its student population and includes courses in the history, philosophy, and social economy of ethnic groups. Such classes help prisoners build a sense of identity with their own communities.

Programs also need to address community political, social, and economic problems from a Latino or Afrocentric perspective. They should acknowledge that people of color will not be allowed, by virtue of our ethnicity, to fit into Eurocentric society and consequently transcend our poverty. Fundamental differences between cultures must be considered and understood in all curricula initiatives, since they concern every aspect of our lives. Programs must take into account "crime generative factors" such as family breakdown, poor health care, substandard housing, undereducation, high unemployment, drugs, teenage pregnancy, discrimination, and prison itself. Without question, these crime-generative factors, which are symptoms of root causes, are the immediate reasons for the disproportionate number of Latinos and blacks in prison. Only when prisoners understand the actual conditions of their communities can they help to confront and overcome racist policies that work against minorities. For example, without political power and financial resources, we cannot fight against redlining practices that keep us from obtaining loans or insurance policies that can help us rebuild our communities. Gentrification, another problem faced by the minority community, is often a result of redlining.[1]

Ironically, funds that could be used by minority communities to improve the quality of life (by improving medical care, building housing and recreation centers, repairing dilapidated schools, and establishing community-based drug and crime preventive programs) are used to build prisons, which the government has selected as its primary solution for contemporary social problems. While $1.5 billion, not including pensions and medical costs, is spent on corrections in New York State and a few years ago Governor Cuomo authorized the State's Urban Development Corporation to issue bonds totaling $2.1 billion to build more prisons, the communities from which most prisoners come continue to deteriorate.

Nor do these communities have input to parole and rehabilitation decisions, even though approximately 95 percent of the prison population when released return to the communities from which they came. Almost half of these people will return to prison (Clark 1991), which suggests that a significant percentage of released offenders are contributing to the crime rate in their home districts. And still these communities have no say in how these problems might be corrected. So long as the justice system fails to allow programs that reconcile the prisoner and the community, successful reintegration of released prisoners into their communities is unlikely. Reconciliation is a primary aim of the Nontraditional Approach being developed by prisoners in several state prisons.

THE NONTRADITIONAL APPROACH

The Nontraditional Approach establishes the ideological framework for a major departure from traditional theories and assumptions about crime and prison by developing Afro-Latino (i.e., minority) perspectives that define and give meaning to our own reality, as we experience that reality. It moves from general approaches and definitions about crime and punishment to one that is minority specific and evolves from the unique cultural norms and socioeconomic conditions of the minority community. It creates the foundation upon which structural changes can be built with minority-specific needs as the primary consideration.

For us and our supporters, "the direct relationship" names the connection between the sixty-eight prisons in New York and the specific communities of the prisoners confined in these prisons. It reveals that, since so many men and women are imprisoned, those communities from which we come are dysfunctional. To correct the problem of crime, a dual approach that addresses the prisoner and the community must be tried.

History

The Nontraditional Approach has its roots in the revolutionary ideals espoused by the radical groups of the 1960s. It is, however, a more benign approach to the problems faced by people of color. The concept began to take form around 1977, when the deputy superintendent of program services, Carl Berry, gave a speech at Green Haven Correctional Facility on the underclass and crime. This speech helped a group of prisoners to see the relationship between prisons and minority communities. This group formed a "think tank" (which included Cardell Shaird and Larry White, and later Charles Gale and Eddie Ellis), the purpose of which was to act as an advisory group. In late 1979, they published the first position paper on the Nontraditional Approach.[2] The members developed and gave lectures from notes or extemporaneously. These lectures took place anywhere prisoners could congregate. Sometimes, it was in the prison yard or in a classroom, when the topic was appropriate. We had no structure, but we were able to gather supporters.

In February 1990, Eddie Ellis, Larry White, George Prendes, executive members of prisoner organizations that supported the Nontraditional Approach at Green Haven, and I finally organized our notes into pamphlet form. These notes still are used to teach prisoners, and they are mailed to prospective supporters of the Nontraditional Approach in our communities. The group's thinking has also been disseminated to other prisons throughout the state when group leaders, perceived by prison administration as a "threat to the security of the facility," were consequently transferred. So far we have established classes at Sullivan Correctional Facility, Eastern Correctional Facility, and Great Meadows Correctional Facility, which has helped us further our objectives.

One outside contact is especially important for the promotion of the Nontraditional Program: the Black and Puerto Rican Legislative Caucus. In order to schedule the first meeting, we established communication with the caucus with the assistance of Alice P. Green, family members, and other outside supporters; thus, we were able to circumvent the prison administration. Our strategy was to contact caucus members directly and ask them to request a meeting through the state's prison administration in the capital. This way, approval for the meeting came from the commissioner's office, and the local prison administrators had little choice but to comply.

The first meeting and subsequent meetings with the caucus have been very important. The caucus permits us to reveal to legislators the direct relationship between prisons and our communities. They hear testimony on the effectiveness of current state policies and programs and on prisoners' efforts to develop programs that improve the life chances of black and Latino prisoners. We are able to establish links with caucus members and gather their support for the Nontraditional Approach.

Two months prior to our first meeting with the Black and Puerto Rican Legislative Caucus (December 1989), Ellis, White, Prendes, and I created the "Conciencia" and "Resurrection" classes and later (about July 1990) the "Liberation" class. I taught the Conciencia class. Eddie Ellis, the principal originator of the Nontraditional Approach and the person who became the founder of the Community Justice Center, taught the Resurrection class. Larry White, cofounder of the Nontraditional Approach, initiated the Liberation class in order to facilitate more students and to provide another perspective that used the Nontraditional Approach.

Description of Classes

We think these classes can serve as models for other prison education programs that address the responsibilities we have to ourselves and our communities. Each of the three classes has its own perspective: Afrocentric (Resurrection), Latinocentric (Conciencia), and Liberation Theology (Liberation). Institutional organizations in sympathy with the perspective of the class sponsor it. For example, here at Fishkill Prison, Conciencia is taught as part of Hispanics United for Progress, a prisoner organization that sponsors cultural events. While all the classes last twenty-five weeks, instructors have developed their own curricula to address the unique needs of each specific group. For instance, I have incorporated five weeks of parenting education into the Conciencia class.

Some aspects of the program are common to all classes, such as the purging stages and culturally specific history segments. The classes include a historical account of how prisons in New York State developed, which teaches an appreciation for the struggles taken on by prisoners in the past. For example, students learn about Martin Sostre, who first litigated prison conditions and about the men who died at Attica. Teaching methods differ too according to needs, but generally we all include lecture and dialogue/discussion.

Throughout the courses, outside speakers are encouraged to participate and provide insight into related issues. We also encourage grassroots groups from the community to assist us in improving what we have developed so far, for we firmly believe there are no prison problems, only community problems that we bring with us to prison. And since it is the community's survival that is at stake, its input is essential.

Students enroll in the class with the perspective that suits their interests by submitting their names to the instructor or the sponsoring organization. Most participants are young prisoners in their twenties. The older ones are those who want to see our program survive because they recognize the problems we have faced, both in prison and out in society. They also want to perceive themselves as useful individuals with a purpose in life; one way to fulfill this need is to help younger prisoners.

Although these classes are not part of any formal schooling, most of the instructors have acquired undergraduate degrees. Some, like Ellis and Prendes, have earned advanced degrees. In addition to validating the program, their educational achievements have earned them the respect of the prison population, who view them as exemplary prisoners.

The three classes take into consideration three principal conditions of the prisoner that the state's traditional approach does not address: (1) the crime-generative attitudes of the prisoner and their origin, (2) the ethnic status and identity of the prisoner, and (3) a sense of community.

The crime-generative attitudes of the prisoner result from the socioeconomic conditions that exist in the community. When a distinct people consistently experience segregation, injustice, inferior education, and police brutality, "making it in society" is best achieved by being tough and mean, or in any way possible. Thus, a disrespect for the rule of law arises. Traditional education fosters the longing to fit the European model. We are taught to value and seek conventional symbols of success, such as money and material possessions, which for most of us can be gained only illegally and often through crime committed against a member of one's own ethnic group. Hence, the attitude that illegal activity is all right becomes a norm, worthy of imitation by community youth who glamorize it as heroic. This places our community members on a collision course with the "white man's law."

Understanding ethnicity as central to the problem of crime must be part of the prison curriculum. The study of ethnicity helps prisoners to deal with the reality of their ethnic status in American society, which is that of second-class citizens. More positively, African American and Latin American history classes identify the role of ethnic groups in American history and instill a natural sense of self-worth that cannot be inculcated through a Eurocentric approach. By combating the self-hatred experienced by us as we fail to "fit in," historical awareness develops the positive self-esteem needed to advance past the stereotypes and stigmas created for us by others. As prisoners acquire positive self-esteem, they acknowledge their strengths and weaknesses and accept their ethnic group as worthy. With increased self-confidence, they improve their ability to learn and apply themselves in a positive manner.[3] Understanding ethnic status also challenges the feeling of powerlessness that keeps us from doing something about our present conditions. Thus, the prisoner who faces discrimination, racism, sexism, or any other exclusionary measure becomes better equipped to handle this type of affront, without resorting to crime.

The final characteristic, the sense of community, is important in our curriculum because it recognizes the direct relationship between the sixty-eight prisons in New York and the specific communities from which prisoners come. Students learn about community politics and social control as the sources of crime-generative factors and their impact on the community, and they learn to see how people are struggling as a community to survive. The prisoner gains insight into how he or she fits into the community, which instills a sense of responsibility toward the community and the people in it.

Accepting responsibility is essential if we are to survive as individual ethnic groups. Though we may still find it difficult to enjoy the same opportunities as the dominant society, addressing our responsibilities puts us in a better position to progress as a community. We prisoners must make ourselves a part of our communities, become advocates for them, and protect them. We must break the prison cycle that threatens future generations.

A Sample Curriculum

The Conciencia curriculum covers six areas of concern. The classes begin with an orientation and overview, followed by five classes on building self-esteem. This first area begins with positive mental attitude and continues with four sessions on cultural awareness. The second area consists of four classes on personal development, in which students are assisted in purging negative attitudes that get in the way of the nontraditional program. Purging stages (emotional, educational, and social) examine the origins and effects of racist, sexist, and hateful emotions; of miseducation that results from narrow Eurocentric learning; and of socially restrictive notions that stigmatize and paralyze whole groups of people within society. The objective is to eliminate, as much as that is possible, negative attitudes in an attempt to "make room" for new information offered by the classes. The purging classes are conducted in rap group style, and open discussion is encouraged. This is followed by the third area, which consists of five classes on family and parenting skills. The fourth area comprises five classes about leadership dynamics. In the fifth and sixth areas, community and prison respectively, the direct relationships among community, ethnicity, and crime-generative attitudes are explored.

Toward that end, we learn about labeling theory in the purging stage. This theory helps us understand that we must be in a position to choose between positive and negative role models, but this cannot be done until we are in a position to identify and understand these role models. An important perspective for us is C. H. Cooley's (1983) theory of the "looking glass self." It suggests just how important it is to understand the labeling process and its detrimental effects on the individual's self-image and the image of the entire community. I believe that just as the individual is affected by the looking glass self, which says that the labeled person behaves as he or she is expected to, so is an entire community affected by this labeling. In a community that has been labeled poor, mean, and dirty, we can expect that outsiders will respond to that community negatively. More detrimentally, we can expect the people of that community to see their community according to the attached label.

The labeling process is reinforced by the traditional educational system. Both the label and the labeling process are made to appear real and natural by the media. We must understand this process and its dangerous effects so that we can begin to redefine our own reality and make concerted efforts toward changing conditions in our communities. In this way, we can become a life-giving component instead of an element that destroys those very communities in which we live and die.

Five-Step Reconciliation

Our program includes recognizing that we have harmed both ourselves and the community and making an honest effort to reconcile ourselves with what we have helped to destroy. We understand that much of the community hesitates to accept us. However, to be allowed to reenter the community and to work within it toward valid solutions are essential if we are going to end the destructive process taking place today.

We do not have all the answers, nor do we pretend to have them. Nevertheless, we have formulated a five-step reconciliation process entailing *recognition* of the problem; *responsibility* for the harm to victims and the community; *reconstruction* through a concerted effort by prisoners and the community to rebuild our relationship to each other; *reconciliation* involving all of the above and a formal statement that expresses and reinforces our unification; and *redemption*, the final step that takes place through our creative acts and the struggle that we engage in together. Thus we redeem ourselves through the conscious efforts we make together. This is a way of saying, "We are sorry and we are willing to struggle along with you." This reconciliation process, which after being explained to students could take place any time throughout the program when the community comes into contact with our classes, attempts to make way for the community and prisoners to create nontraditional approaches to the problems of crime and criminal justice.

Meaningful working relationships could be developed between community and prisoners through workshops designed to that end. For example, I have proposed a "Victim Confrontation Program" whereby professional community people involved in the fields of psychology, social work, and criminal justice would be able to bring victims of any crime into the prisons to confront offenders, vent their anger and frustrations, and express the consequences of crime. This program is intended to help victims get on with their lives and to help prisoners realize the impact of their behavior. It would also be an excellent vehicle for the reconciliation process.[4] The community group could evaluate the progress of the prisoners involved in the project. Over a period of time, the community would learn about a prisoner's personality, aspirations, weaknesses, and strengths. Ideally, community groups would monitor and make valuable recommendations for releasing prisoners they considered ready for release. Thus, the communities which are most affected by crime would become involved in the transformation of prisoners and their reentry into society.

OPPOSITION

Finally, I wish to point to the resistance experienced by those of us implementing the Nontraditional Approach. The opposition comes from both prison officials and prisoners.

The prison administrator's primary reason for opposing prisoners' programs is the need to maintain an image of control within the prison walls and to appear competent in the public's eye. Prisoners must be viewed as dependent on state programs, which are created by the experts employed by the criminal justice system. Anything short of a state-run program is viewed with skepticism. This is especially true if the program is radically different, like the Nontraditional Approach. Some correctional officials believe in punishment rather than rehabilitation, and they view prison programs, especially those created by prisoners, as ways to manipulate the system. Racist attitudes, camouflaged by the correctional uniform, form the basis of some opposition.

Opposition also comes from prisoners who have defeatist attitudes about challenging the status quo. These prisoners believe that nothing will ever change to their benefit, a form of learned helplessness inculcated after many years of frustrated attempts to make changes within the walls of confinement, or from observing the foiled attempts of others. Other prisoners believe that a nontraditional method will not work because it is too radical and that in order to accomplish something we must work within the parameters established by the system, whether that system is correctional or political. For example, certain members of the NAACP chapter in the Fishkill Correctional Facility believe that the Nontraditional Approach will not work in a capitalist society. Yet, a close look at the Nontraditional Approach reveals that the goal is to work within communities, which obviously exist in a capitalist society but which do not reap the same benefits as the rest of society. In fact, we are committed to reeducating the community and prisoners alike on how to utilize those agencies, organizations, and political groups that exist in our communities and to make them accountable.

Another form of opposition comes from what some prisoners call the "green syndrome," the attitude of prisoners who think that they cannot learn anything from another prisoner because he or she is also wearing greens (prison garb). This perspective, common inside of prison, contributes to the defeatist attitude of those prisoners trying to learn and to teach. Consequently, both fall back on their individual resources, forsaking the greater goal of helping one another.

Racism among prisoners is a perennial reality inside of prison. Ideally, I would like to see a united front where each ethnic group can learn from each other's historical struggle, whether that struggle took place in Europe or in America. Surely we would find that Italians, Irish, and Jews faced their own forms of discrimination here and abroad, but since that ideal is not within reach at this time, we need to concentrate on what is practical for us as the minority. Contrary to popular belief, in New York prisons violence breaks out more within one's own ethnic group than it does with an outgroup. Although the white prison population in New York obviously accounts for a much smaller percentage than either the Latino or black population, violent conflicts are not experienced between whites and other ethnic groups as often as the public is led to believe. In fact, such progressive white prisoners as David Gilbert, Chett Shanholtzer, and Shakoor, whose political and social perspectives are not popular among many white prisoners, are usually found in the midst of the Latino and black progressive prisoners, whose ideologies are in agreement.

Our program has experienced problems conducting classes when over-zealous correctional officers have canceled classes as a form of punishment for unrelated incidents. For example, at Fishkill Correctional Facility, a clerk of the organization which sponsors the Conciencia class is under investigation for gambling. Although this prisoner is not a student in the class, and his alleged involvement in gambling occurred outside of the sponsoring organization, security canceled our classes.

Another problem confronts participants. Currently, students risk getting put in segregation if caught with Latin American literature. Although this practice was instituted to discourage gang membership, it has become a persecutory policy against Latino prisoners who may possess Latin American literature. This then becomes a discriminatory act that discourages students from participating in a program designed specifically by and for them. No one would assume that because an Irish-American prisoner read Irish historical literature that he or she is necessarily affiliated with the Irish Republican Army, but such absurd conclusions are made when we have copies of our literature. In effect, rather than promote voluntary self-change, incidents such as this thrust prisoners into coercive state programs that are designed not in the best interest of the community, but to create the perception that something is being done about drugs and crime.

CONCLUSION

The Nontraditional Approach advocated here recognizes the direct relationship between the prisoner and the community and the importance of Latino and Afrocentric perspectives to understand the current situation of minorities. The aim of the program is to help prisoners to embrace a new vision of themselves, to transform their criminal attitudes into socially and politically conscious ones, and to return them to their communities equipped to rebuild them. The program works too to reconcile the prisoner and the community because a productive relationship has the greatest chance for success.

Outside prison, the Community Justice Center (CJC), established in 1993 by Eddie Ellis, an ex-offender who spent twenty-three years in prison and a founding member of the Nontraditional Approach, attempts to generate community support for the Nontraditional Approach. Among other things, this not-for-profit community-based agency works to make known its analysis and solutions through community education. Emphasizing the need for children-first initiatives, the center teaches the tenets of its program to community youth before they get in trouble with the law. It calls for a reevaluation of state criminal and social justice policies, with an emphasis on prisons, and for a redistribution of state budget expenditures in accord with the community-specific approach.

Following its commitment to helping develop the community, CJC has purchased an abandoned building from New York City. They gutted and renovated it. They hired ex-prisoners to do most of the labor, thus providing them with training and employment, which ultimately aids the community and the ex-prisoner.[5]

Through the initiatives of CJC, the Nontraditional Approach is beginning to gather support from the community and from locally elected officials. Recently, the CJC received an offer from the Housing Authority in New York City to conduct nontraditional classes similar to the Conciencia and Resurrection classes for young people in the community. We believe these classes will succeed in instilling a sense of community that is so crucial to addressing the problem of crime.

We encourage anyone who is interested and able to assist us in enhancing these classes and our curriculum, as well as anyone who wishes more information concerning our program, to contact us at the Community Justice Center, located at 54 Macombs Place, New York, New York 10039.

NOTES

1. Redlining is a pattern of discrimination in which financial institutions refuse to make mortgage loans, regardless of the credit rating of the applicant, on properties in specified areas due to alleged deteriorating conditions. At one time, lenders actually outlined these areas with a red line, thus the name. Although the practice is illegal in the United States, it is still practiced.

2. Reverend Edwin Muller, a man sympathetic with liberation theology, became the staff advisor to the group and helped us advance its ideas.

3. At the Green Haven Correctional Facility, we have observed that prisoners who attended both the African American and Latin American history classes acquired a GED diploma and went on to enroll in the Dutchess or Marist College with greater success than those who did not attend either class. Although we have not conducted an empirical analysis of the success rate of those students who have taken the African American or the Latin American history classes, we believe the classes capture the students' interest and stimulate their learning ability.

4. I created this program with another prisoner. Neither one of us was aware that a similar program had been created by the Mennonites. We were discussing our project with the deputy superintendent of program services of Fishkill Correctional Facility when, unfortunately, the superintendent suffered a heart attack,

which forced his retirement. It is unlikely that the new deputy will be receptive to our proposal.

5. The CJC has one building located at 299 W 155th Street, New York, NY. Three other buildings are targeted for management, two in Harlem and one in Brooklyn. Anyone interested in obtaining more information should call Eddie Ellis at the Neighborhood Defender of Harlem (212) 876–5500. People like Eddie Ellis and George Prendes, members of and speakers for CJC, exemplify the value of the Nontraditional Approach. They have given numerous speeches in Albany and throughout the New York City area on the problems of crime and poverty in the minority communities and on the Nontraditional Approach as a viable solution.

12

The Santa Cruz Women's Prison Project, 1972–1976

Karlene Faith

> The desire for education . . . is a desire which springs from no conceit
> of cleverness, from no ambitions of the prizes of intellectual success as
> it is sometimes falsely imagined, but from the conviction that for many
> women to get knowledge is the only way to get bread, and still more
> from the instinctive craving for light which in many is stronger than
> the craving for bread. (Butler 1868, 7–8)

On weekends during the years from 1972 to 1976, graduate students,
instructors, professors, law students, artists, performers, and community
activists converged at the California Institution for Women (CIW). Situated
sixty miles east of Los Angeles, it was, with 600 prisoners, the world's
largest prison for women. The purpose of these gatherings was to offer
university courses, cultural workshops, and artistic performances to imprisoned women. The program was coordinated by the community-based
Santa Cruz Women's Prison Project (SCWPP), with sponsorship by the
History of Consciousness graduate program and Community Studies at the
University of California, Santa Cruz.[1]

Radical and Black Power politics in the United States during the late
1960s and early 1970s, as well as a series of uprisings in men's prisons across
the continent, encouraged new, critical analyses of prisons, the creation of
prisoners' rights organizations and unions, and new communications
among prisoners, academics, and community activists. By the early 1970s,

prisoners' writings were required reading in numerous university courses, and some universities began teaching courses inside prisons. In California, much of this activity was centered on African-American male prisoners, who were (and are) seriously overrepresented in the imprisoned population. African-American women were similarly overrepresented at 40 percent of the California female prison population, although they constitute only 10 percent of the female population in the state. Yet women in prison had received virtually no attention from activists: They constituted less than 4 percent of all state prisoners, they were not as politicized as the men, and they did not engage in the kinds of protest actions that aroused media attention.[2]

In 1970, while teaching a political science course with prisoner-students at the Soledad maximum security men's institution (Faith 1975), I was startled to discover that they knew nothing about women in prison, not even the location of CIW. These men knew about the dozens of state and federal men's prisons which dotted the state; they had served time in these institutions. But female prisoners were as invisible to them as they were to the broader public.

Out of frustration that there was so little awareness of incarcerated women, I turned my attention to women behind bars. Beginning in the spring of 1972, I virtually lived at the women's prison during the week for a five-month period to conduct participant-observation research, as well as life history interviews with 100 women and many small-group interviews to learn about the experience of incarceration. A recurrent complaint expressed by these women was the lack of programs with relevance to their own life experiences. Some wanted to know about "women's lib," then a hot topic in the media. Thus began the work of organizing the first university-level course to be taught in a women's prison, on the topic of "Women in Society."

A friend, Jeanne Gallick, worked with me to organize and teach the course. The university's Community Studies Department and the Extended Studies Division provided credit and registered the women as "mature students." On the first day for registration, the fifty spaces were filled by women who represented a cross-section of the prison population. About half were African-Americans, and some were Latina, Asian, and Native. They were serving sentences from two years to life primarily for theft, fraud, and drug offenses. A few were serving their first prison sentence; others had been in and out of prison from youth. Most had grown up with poverty and had not completed high school.[3]

The readings for this course included virtually everything that had been published by "second wave" feminists to that time. The topics centered on the family, schooling, women and the law, "myself as woman," and how attitudes based on racial identity worked to divide women within the prison and to obscure their common experiences. Many students were critical of the "white middle class" perspectives found in the literature, but they believed in the importance of "women's liberation" as they came to understand it on their own terms. Indicative of the positive response to this course are these two excerpts from students' course evaluations.

Through this class I have seen something happen. I've done so much time and I've never seen a group of convicts hang in with each other in so much unity. It's been beautiful, a spiritual experience really. You walk past people every day in the institution and you don't know they've got all this in their head or in their heart and we came together in this classroom and there it all was.

I saw sisterhood in action for the first time. I was in with a group of women of all different types and we all became one. It's the first time I have ever been with a group of people where I felt completely free to say whatever I thought or felt. It was something very beautiful.

We were satisfied that the course was a success, and the students urged us to continue with an expanded program. The university and prison administrators agreed.

The Santa Cruz Women's Prison Project (SCWPP) rapidly evolved from a single women's studies course to a statewide educational, political, and cultural network which converged at the women's prison most weekends for four years, involving hundreds of volunteers over time. Through the project's first year, the prison's administrators were publicly appreciative that the university was making it possible for women inside to take university-level courses. This was a first in the history of women's prisons, and the CIW administration was glad to take credit for it. The California Department of Corrections was similarly supportive, especially because the work was donated entirely through the university, with volunteer labor.

However, the attitudes of the prison guards toward the program were always mixed and often hostile. Among the few guards who had themselves gone to college there was some support for the program. But the majority were disdainful of trying to educate "stupid convicts" and outwardly resentful that "inmates" would be able to get college credits, which they perceived as rewarding prisoners for committing crime. In one of my first meetings with the warden, she identified herself as someone who shared the goals of the women's liberation movement and who looked to social causes of crime, rather than individual pathologies, to understand prisoners' situations. Over time, however, it was clear that many members of her staff, especially male guards, were contemptuous of anyone who did not regard "criminal women" as a breed apart.

After the first year of SCWPP, we experienced increasingly overt expressions of resentment by those guards who wanted us out of there. This resulted in periodic, temporary expulsions of the program from the prison.

On those occasions when the program was barred as a punishment for some breach of prison regulations, the program coordinators and volunteers used their energy to do public education and fund-raising through protest rallies, community meetings and forums, the media, and cultural events. The prisoners, meanwhile, were protesting from inside, circulating petitions, holding work strikes, and meeting with the administration to urge that SCWPP continue. Thus, much of this chapter is about resistance: about ways in which our work was obstructed by staff who opposed us and about our constant struggle to keep the program active.[4]

Here, then, is an account of the first university-level program for women in any prison, conducted at the California Institution for Women between 1972 and 1976.

THE SANTA CRUZ WORKSHOPS

Both academic classes and noncredit workshops were known generically in the prison as the "Santa Cruz Workshops." The work of the project was coordinated as a collective by women who were located in Santa Cruz, Los Angeles, and San Francisco. All of them worked with local support groups.[5] Basic organization, scheduling, curriculum planning, and liaison with the university rested with the Santa Cruz group. The San Francisco group, which consisted of women in law school, handled the legal education component for the four-year duration of the program. The Los Angeles group, with the closest proximity to the prison, organized special events and ongoing art workshops and was closely involved with the Santa Cruz group in planning and logistics. The Los Angeles group also sponsored a major public forum on women in prison and organized a group called the Organization of Family and Friends of Women in Prison.

The coordinators from all three locations cooperated with each other's initiatives, and although we did not always arrive at a consensus concerning program policies and often had to make compromises, we avoided most of the problems that subvert the principles of collective decision making. We did not intentionally model ourselves after any existing program, but we resembled (and sometimes worked in coalition with) the People's Colleges and Universities Without Walls which operated out of storefronts in the San Francisco Bay Area during this period. Apart from very small grants and the occasional donation, we received no funding. Volunteers who could afford it would sometimes contribute a few hundred dollars to assist with travel expenses, postage, and teaching materials.

Through the grapevine of the women's movement, people heard about the project and became volunteers. From the beginning, the volunteers included many feminists and activists on the cutting edge of post-1960s cultural and political resistance movements. Some had spent time in jail, or would in the future, for actions against the Vietnam War and in support of other radical causes. Many were working class and a number of women were single parents. Most of us brought a certain understanding of class consciousness to our work and considered ourselves leftists of one stripe or another. Among us there were whites, African Americans, Natives, Chicanas, heterosexuals, gays, and lesbians. We included a wide age range, people inexperienced with the criminal justice system and former prisoners, people who lived communally or in a nuclear family or alone. In the first years of the project, both men and women were involved, but by the end most participants were women.

The credit courses consisted of a series of from four to twelve all-day workshops, held in the school building on weekends so they would not interfere with the prison work assignments. In addition to the classes, special entertainment events (celebrations) were held on Friday and Saturday evenings. Noncredit workshops were generally one-time events which engaged the interest of women who were not initially interested in taking courses for credit but who, as a result of contact with the program, gained confidence and often enrolled in credit courses in subsequent terms.

Outside volunteers worked with students to design accredited courses and to organize poetry readings, concerts, dances, and other cultural events. The coordinators provided academic advice to prisoners enrolling in the program, assisted students when they were released on parole to find support contacts, wrote admission recommendation letters, and arranged transfer credit for parolees enrolling in other colleges and universities. We worked on projects with prisoners' groups (e.g., a Black Culture Marathon cosponsored by the African-American sisterhood), cosponsored events with self-help groups (e.g., the Long-Termers Organization's in-prison public forum on alternatives to incarceration, which was attended by over 200 guests from the outside), and supported projects such as "family days" and the construction of a playground through the mothers' support group. The volunteers also worked with groups on the outside to introduce people to the project. This included writing grant proposals for modest funding from progressive social change foundations, organizing prisoners' rights benefits in collaboration with diverse community groups (e.g., Women Against Rape), and maintaining contact and doing coalition work with a myriad of political activist groups around the state. Throughout the project's history, we had to balance our goals for the program with the demands of the university, the prison authorities, and the prisoners' own priorities.

Prior to each new term, posters were placed in each of the cell blocks and the work, school, and recreation areas to announce upcoming courses and cultural events. Every woman was eligible to enroll unless her security level did not permit her to be with the open population. About 100 women at any given time would be involved in courses for credit. The courses offered to women enrolled in the academic component of the Santa Cruz Workshops changed from one year to the next, depending on availability of instructors and students' interests. As an example of the subjects and instructors, here is a brief description of the courses offered during the 1973–1974 term.

Women and the Law was developed by Tanya Neiman, Abigail Ginsberg, Ann Grogan, Chris Epifania, Mary Morgan, Wyanne Bunyan, and other law students. A boon to jailhouse lawyers at CIW, this course included units on criminal procedure, sentencing, prisoners' legal rights, postconviction remedies, legal aspects of health care, women and family law, and legal aspects of landlord-tenant relations, discrimination, welfare, and consumer risks. This course was successful in demystifying the reasons so many of the women were in prison.

Ethnic Studies was taught by Bill Moore, a leader in the Bay Area African-American community, with seven assistants. This course included historical and sociological perspectives on Third World women in the United States, including Native women, Chicanas, Asian Americans, and African Americans. This was an exceptionally popular course, in part due to the high ratio of minority women within the prison. One of the most popular units, among black and white students alike, was the history of black music and its influences on American culture, taught by media and music scholar Bill Barlow.

Radical Psychology was taught by a progressive Santa Cruz therapist, Theo Alter, with three female assistants. This course examined assumptions and practices of dominant schools of psychology and psychotherapy, including Freud, Jung, Transactional Analysis, Gestalt and Reality Therapy. A guiding principle of both radical psychology and feminism in the 1970s was that "the personal is political"; thus psychological problems were examined in the context of the political economy as it affects society's "mental health." The course was designed to provide a safe and nurturing learning environment in which women could identify troubles in their own emotional lives and gain insights into how best to resolve them with appropriate support.

Politics: U.S. Institutions and Political Consciousness was taught by Michael Rotkin, a political mentor to many of us involved in SCWPP and to the Santa Cruz community at large. In 1979 he was elected to the city council and later became the first self-declared socialist-feminist city mayor in the United States. For this popular course Michael had five assistants, including economist John Isbister and sociologist William Domhoff. They challenged students to formulate analyses of capitalism as the underlying institution of North American political structure, with attention to the evolution of monopoly capitalism and economic stagnation in the twentieth century. Critical analysis focused on the role of the state in setting and implementing social policy relative to schools, the family, prisons, welfare, tax structure, and income distribution. This course was particularly satisfying to those few women, generally well educated, who were serving time for political crimes and who welcomed the opportunity to engage in dialogue and analysis with other critical thinkers.

Creative Arts was taught and organized by Catherine Cusic and Debra Miller, key coordinators of SCWPP, who offered a broad survey of the creative arts to introduce the women, many of them artists themselves, to some of the woman-identified art and culture that was proliferating at the time. Units focused on music, dance, drama, art, photography, film, mime, and puppetry with over thirty guest performers and speakers. For their final assignment, students created their own paintings, sculptures, ceramics, photographs, music, and dramatic presentations.

On Being a Woman was taught by Jeanne Gallick, one of the founders of SCWPP, and thirteen assistants plus members of the Berkeley-Oakland Women's Union. With slides, films, poetry, and music the course presented a potpourri of cultural, economic, and political dimensions of being a woman. Specific topics included women and their bodies, Third World women and human rights, depictions of women in literature and the media, class analysis of the women's movement, and feminism as political ideology. This course presented a powerful array of new ways of thinking about women and their many identities.

Drug Use in U.S. Culture was taught by Josette Mondanaro, Director of the California Health Department Substance Abuse Programs. Almost half the women had been convicted of drug offences, which made this course very relevant to their preoccupations. Topics included the politics and economics of drug distribution and use; effects on babies born to mothers addicted to heroin or methadone; the physical effects of alcohol and other drugs; the relationship of drugs to prostitution (with Margot St. James, founder of COYOTE—Call Off Your Old Tired Ethics—as a guest speaker); issues of race, sex, and class relative to drug use; the analysis of drug abuse treatment programs; uses of law and the criminal justice system in responding to drug use; and confronting addiction.

Creative Writing and Literature was one way for some women in CIW to maintain their sense of private space or "sanity." Students kept prison diaries and wrote poetry or short stories for the prisoner newsletter, *The Clarion*. This course, which was team taught on a tutorial basis and coordinated by Ellen Rifkin (Fischman), encouraged this writing activity. It focused on writing skills for articles, poetry, short stories, plays, essays, and autobiography. Tutors offered critical feedback, and the students shared their writings and discussed and evaluated one another's work in a supportive classroom environment. The course introduced the students to literary analysis and criticism, including modern fiction, writers of different ethnic and cultural backgrounds, primal myths, and a study of preliterature stories of gods and goddesses.

A series of workshops on video production, taught by women from the University of California film school, had an influence far beyond the prison.

The students produced a documentary on life in this women's prison, titled *We're Alive*. In addition to becoming a major fund-raising tool for SCWPP, the process of producing the video provided an occasion for the students to reflect on and then document their experiences of incarceration. As individual women were released from prison, they would attend public showings of the video and afterward speak about their own experience and take questions from the audience. The dehumanizing effects of prison, with the loss of identity that afflicts so many prisoners, were countered by this opportunity to validate their experiences and to convey their own image of themselves to the thousands of people who viewed their video and were moved by it.

One of the most dramatic experiences for many of the volunteers was an opportunity to bring workshops to women in the Special Security Unit. This small, isolated building had served as Death Row until 1972, when the United States Supreme Court temporarily abolished the death penalty. The unit was occupied by three young, intelligent, and unexpectedly endearing and vulnerable women who had been convicted in the Charles Manson murders. After waiting three years to be executed, they were now condemned to life in prison. Over the four years of the program, we conducted workshops and special events in this unit.

Overall, the responses of the students to the courses and other activities were positive, as indicated in the following excerpts from their evaluations.

You have allowed us to grow and expand through this class and that was a real compliment to us. We don't usually grow in here. We die in here. This has been fantastic.

The "Black Studies" workshop introduced me to a man for whom I have the deepest esteem. Also the "Women in Film" workshop was very meaningful to me—informative and enlightening. The books you bring in are very much desired and appreciated. All the material is stimulating and gives us things to think and talk about with each other.

You all have inspired us to start thinking positively about continuing our education on the outside. With these classes we come alive. I began to realize where I was and what a predicament I had let myself fall into. I began picking up on the real strength of the women I was coming into contact with. Every week day I am so damned impatient waiting for the weekend to come and the workshops. I draw strength and courage from them.

The workshops kept me from flipping out. I seemed to be able to make sense out of things that had never made sense. I was able to get information about racism and to air some feelings and meet with Black sisters on calmer ground.

The program just described broke with all assumptions of traditional penal philosophy. We did not assume that the women were in need of rehabilitation. We understood crime as a socially constructed condition, and criminal justice as a discriminatory system that criminalized people from the least socially empowered groups. We rejected patriarchal and class-based assumptions which stereotype women in conflict with the law as nonconformists to feminine standards. As program planners we did not presume to know better than the women inside what they needed to make sense of their lives. We recognized that women in prison are adults who are no less aware of the world they live in than anyone else, and, despite popular mythology, no less intelligent by any discernible standard.[6]

It was at the urging of interested prisoners that we developed SCWPP, and in the collective process of designing the curricula, we gave priority to courses that reflected directly on the students' articulated concerns. In contrast with the existing vocational and school programs in the prison which offered instruction in sewing, hairdressing, office work, or grade twelve equivalency, we introduced the study of critical theory and substantive social issues affecting women's lives. We thus developed, in this unlikely circumstance, what became in effect one of the nation's earliest women's studies programs.

A minority of the instructors in the program took conventional pedagogic approaches to teaching, but most adhered to a philosophy of education that was holistic, student centered, and praxis oriented, whereby theory was informed by practice with an explicit commitment to social change. Several of the organizers had been involved in grassroots, multicultural community schools, and had studied the work of Paulo Freire, Ivan Illich, Paul Goodman, and other liberationist educators. Those of us who were graduate students were influenced by the interdisciplinary methods of our History of Consciousness professors at the University of California at Santa Cruz.[7]

Most of us believed that to teach was to ask critical questions, examine the androcentricity of conventional texts, make political sense of social reality, and effect changes in the construction of knowledge and the analysis and "ownership" of experience. Circle discussions, exercises in communications, and open critiques of one another's work replaced conventional, hierarchical student-teacher relationships, methods of evaluation,[8] and lecture formats. In these "student-centered" groups, the prisoners themselves often took initiative for material to be covered or for presentations drawing on their experiences prior to or during incarceration. In our teaching methods, as in our approach to planning and our concept about the project and its relationship to ourselves and students, we were as unlike any traditional prison schooling (or "treatment" program) as we could be.

INSTITUTIONAL RESISTANCE

It was perhaps inevitable that problems would erupt. In a political climate that drew negative attention to the state's prison system at large, any outside group seen to be challenging penal ideology was perceived as a potential threat to institutional routine and the authority of the guards. Many participants in our group were identified as radical rabble-rousers, and although some of the staff (especially, but not only, female staff) strongly defended our presence, others were unrelenting in their intolerance. That we were affiliated with a university and had the support of liberal state officials, as well as the prison's administration, only served to exacerbate guards' resentments of the group as a whole.

Everyone entering the prison was subject to prior security clearances. Routine body searches reminded us of the necessity to obey all prison regulations and to acquiesce without argument to any order given by the guards. While there was an agreement with the administration that course content would not be censored, this did not extend to the literature we brought to the prison. The guards often censored books whose covers suggested a radical content, especially those authored by Karl Marx, George Jackson and other prisoners, or any writer publicly associated with Left or Black Power political perspectives. After observing that the guards did not examine the content of books without covers, we tore off the covers of all paperbacks we brought to the prison.

Efforts not to rock the boat extended to wardrobe, at a time when hippie garb, blue-collar work clothes, and African dashikis were in popular-radical fashion both in the prison and in the outside world. Some of us tried to be more conventional in dress and appearance so as not to offend the guards' conservative sensibilities, but some of us were unavoidably "offensive" unless we cut our hair, shaved our legs, or disguised our Jewishness. Most of us, for one reason or another, simply did not fit the stereotype guards held for respectable university professor types; indeed, even those who appeared very proper were tainted by association.

The forms of institutional resistance and surveillance were many; some were precipitated by trivial incidents and issues. Some incidents led to the program being suspended and resulted in protests by prisoners, volunteers, and activists associated with the social movements of the time. What follows are descriptions of a representative sample of the incidents that disrupted the project. In retrospect some of these incidents seem almost comical, more akin to guerrilla theatre than to a serious academic and cultural program. However, at the time, each was taken very seriously given the repercussions for the program.

During the first year of the program, I was temporarily banned from the institution, and the program was temporarily suspended, because I had ended a letter to a prisoner with the word *Venceremos*, a then popular colloquialism which signified the overcoming of obstacles to freedom. However, the guard who had read the letter (a standard procedure on all incoming mail) concluded that I was connected with a group called "Venceremos," which had claimed credit for assisting with an escape from a neighboring men's institution. The warden telephoned me to explain what had happened, and she readily accepted the truth that I had no connection with that group. However, she also warned me that, given the seriousness of the charge, an associate warden in charge of security would not be satisfied until an investigation was completed; meanwhile, I would not be permitted to return to the institution.[9]

While I was barred, women in the prison who had been working with me and Jeanne Gallick on curriculum plans for the project organized a strike. They refused to work and sat on the ground in front of the warden's office until herded off to their cells. Only after a thorough investigation of my background, one of many, was the warden able to officially assure the staff that I did not represent a (violent) political threat to the institution, and I could be trusted to proceed with the university program.

Another disruption resulted from the prerogative of the security staff to search not only the bodies, clothing, and briefcases of volunteers when they entered and departed from the institution, but also to search thoroughly our vehicles left in the prison parking lot. On one occasion, while rifling through suitcases in the trunk of a car, they found a small amount of marijuana. The young woman who owned the suitcase had been a guest contributor to one of the workshops. Nonetheless, the entire program was suspended following a dramatic show of force by the administration: A helicopter circled above the prison grounds, three state police cars arrived on the scene with their sirens at full volume, and the sheriff arrested the woman. The volunteers inside were routed out, searched, and sent home when nothing more was found on their persons or in their cars. The prisoners, we learned later, were sent to their cells in a state of agitation because they did not know what was happening. As it turned out, the woman's boyfriend was the son of the head of the state parole board. When this official heard the story he was as annoyed with the prison administration for their overreaction as he was with the woman, and after negotiations with senior officials the program was reinstated.

Most of SCWPP's episodic expulsions from CIW lasted no more than a few weeks, and were resolved informally. A more serious and telling incident occurred in our second year in conjunction with an academic exercise, which resulted in a month-long break in the program and our first major concern as to whether the program could continue at all. In this case, Nancy Stoller, a medical sociologist, and her assistant Laurie Hauer were teaching a course on women's health issues, which included units on nutrition and medication. As basic data for an overall health analysis, a questionnaire was distributed to the fifteen students in the course. They were asked to keep a record for one week of food and beverage consumption, cigarette smoking, medication and vitamin intake, exercise, work environment, and sleep patterns.

The health officers did not want to risk having information on overdrugging (for the purpose of maintaining a placid population) recorded and made public, and so it was predictable that the authorities would censor questions about this aspect of the prison regimen. However, the administration also made it clear to us that we had overstepped our boundaries by inquiring about the food. Women routinely complained about their overcooked, high-starch, low-protein diet and the lack of fresh fruit or vegetables. No one defended the diet, including the authorities, who blamed the problem on an inadequate budget. Thus, we were taken by surprise when this component of the questionnaire was treated as a major subversive action. After more than two months of negotiation—complicated by changes under way in the administration—the new warden canceled the health course. The rest of the program was able to resume its activities under pressure from university and state correctional authorities.

A noncredit workshop organized by a professional masseuse to teach techniques of therapeutic massage also caused problems. The workshop was offered to train women to give one another foot and neck and shoulder massages, as an alternative to the routine use of drugs as treatment for the profound tensions that pervaded CIW. There was certainly no thought of appealing to prurient interests. The intent was to impart in a straightforward way some simple methods of relaxation. After a brief lecture on the history and therapeutic value of massage techniques to the approximately two dozen women in attendance, the therapist organized the women in pairs to take turns practicing foot massage. She turned out the harsh fluorescent classroom lighting and lit candles to produce a soothing atmosphere. She lit a stick of incense and turned on a cassette tape of gentle music. From the moans and sighs of satisfaction that ensued, and the candlelight glow of relaxation on women's faces, it seemed to us that the massages and the overall peaceful ambience were having the intended effects. However, to a passing guard, the scene smacked of a "sex orgy," and he reacted with a show of fury that brought the workshop to an abrupt end. The SCWPP coordinators were again subjected to what, by now in our third year, had become a routine disciplinary meeting in which we were scolded by irate prison administrators. It was "admirable" for us to bring university courses to the prison, and the concerts and other cultural events were "nice for the girls," but we could never under any circumstances encourage the women to touch one another. Once again, the program was temporarily suspended.

A problem of a different kind, but no less a threat to the integrity of the project, was an attempt to link participation in the program to the parole system. For a short period at the beginning of the program, course completion could positively affect prisoners' chances for parole. Whereas some of the guards were skeptical of or disturbed by our course topics, some members of the state's parole board valued the education and some women serving indeterminate sentences were receiving release dates because they had gained academic credit. Meanwhile, others were being denied parole on the grounds that they had not yet completed courses in which they were enrolled. This practice stopped when the project's coordinators protested on the grounds that our purposes would be defeated if parole was contingent on course participation and completion. Such a contingency would have had negative implications not only for women enrolled in courses but particularly for women who were not enrolled.

Each incident discussed here was resolved through negotiations among prison authorities, the project coordinators, and outside officials (from the university or the state), with support from grassroots communities. It is also important to register that, with every suspension, the students would organize among themselves to assert pressure on the authorities to let the workshops continue. A woman who had served a long time in prison got a letter out to me during one of these breaks, and she wrote:

I witnessed something I would have believed [three years ago] was impossible. We had an [illegal] meeting where Black and White were united, under one common cause. There were women there who in the past would never have spoken to each other but here they were standing together, agreeing, touching shoulders. The tone of the meeting was not loud or wild. It was a confident approach to bringing back the workshops. It is something we all want. It was beautiful. We elected a six-woman committee to speak for the group. We are not afraid. Everything is in a suspended state pending the outcome of the [coordinators'] meeting with [the administration]. We're ready to act.

There was no single incident that resulted in the final demise of the project. If pushed to attribute the cancellation of the project to one cause, it may be attributed to a combination of political and organizational shifts. For instance, a newly appointed warden—a former department store marketing director with no prior experience in prison management—decided that outside volunteers were simply more trouble than they were worth. Simultaneous with the final expulsion of the SCWPP in 1976, at least a dozen other community volunteer groups were likewise forced to cease their in-prison work at CIW, including conventionally conservative religious groups. A special committee of the legislature, celebrities, attorneys, and professors joined their voices to the outcry of prisoners, ex-prisoners, project volunteers, and grassroots activists to demand closer scrutiny of the administration of prisons. The director of the Department of Corrections and his associates went through the motions of listening to the complaints, but they did nothing to implement a practical means of integrating the work of outside groups with the day-to-day life of women in prison.

Even if we had not been officially expelled, those of us coordinating SCWPP would have had to reduce our activity. After four years, many of us were close to burnout, and the logistical complications of commuting

500 miles for weekend work were taking a toll on our personal lives and our pocketbooks. Prior to the final expulsion from the prison, several of the project coordinators had been meeting with faculty and administrators at community colleges within easy commuting distance from the prison to ensure that, when it was time for us to leave, the women committed to their studies would not be left without a program. We also organized a College Program Advisory Council at the prison, with the support of the authorities, to assist with the future coordination of higher education at the institution. Several of these colleges had begun offering courses by the time we left. They developed more limited and conventional programs than those offered by the Santa Cruz Workshops, and fewer women participated. But given the demonstrated commitment of a solid block of women to academic work, the viability of higher education in a women's prison was no longer an issue.

POLITICAL EDUCATION IN PRISON

No one expects a prison to be an easygoing environment, but volunteers with SCWPP who were novices to the prison system were invariably shocked at the level of power held by guards and the perceived pettiness of their concerns. SCWPP extended to women in prison the benefits of higher education and the empowerment that accrues from gaining political knowledge, recognizing constructive life choices (despite structural limitations), and acquiring skills to act on them. We also developed a strong support network for women on parole. Five years following the completion of the program, only five out of approximately 100 women who had been released had returned to prison for a new crime or parole violation. This is compared to the usual recidivism rate at CIW of approximately 80 percent.

Moreover, the program had at least as much educational value for the volunteers as it did for the women. The volunteers came to understand *who* is in prison, and *why*, beyond the fact of having broken a law. The volunteers also received an education in the power of the state to delimit options for those judged to be criminals. Most had never encountered such utter lack of control over one's own environment as we witnessed in the prison. But we also saw prisoners demonstrating exceptional strengths. As indicated by these excerpts from instructors' evaluations of their experience, it was an education in the politics of punishment and in the significance of education in this context.

I got far more out of this work than the prisoners. As a person who genuinely likes teaching, it was a dream come true. These students gave back at least as much, really more, than they got. They were creative, thoughtful, analytical and forceful, capable of warmth, cooperation and amazingly enough, ambition. I really felt this to be one of the most powerful experiences of my life.

I had some fears about going to the prison and was surprised to see they looked like an ordinary group of women, sitting in a circle and talking about ordinary things. All the faces were familiar. I had seen them everywhere I had ever been.

We learned an enormous amount about how the state operates and the potential strength of women's resistance. The women at CIW made me understand how those women who are the most oppressed by this imperialist society—Blacks, Latinas, Native Americans and poor whites—can be the strongest and clearest force for change.

The classes brought a good analysis to the prison. We set a context which helped people move from anger at themselves, individual guards or the prison, or even the "middle class," to an understanding of the system of capitalism, its relations to other institutions and what might have to be done to overcome it. In balance, we probably eased day-to-day tension in the institution by increasing long range radicalism against the broader system.

The more effective you are politically in a prison, with community back-up, the more likely you are to get kicked out. The women learned to write their own writs and became educated about their own skills. The more you really develop collaborative learning, and people effectively take power over their lives, the less likely they are to go to or stay in prison.

Politically this work is more sensitive, fragile, ugly, awkward, beautiful and compelling than any I have known. I was so relieved to be at the prison with so many rebellious women [in contrast to] the straight world—that part I loved. But then I'd see things that made me feel horrible—my heart would break. Some of the classes were gripping. We would all be totally there, completely involved in each moment, every antenna alert. That kind of concentration is exhilarating and sustaining.

One of the values of the program was that it linked those associated with one of the most elite institutions with those held in one of the most disreputable institutions and located common denominators among them. It created a bridge across which people from very different social elements could meet and engage in discourse related to social change. In the prison environment, potential antagonisms based on real differences of culture, class, ethnicity, age, gender, sexual orientation, and social status were deconstructed through the unifying processes of building the program. The women inside either initiated or were consulted about every decision concerning academic curriculum and cultural workshops; their priorities affected and often dictated the program's direction. It was a collective investment, and whenever the program's continuity was disrupted for another investigation or penalty, everyone's education was at stake. At no time did the volunteers assume that they were giving more to the women inside than they were receiving from them. A volunteer spoke for all of us when she wrote:

I was inspired by how the prisoners organized demonstrations whenever there was a possibility they would not be able to have the Santa Cruz project coming in. . . . Both personally and politically it was incredibly important work. I think I learned more and grew more in my political awareness faster than ever before, being thrust into the kind of intensified experience that is prison work.

CONCLUDING COMMENTS

State policies, particularly those engendered by criminal justice systems, rarely empower the least privileged populations in any meaningful way. It is also dubious whether educators who receive substantial grants for prison education or research programs are likely to promote empowering, grassroots initiatives. The liberal democratic state educates not for independence, freedom, and equality, but for the duties of citizenship accorded to one's (usually inherited) social position. However, the state is not a singular, omniscient entity containing unitary power. It is a network of agencies dispersed through a body politic with conflicting priorities and abundant contradictions.

Within individual institutions these same contradictions are played out. Those at the top are concerned with public image and relations, especially as it affects funding, and they must be sensitive to contemporary thought and exercise diplomacy with both liberal and conservative trendsetters. As decision makers they must accommodate these trends while at the same time sustain the power relations upon which their own positions are dependent. Middle management, for its part, must juggle the expectations of senior officials with the requirement to sustain order among those who work at the bottom. They must be seen at once to be open to change while capable of preserving the status quo in order to keep things running with minimal bureaucratic disruption. In prisons, those at the top are invariably more aware of and at least superficially in support of changes that will appease public opinion. Middle management will speak the language of reform while resisting wardens who "rock the boat." Prison guards are the underlings in this class-based chain of command. The only real powers they possess are resistance to middle management and the power to abuse those who are subordinate to them, the prisoners.

At the onset, the Santa Cruz Project received the full support of a liberal warden and liberal officials in the state capitol, including some members of the parole board. The project could be interpreted as an innovative approach to rehabilitation through education. At the same time, the project explicitly challenged the class privilege which normally excludes the women who benefited from this program from participating in higher education. Meanwhile, during the four years that the project survived, the prison lost one warden after another. In less than two years, the position changed hands four times, as a consequence of political maneuvering within the "correctional enterprise." As the prison's administration fell into disarray, guards—especially male guards—became more authoritarian and inflicted more arbitrary discipline upon prisoners and outsiders. The most reactionary guards demonstrated their objection to women enjoying class privileges denied to them.

There were moments in the history of the program when our relationships with the guards might have been otherwise. When the Santa Cruz Project was just forming, one of the CIW guards had asked if our group would be willing to let staff take the classes for credit. We said no because the women wanted a program that was independent of the custody, security, and punitive functions of the institution. We knew that if guards attended the classes the prisoners would not enroll. In retrospect, I regret that we did not set up a separate program for the staff, or appeal to the women to open up certain classes. Certainly, in the broader picture, the guards were not our enemy, and if they had had a vested interest in the program's continuance, more of them would have supported it. It would have been a process of genuine demystification if the guards and volunteers had gotten to know one another within a study environment.

In the spirit of Paulo Freire (1970), who introduced the idea of the "pedagogy of the oppressed," I witnessed women in dialogue with one another, and with their teachers, locating and naming themselves within the social context of their lives beyond the prison. They refined their understandings (consciousness) of how society is constructed, and they gained insights into how they could individually and collectively challenge their exclusions through political (as opposed to criminal) activism. Together we demystified a theoretically complex process. African-American women who studied African-American history became advocates of Black Power. Women who wore the cloak of lifetime poverty gained class consciousness and an energizing commitment to social change. Women who had been raped and battered gained feminist consciousness and a basis for unity with other women. Women who were mute from years of silencing found their voices.

The Santa Cruz Workshops came to symbolize resistance by insiders and outsiders alike to shame, blame, condemnation, labeling, and powerlessness. Cumulatively and collectively, the workshops, through the conduits of knowledge sharing, culture, artistry, and friendship promoted analysis in place of shame, responsibility in place of blame, solidarity in place of condemnation, unity in place of labeling, and the nurturance of power *with* (contra power *over*) in place of perceived powerlessness. Outsiders who came in with stereotypes of people in prison cast them off. Insiders who held stereotypes of professors, students, socialists, feminists, and Jews likewise "turned their heads around." The most authoritarian of the guards, in turn, resisted a program that symbolically weakened their own authority, legitimacy, and indispensability.

For those who participated, the Santa Cruz Workshops generated a spirit of community and solidarity. Many of us, students and instructors alike, are still in touch with each other, and we still enrich one another's lives. Most of us, whatever our occupations, are still political activists who have not abandoned our ideals and who look back on our work at the prison satisfied that, on a micro-level, it was useful work. Many of us have continued to work with prisoners in various institutions, to sit on committees working to reduce the numbers of people sent to prison, to improve conditions for those who are incarcerated, to do research, teaching, and public education on criminal justice, and to otherwise put to use the knowledge we gained from and with women in the California prison. The prisoners, for their part, have similarly continued to show their commitment to the beliefs that were collectively developed through the project and to use their experiences to educate others. Most of them were paroled and have never returned; many are living interesting and creative lives in a wide range of occupations. A number of them completed college degrees on the outside. These women and others gained a sense of community and became important allies in social change work. Not every story has had a happy ending, but most of our lives, insiders and outsiders alike, were changed for the better through our shared work.

Education for liberation and empowerment of confined groups, wherever and however rarely it occurs, is an exercise in counter-hegemony which calls for a more equitable and transformative share in social power and decision making. As coordinators Catherine Cusic and Debra Miller summed up our work, we engaged in "education as the practice of freedom, as opposed to education as the practice of domination" (SCWPP 1974). People sent to prison may have offended society, but by virtue of their incarceration (together with inmates of mental illness institutions) they signify the least socially empowered of all adult groups. When these people are also women, they are the least visible and the most silenced of all. As women and men who in the early 1970s were finding our voices as feminists and feminist allies, we could do no better for ourselves than to support their reclamation of their lives.

NOTES

An earlier version of this chapter appears in K. Faith, *Unruly Women: The Politics of Confinement and Resistance*. It is reprinted with the permission of Press Gang Publishers, Vancouver, British Columbia, 1993.

1. For an account that provides more detail on the individuals who participated in SCWPP, see Faith (1993).
2. Women's experience of prison education has also been all but ignored in the literature. Of the 1,250 references cited in a recent annotated bibliography on

prison education, only 31 are concerned with women (Duguid, Fowler, and Shew-felt 1992).

3. In addition to the course, Jeanne Gallick tutored women who required specific academic skills.

4. It may go without saying that this struggle occurred within a particular historical and political context—California in the 1970s—through a specific convergence of women's liberation and prisoners' rights movements. In 1976, following the final expulsion of SCWPP from the prison, over 1,000 women and their male supporters marched on the state capitol in Sacramento for a rally to call attention to abuses against incarcerated women, and to address a special legislative committee investigating prison conditions (Faith 1976). In support of these actions, 10,000 individuals signed petitions demanding greater public access to prisons. The stimulus for this action was the prison administration's decision to cancel a concert at CIW produced by Women on Wheels, a feminist cultural production company, with performances by Margie Adam, Meg Christian, Holly Near, and Cris Williamson. The rally was cosponsored by SCWPP with considerable input from the Bay Area Legal Education group, the Women's Prison Coalition, the United Prisoners Union, the Berkeley-Oakland Women's Union, and the National Alliance Against Racist and Political Repression.

5. The primary coordinators included Catherine Cusic, Jeanne Gallick, Debra Miller, Nancy Stoller, Francis Reid, Mary K. Blackmon, Ruth Marance, Marilyn Stamos, Tanya Neiman, Ann Grogan, and myself.

6. A review of IQ scores in 100 randomly selected files on women at CIW indicates an average of their Stanford-Binet IQ test score of 110, a score that is at the high end of the norm. It is plausible to suggest that the average may have been higher if one takes into account the stressful conditions under which the tests were administered.

7. Our professors included historian Page Smith, philosopher Norman O. Brown, poet Robert Duncan, and psychologists Bert Kaplan and Ted Sarbin. Scholars later associated with the program include Bettina Aptheker, Gregory Bateson, James Clifton, Angela Davis, Barbara Epstein, Donna Haraway, Stephen Heath, Teresa de Lauretis, Gary Lease, Jerry Neu, Paul Niebanck, Herbert Marcuse, Hayden White, and Sheldon Wolin.

8. A unique feature of the University of California, Santa Cruz, is a Pass/No Record marking system by which students either receive a Pass and credit for their work, or, if they fail to complete the work at an acceptable standard, nothing appears on their record. Although standards for admission are higher than at other universities, once admitted the students do not have to compete with one another for a letter grade. Instructors write detailed narrative evaluations for each student, giving clear indications of strengths and areas needing improvement. The benefits of this system are that students strive to achieve their "personal best," students learn the value of cooperative learning, "cheating" is virtually unknown, students are spared the constant tensions and anxieties of a competitive environment, and the rewards of study are more intrinsic when learning is not measured by an external ranking system. Although traditionalists were initially skeptical as to the viability of this system, it has proven highly successful, not only in the arts but also for students in professional programs such as pre-med studies. As the Santa Cruz campus goes toward its fourth decade, the system remains intact. This system was

particularly useful to women in the prison, where competition for marks would have defeated the purpose of the program.

9. The warden, who had been our strong ally from the beginning, suddenly "resigned"; this particular associate warden, an authoritarian man who had worked his way up from the line staff, became one of a series of temporary wardens and years later he proved to be the nemesis of the Santa Cruz project.

13

Jailhouse Lawyers Educating Fellow Prisoners

Julian Stone

I have been a "jailhouse lawyer" since 1970. A jailhouse lawyer is a prisoner who has learned how the law operates and who advises other prisoners about their legal rights and options. They often help prisoners prepare appeals of their convictions. Prisoners in the United States were given the authority to assist fellow prisoners in legal matters by the United States Supreme Court in *Johnson v. Avery*.[1]

I am a prisoner serving a life sentence in Massachusetts for first degree murder. I was sentenced to death in January 1969 and confined on death row until 1972, when the United States Supreme Court vacated the death penalty and death sentences were commuted to sentences of life imprisonment (*Furman v. Georgia* 408 U.S. 283, 92 S. Ct. 2726, 33 L. Ed.2d 346 [1972]). While still on death row, I discovered that the judicial system does not offer much assistance to an accused prisoner, especially once he or she has been convicted. The court appointed an attorney to me only thirty days before my trial was scheduled to begin, during which time the attorney visited me once. After my conviction, he never discussed the appeal with me personally. He filed a routine Motion For A New Trial, arguing that there was insufficient evidence. After that, my letters to him were never answered. I also wrote to the clerk of the county court in which I had been convicted and to the trial judge, but found no relief. Much to my horror, I learned that my only appeal had been dismissed because my attorney had failed to file the appropriate briefs within the time period set by the court. My experience was not unique.[2]

It became clear that I had to depend on myself, and I decided to learn as much as possible about the law and the legal system. Fortunately I knew a jailhouse lawyer, who advised me to read an introductory guide to the law. We met at the prison chapel each Sunday morning when he answered my questions and lent me other books on law. After studying the law in this fashion for some time, I realized that I wanted to share this knowledge with anyone who was interested. I did not have that chance until I left death row and was placed in the general prison population at Walpole Prison in Massachusetts.

The first problem I faced was that Walpole did not have an adequate law library. Essential texts were not available, and those that were had to be requested a week in advance. Several former death row prisoners and I prepared a suit against the Department of Corrections, arguing that we were entitled to a law library. An agreement was reached which brought to the prison most of the law books needed to prepare cases and have access to the courts.

About the time the law books arrived, I was transferred to Norfolk, a medium security prison which had a law library and a system of prisoner self-governance conducive to teaching law courses to fellow prisoners. It is useful to take a moment to describe this context.[3] Norfolk operates under the provisions of its own constitution, which was authorized by the governor of Massachusetts following the Attica insurrection of 1971 and various strikes by prisoners. This constitution provides for a Resident Council to give prisoners a "voice" in the institution's management. Chairmen are elected by the general population, and each housing unit elects its own representative to the council. The council's members chair special committees (e.g., Medical, Black Rights, Spanish Rights) that provide services to the general population. One of these, the Legal Advisory Committee, which provides basic legal assistance to fellow prisoners, became the vehicle for the development of a law class.

Locating the law class within the structure of the Resident Council was crucial because it kept the class outside the authority of the prison's education department, which was directly responsible to the warden and, through him, to the Department of Corrections. If the class were part of the prison school, its principal would be in a position to dictate what materials would be used to teach the course, who would be suitable students, how the class would be organized, who would teach, and how students would be evaluated. With the course sponsored by the Legal Advisory Committee, these decisions were made by a group responsible to fellow prisoners, not by the administration. While this arrangement did not make the class fully independent of the warden's office, it provided a degree of autonomy that proved to be essential for the development of the course.

Taking suggestions from the members of the committee, I decided to set up the law class in two parts, basic and advanced. The content of the basic course was in part defined by the legal needs of the general population. To determine these needs, I talked with a number of prisoners who knew little about the law to learn generally what was the level of legal knowledge. When I felt that I had a sense of how well the law was understood, I formulated the course's content. It aimed to teach students the organization of the federal and state governments, the jurisdictions of each court, and the rights guaranteed by the constitutions of the United States and Massachusetts. The students would also learn how laws were passed, how to read and understand decisions rendered by various courts, how to apply fact to the law, how to do legal research, and how to determine whether there exist judicial remedies for violations. The basic course would include ten sessions. Those who completed it successfully would be allowed to enter the advanced course.

The criteria for passing the course also had to be determined. Ultimately, I wanted students to show that they knew how to use all the books in the law library. They would be given questions that required the use of various legal resources. Through written responses and class discussion, they would demonstrate their understanding of the exercises. Anyone who had difficulties with the material could see me outside of class for extra help. No one who could not effectively use the resources in the law library would receive a certificate for completing the basic course. However, anyone who found himself in this position would be encouraged to repeat the basic course in order to accomplish his goal.

I arranged for the course to be taught in the law library where students could familiarize themselves with each resource as it was discussed. Pencils and paper were supplied by the Resident Council so that students would not have to spend their own money. Once content, assignments, and facilities were in place, I advertised the course, putting out flyers to the general population. About 40 men signed up out of a population of 650.

The first class was a challenge. I felt nervous since I did not know how the students would react to being taught by a fellow prisoner. Being shy and apprehensive about speaking before a large group, I worried about being effective or making mistakes and being embarrassed if a student corrected me in class. In anticipation, I showed up an hour before the class was scheduled to begin. I was pleasantly surprised to see the students arriving a few minutes ahead of time. This gave me an opportunity to introduce myself to those I had not met, and this eased my nervousness.

Most students had no prior knowledge of the judicial system except for their experience as defendants. As planned, I started the course with basic information about American government at the state and federal levels, the three branches of government, and their separate functions. Focusing on the judicial branch, I discussed the court system, paying close attention to those courts that were important to my students, the district courts, superior courts, and appeal courts within the state of Massachusetts and the federal court system. I also touched on courts they may not have known about (e.g., probate courts). Several students were eager to discuss the law per se, and so I had to explain that this information was fundamental to an understanding of the legal system. This completed my first class.

Next I wanted the students to start to become familiar with the law books. I gave an overview of the books and their contents. The first text we worked with in depth was the U.S. Constitution, in particular the Amendments which delineate the rights of citizens. These rights directly affected us as prisoners and may have been violated at the time of arrest, trial, and appeal.

Basic constitutional rights remained a topic of discussion throughout the course. The students learned how the Amendments could be used to challenge violations during arrest and trial. They also learned about protection offered by the Massachusetts Constitution which exceed those guaranteed by the U.S. Constitution in areas such as search and seizure warrants and the right to counsel. The federal and state constitutions are the first source to use when doing research on the violation of rights since they refer the reader to cases in which a particular argument was either supported or rejected.

Other sources that the students learned to use included *West's Case Digest, United States Code Annotated, Black's Law Dictionary*, and several secondary books that expedite research. They were assigned cases to read outside of class. Then class discussion focused on distinguishing the facts, issues, decisions, and reasoning of each case. Students were taught how to use *Shepard's Citations* to identify court decisions that refer to previous case citations. If an earlier court decision is no longer accepted by the courts, this too can be determined using *Shepard's*.

For three classes we studied the Massachusetts General Laws and the accompanying cases that have resulted in court opinions, which interpret these laws. In this way we covered information that would help students determine whether their rights had been violated during the arrest, trial, or appeal of their conviction. Students learned to recognize examples of violations and to cite case law that supported their contention that basic rights had been violated.

After I had tested the students to see whether they understood how to research the various issues, the class was ready to apply what they had learned. For instance, I gave the class a case study, including a series of facts, and asked them to apply the law using a Memorandum-of-Law format. Working in teams of five, the students decided what rights had been violated and found cases to support their decisions. After an hour, the groups came together and argued their positions. This gave me an opportunity to point out the fine distinctions that separated the facts I had originally given them from the facts found in the cases they used to defend their arguments.

Students were given a written test at the next to the last class. The correct answers to fifty questions required the effective use of specific reference texts. Student also had to quote particular case citations that could be found only if they knew how "to shepardize." Some questions made students go back to specific chapters in the Massachusetts General Laws. Other questions on tenant rights, landlord duties, and consumer protection laws ensured that students could use the various indices to law books.

I corrected their written exams in time for our last class meeting. It was critical that each student understood the correct answers and where the answers could be found. Overall, the class performance was good although some misunderstood questions or carelessly transcribed case numbers. I talked to the students who had not been able to answer many questions in order to determine whether they did not understand the material or had "frozen" during the test. Since they could not show that they understood the material, we discussed their expectations and agreed that they would repeat the basic course.

During the final class, I asked oral questions of those students who had made mistakes on the written exam. In this way, students had every opportunity to demonstrate their competence, and I could further clarify my assessment of them. I thought too that oral testing would prepare the students for questions asked by others who were knowledgeable about law.[4] After lengthy discussion, I was convinced that these students understood the material and had successfully completed the course.

The students had reason to be proud because, from the beginning, I had made it clear that the course would have the same expectations of accomplishment as a regular college course. I expected from students a very high level of achievement because, whether they did legal work for themselves or their fellow prisoners, often they would be concerned with matters of survival. They needed to have in hand some proof of their legal knowledge, assurance to prisoners seeking legal assistance that their needs would be met competently. Thus it was decided that certificates which endorsed the bearer as proficient at the level stated would be given to graduates. I put my reputation on the line each time I signed a certificate, and I took this very seriously.

Obtaining certificates for graduation is a story in itself. As the basic course was coming to an end, the Legal Advisory Committee and I drafted a document that recognized the accomplishments of the graduates. Since having the certificates printed would necessarily be a clandestine affair, the "right" prisoner working in the print shop had to be consulted. I found that person and showed him what we needed. He agreed, although he risked losing his job and receiving disciplinary sanctions had he been caught printing them. He did not want any compensation for the work, but I gave him a couple of cartons of cigarettes (standard prison currency) as an expression of my appreciation.

In addition to awarding certificates, I wanted to put on a graduation ceremony for the students. I invited the prison superintendent to say a few words and pass out the certificates in order to lend dignity and credibility to the event. He also agreed to cosign the certificates, never asking how I had gotten them. At the ceremony, he recognized the dedication the students had shown by completing the course, and I expressed my appreciation to them for their commitment to the class. I felt sincere pride in my students as I called their names and each received his certificate from the superintendent. Afterward we celebrated with cookies, donuts, and coffee (purchased from the prison canteen) and sat and talked informally. The evening proved to be an unintended opportunity for the superintendent to get to know firsthand each of the students and the work they were doing.[5]

The advanced law class started the following week. Fifteen students had signed up for the forty-week course, which ran for two hours every Friday evening.[6] My objective was to teach the students to prepare legal actions in both criminal and civil cases, to access and extract information from law books necessary to support actions, and to prepare and serve documents exactly as the rules of the court required. Weekly attendance was mandatory, except in cases of emergency. As I explained to the students, learning the information taught in each class depended on an understanding of the content of the preceding classes. In studying law, students need all the pieces to make sense out of the puzzle. Most of the course concentrated on aspects of criminal law which, when violated, open the way for a challenge to the legality of a conviction. Thus, we examined what constitutes legal arrest (including probable cause for arrest, warrantless arrests, and the Miranda rights), search and seizure, confessions, and evidence. Student discussion was always active. In fact, I would usually reserve a half-hour at the end of class to answer questions about violations since, if I allowed discussion during class, the evening's topic would never get covered. Students' questions drew on their own experiences, and on those of fellow prisoners, to determine whether violations had occurred and whether conviction could be challenged based on these violations. Within a prison, criminal law is seldom theoretical. Information has real and immediate importance to students that can mean renewed freedom.

Because I wanted students to be able to compete as paralegals once they were released from prison, they had to understand civil law as well as criminal. We examined family laws concerning divorce, child custody, and visitation rights. We also discussed laws involving wills, and students learned to prepare a will after seeing samples. They became familiar with complaints against landlords, suits of negligence, and cases of professional malpractice, and they learned about evidence needed to win such cases. The class also studied the federal laws of civil procedure and the exact preparation of necessary documents, since errors in these could result in automatic dismissal.

As the course progressed, students began to drop out. I felt compelled to know why, and so I tracked each of them down. Some found the workload overwhelming, that it meant they did not have time for their college courses (many were students in programs offered by the University of Massachusetts and Boston University), for playing sports, or for other forms of relaxation. I had to agree that the assignments were very demanding and that the course required solid commitment. By the fifteenth week I had only eight students, but they were sincerely dedicated to learning how to be jailhouse lawyers. For them, knowing about the law was the key to release through the court system.[7]

So small a group brought out the personalities and motives of individual students. Reggie, for one, was a young black man who came from a middle-class family. His father was a doctor and his uncle a college professor. Reggie was "a string-bean," who was very shy. He felt that he had been falsely convicted of a crime and wanted to overturn his conviction. He was also very concerned about others who he felt were victims of the police and the judicial system. His questions were usually related to a particular person's situation and the potential for legal redress. Over the weeks, he grew from a shy, awkward person with no confidence into an assertive person who demanded his rights.

Another student, Jerry, was my "wonder student." He was a short, stocky man in his late twenties, bearing the rough appearance of a "biker." He looked out of place in the classroom and was no different from his wild friends, except that he wanted to learn about law. He attended every class and took notes constantly. He clearly studied all the handouts because he was able to answer any question put to him. He also stood out because he came to each class high on home brew, marijuana, or some sort of pills. This bothered me at first, but when he nevertheless proved to be my best student, I decided that students' habits were not my concern as long as the class was not disrupted.[8] Eventually I learned that Jerry wanted to help bikers, many of whom were targets for prosecutions based on their appearances and on stereotypes promoted by the media and law enforcement personnel.

I found the classes rewarding as I watched the students develop their skills. They increasingly challenged me and began to ask concise questions that demonstrated their growing understanding of the topics. My role as teacher shifted; I asked questions, and they formulated answers based on extensive research. Compared to the basic law class, where students spoke emotionally about fairness, the advanced class discussions drew on distinctions made by the courts. These students could point to specific violations and cite case law to support their interpretations.

As a final test, each student received a set of facts and was allowed one week to identify the issues and pertinent laws and to write a formal brief, in accordance with the Rules of Appellate Procedure. Although some students put too many or too few facts into the argument and some included case law that was redundant, each brief was sufficient since all students correctly identified the constitutional violation and cited the appropriate case law as support. The advanced class was ready for graduation.

Again certificates were prepared, and the superintendent was invited to participate in the ceremony. I also invited several defense lawyers to meet the students and to talk about the paralegal profession. Ideally I had wanted the law courses to train the students so that they could work as paralegals upon release from prison. In addition, establishing a rapport with lawyers was important for the graduate's future as a jailhouse lawyer, who often works between prisoners and court-appointed lawyers.[9]

I was interested in knowing how my courses compared to law courses on the outside. Through discussions with law students from Northeastern University and Boston College (many of whom come to the prison to participate in the Lifers Group), I was able to make a comparison. Differences in course content reflected different goals. The university law schools concentrated on civil law; criminal law constituted less than 20 percent of the course work required for a law degree. Much time was devoted to courtroom rehearsals. As I have indicated, my syllabus was concerned primarily with criminal law and especially with students learning to spot situations that warrant new trials.

Teaching the law courses was very time consuming and mentally demanding. Although I had hoped to wait several months before beginning again, many prisoners were keen to take the courses, and the reward of seeing the students succeed convinced me to advertise after a two-week rest. This time, I invited graduates of the law courses, members of the Legal Advisory Committee, and lawyers to speak as guest lecturers. This afforded the students a wider range of perspectives and experiences than I could offer, and it gave me a chance to observe the classroom dynamics.

I have to date successfully taught both law courses in a number of institutions where I have been imprisoned. Prisoners have responded favorably to them. Many prison administrators and guards too have approved of my efforts, and if any of them disapprove, no one has attempted to disrupt our work. Perhaps my ability to launch successful suits has restrained resistance.[10] However, I believe the courses have been accepted because I have tried to demonstrate to prison personnel that the courses are in their interest. Legal education helps prisoners to identify legitimate grievances and to rectify the matters within courts of law. The stability of the institution is more easily maintained when grievances are taken seriously, and prisoner frustration is lessened when there are means to demand one's rights. Hopefully, when prisoners are informed about recourse to legal action, guards and administrators must learn to restrain from serious violations of prisoners' rights.

NOTES

1. In a concurring opinion, Justice Douglas stated, "Where government fails to provide the prison with the legal counsel it demands, the prison generates its own. In a community where illiteracy and mental deficiency are notoriously high, it is not enough to ask the prisoner to be his own lawyer. Without the assistance of fellow prisoners, some meritorious claims would never see the light of a courtroom" (*Johnson v. Avery*, 393 U.S. 483, 496–497, 89 S.Ct. 747, 754).

2. This attorney had abandoned two other men on death row. It took several years to undo the damage caused by his inaction. One prisoner received a new trial which resulted in the indictments against him being dismissed because his rights had been violated [*Commonwealth v. Harris*, 371 Mass. 462, 471 (1976]. The other prisoner and I are still pursuing justice.

3. The history of Norfolk is worth noting in relationship to the development of this course. On Norfolk in the context of practices of imprisonment during the Progressive Era, see Rothman (1980).

4. For example, the superintendent of Norfolk Prison taught a criminal justice course at a community college.

5. Inside prison, such personal contact can help a prisoner when asking, for example, for approval to be transferred to a lower security institution. Most prisoners do not have a forum that allows them to talk informally with the superintendent, where he can make personal observations and judgments. To receive a transfer, a prisoner must convince the administration that he is a worthy candidate. By participating in programs with positive results, the prisoner demonstrates that he is trying to change. Let me stress that this was an unintended consequence of the law course. Students did not know that the superintendent would be at the graduation until that night. They took the course to learn law, not to receive good conduct deductions or other benefits.

6. The school's principal at Norfolk helped arrange for the use of a classroom. I had worked for him as a television repairman when I first arrived there and, since I was also a Boston University student, we had a good working relationship. He was always supportive, even going out of his way to get materials that were otherwise not available to me.

7. Note that students would receive no college credit for their work, and their participation was not considered by classification or parole boards.

8. It seems likely that a teacher hired by the state to teach in prison would have removed him from class and filed a discipline report, which would have put him in isolation or resulted in his transfer to higher security.

9. Without question, a student's criminal record would be a substantial obstacle to employment as a paralegal after release. Still, a jailhouse lawyer has the opportunity to build a reputation with individual lawyers and law firms as a skilled researcher through his work on behalf of other prisoners.

10. It may be that guards support the law classes because the students learn how to file suits against the prison administration. Many guards believe the administration is "antiguard," and any form of harassment, even by prisoners, may be looked upon with glee.

References

Abbot, J. (1990). *In the belly of the beast: Letters from prison*. New York: Random House.

Acoli, S. (1992). A brief history of the new Afrikan prison struggle. *Sundiata Acoli Freedom Campaign*. Harlem, NY: Sundiata Acoli Freedom Campaign.

Amnesty International. (1987). *Allegations of ill-treatment in Marion Prison, Illinois, U.S.A.* Report distributed by Amnesty International.

Arbuthnot, J., & Gordon, D. A. (1988). Disseminating effective interventions for juvenile delinquents: Cognitive-based sociomoral reasoning development programs. *Journal of Correctional Education, 39*, 48–53.

Arcard, T. E., & Watts-La Fontaine, P. (1983). They're here to follow orders, not to think: Some notes on academic freedom in penal institutions. *Journal of Correctional Education, 34*, 119–121.

Aronowitz, S., & Giroux, H. A. (1991). *Postmodern education: Politics, culture, and social criticism*. Minneapolis: University of Minnesota Press.

Atkins, B. M., & Glick, H. R. (Eds.). (1972). *Prisons, protest and politics*. Englewood Cliffs, NJ: Prentice-Hall.

Auerbach, B., Lawson, R. H., Luftig, J., New, B., Schaller J., Sexton, G. E., & Smith, P. (1969). *A guide to effective prison industries*, Vol. l, *Creating free venture prison industries: Program considerations*. Philadelphia: The American Foundation.

Baker, L. (1983). *Miranda: Crime, law, and politics*. New York: Atheneum.

Ball, S. J. (Ed.). (1990). *Foucault and education: Disciplines and knowledge*. London: Routledge.

Bank robber makes prison an asset, earns a degree. (1985, June 6). *Standard-Times*. New Bedford, MA.

Bayley, D. H. (1976). *Forces of order: Police behavior in Japan and the United States.* Berkeley: University of California Press.

Becker, G. (1964). *Human capital.* New York: Columbia University Press.

Becker, H. (1963). *Outsiders: Studies in the sociology of deviance.* New York: Free Press.

Benidt, B. (1985, June 16). Prisoner-run program gives inmates education and hope. *Minneapolis Star and Tribune*, p. 10.

Berger, P. L., & Luckmann, T. (1966). *The social construction of reality.* Garden City, NY: Anchor Books.

Black, D. (1976). *The behavior of law.* New York: Academic Press.

Boston Globe. (1984, June 7), Graduation with honors—underguard. p. 67.

Bowles, S., & Gintis, H. (1976). *Schooling in capitalist America: Educational reform and the contradictions of economic life.* New York: Basic Books.

Boyer, R. O., & Morais, H. M. (1955). *Labor's untold story.* New York: United Electrical, Radio & Machine Workers of America.

Braithwaite, J. (1994). *Crime, shame and reintegration.* Cambridge, England: Cambridge University Press.

Breed, A. F. (1991). What are the "top three" issues for the correction system in the United States? In *International symposium on the future of corrections: Program.* Ottawa, ON: Correctional Service of Canada.

Brown, R. "Bo." (1993, May/June). The white North American political prisoners in the U.S. *Prison News Service.*

Bureau of Justice Statistics (BJS). 1992. *Sourcebook of criminal justice statistics—1991.* Washington, DC: U.S. Department of Justice.

Buswell, C. (1980). Pedagogic change and social change. *British Journal of Sociology of Education*, 1(3), 293–306.

Butler, J. (1868). *Education and the employment of women.* London: Macmillan.

Callwood, J. (1990, January). Reading: The road to freedom. *Canadian Living*, p. 7.

Carter, S. A. (1991). The future of corrections in the 21st century: Broadening our vision by narrowing the focus. In *International symposium on the future of corrections: Program.* Ottawa, ON: Correction Service Canada.

Cervero, R. (1980). Does the Texas adult performance level test measure functional competence? *Adult Education*, 30(3), 152–165.

Chambliss, W. J. (1978). *On the take.* Bloomington: Indiana University Press.

Chambliss, W. J. (1988). *Exploring criminology.* New York: Macmillan.

Chaplin, R. (1948). *Wobbly.* Chicago: University of Chicago Press.

Christie, N. (1991). The purpose of corrections: The eye of God. In *International symposium on the future of corrections: Program.* Ottawa, ON: Correctional Service of Canada.

Clark, D. D. (1991, August). *Analysis of return rates of inmate college program participants: Executive summary.* Albany, NY: State of New York Department of Correctional Services.

Clarke, R., & Cornish, D. (1983). *Crime control in Britain: A review of policy research.* Albany: State University of New York Press.

Clarke, R., & Cornish, D. (1987). Understanding crime displacement: An application of rational choice theory. *Criminology*, 25, 933–947.

Cleaver, H. (1979). *Reading Capital politically.* Austin: University of Texas Press.

Clemmer, D. (1958). *The prison community.* New York: Holt, Rinehart, and Winston.

Cleveland, W. (1989). The history of California's art-in corrections program. In S. Duguid (Ed.), *Yearbook of correctional education* (pp. 175–191). Burnaby, BC: Institute for the Humanities, Simon Fraser University.

Cline, F. X. (1992, December). Lifers argue for early parole for good behavior. Special to *New York Times. DOCS/Today*, pp. 6, 10, & 11.

Cloward, R., & Ohlin, L. (1960). *Delinquency and opportunity.* Glencoe, IL: Free Press.

Cloward, R., & Piven, F. (1977). *Poor people's movements: Why they succeed, How they fail.* New York: Pantheon Books.

Cohen, A. K. (1955). *Delinquent boys.* Glencoe, IL: Free Press.

Coleman, J. W. (1989). *The criminal elite.* New York: St. Martin's Press.

Collins, M. (1983). A critical analysis of competency-based systems in adult education. *Adult Education Quarterly: A Journal of Research and Theory, 33*(3), 178–183.

Collins, M. (1984). CBAE and variations on a theme: A reply to my critics. *Adult Education Quarterly, 34*(4), 240–246.

Collins, M. (1987). *Competence in adult education: A new perspective.* Lanham, MD: University Press of America.

Cooley, C. H. (1983). *Human nature and the social order.* New Brunswick, NJ: Transaction Books.

Correctional Association of New York. (1993, March). *Trends in New York State prison commitments.*

Curtis, B. (1988). *Building the educational state: Canada West, 1836–1871.* London, ON: Althouse Press/Barcombe (Lewes).

Davidson, H. S. (1988). Meaningful literacy education in prison? Problems and possibilities. *Journal of Correctional Education, 39,* 76–81.

Davidson, H. S. (1991). *Moral education and social relations: The case of prisoner self-government reform, New York (1895–1923).* Unpublished doctoral dissertation. University of Toronto.

Davidson, H. (1993). Toward a historical sociology of needs and needs assessment in adult and continuing education. A paper presented at the Canadian Association for Studies in Adult Education. *Learned Societies Meetings.* Ottawa, ON: Carleton University.

Department of Correctional Services. (1988). Increasing parole success. *DOCS/Today, 1*(9), 8–9.

Deutsch, M. E., & Susler, J. (1991). Political prisoners in the United States: The hidden reality. *Social Justice, 18*(3), 92–107.

Deutscher, I. (1968). *The non-Jewish Jew and other essays.* Boston: Alyson Publications.

DiIulio, J. J., Jr. (1987). *Governing prisons: A comparative study of correctional management.* New York: Free Press.

DiVito, R. J. (1991). Survey of mandatory education policies in state penal institutions. *Journal of Correctional Education, 42,* 126–132.

Doob, A. N., & Roberts, J. (1988). Public punitiveness and public knowledge of the facts: Some Canadian surveys. In N. Walker & M. Hough (Eds.), *Public attitudes to sentencing* (pp. 111–133). Aldershot, England: Gower.

Dowker, F., & Good, G. (1993). The proliferation of control unit prisons in the United States. *Journal of Prisoners on Prisons, 4*(3), 95–110.

Duguid, S. (1979). History and moral development in correctional education. *Canadian Journal of Higher Education, 4*(4), 81–92.

Duguid, S. (1981). Rehabilitation through education. In L. Morin (Ed.), *On prison education* (pp. 43–55). Ottawa, ON: Canadian Government Publishing Centre.

Duguid, S. (1983). Prison education: A case for the liberal arts. *Adult Education Research Proceedings.* Montreal, Que.: University of Montreal, 87–92.

Duguid, S. (1986). Selective ethics and integrity: Moral development and prison education. *Journal of Correctional Education, 37,* 60–64.

Duguid, S. (1992). "Becoming interested in other things": The impact of education in prison. *Journal of Correctional Education, 43,* 38–44.

Duguid, S., Fowler, T. A., & Shewfelt, J. (1992). An annotated bibliography on prison education. In S. Duguid (Ed.), *Yearbook of correctional education* (pp. 139–420). Burnaby, BC: Institute for the Humanities, Simon Fraser University.

Duguid, S., & Hoekema, H. (Eds.) (1986, November). *University education in prison: A documentary record of the experience in British Columbia 1974–1986.* Burnaby, BC: Simon Fraser University.

Dunne, B. (1993). Dungeon Marion: An instrument of oppression. *Journal of Prisoners on Prisons, 4*(2), 95–110.

Editors. (1976). The politics of street crime. *Crime and Social Justice: A Journal of Radical Criminology, 5,* p. 2.

Eggleston, C. (1991). Elmira reformatory programs: Correctional education in the nineteenth century. In S. Duguid (Ed.), *Yearbook of correctional education,* (pp. 167–187). Burnaby, BC: Institute for the Humanities Simon Fraser University.

Eggleston, C. (1992). Correctional education teacher preparation: An overview and a look toward a third generation. *Issues in Teacher Education, 1*(2), 7–15.

Ellis, D. (1979). The prison guard as a carceral luddite: A critical review of the MacGuigan report on the penitentiary. *Canadian Journal of Sociology, 4*(1), 43–64.

Erikson, K. (1962). Notes on the sociology of deviance. *Social Problems, 9,* 307–314.

Faith, K. (Ed.). (1975). *Soledad prison: University of the poor.* Palo Alto, CA: Science and Behavior Books.

Faith, K. (1976). *Inside/Outside.* Los Angeles: Peace Press.

Faith, K. (1993). *Unruly women: The politics of confinement and resistance.* Vancouver, BC: Press Gang Publishers.

Fingeret, A., & Jurmo, P. (1989). *Participatory literacy education.* San Francisco: Jossey-Bass.

Fogel, D., & Hudson, J. (Eds.). (1981). *Justice as fairness: Perspectives on the justice model.* Cincinnati, OH: Anderson Publishing.

Foucault, M. (1977). *Discipline and punish: The birth of the prison.* New York: Pantheon Books.

Foucault, M. (1981, Spring). Questions of method: An interview with Michel Foucault. *Ideology and Consciousness, 3,* 3–14.

Freire, P. (1970). *Pedagogy of the oppressed.* New York: Continuum.

Freire, P. (1978). *Pedagogy in process: The letters to Guinea-Bissau.* New York: Seabury Press.

Freire, P. (1981). *Education for critical conscious.* New York: Continuum.

Freire, P. (1985). *The politics of education: Culture, power, and liberation.* South Hadley, MA: Bergin & Garvey.

Gaither, C. C. (1982). Education behind bars: An overview. *Journal of Correctional Education,* 33, 19–23.

Garland, D. (1991). Punishment and culture: The symbolic dimension of criminal justice. *Studies in law, politics, and society: A research annual,* 2, 191–222. Greenwich, CT: JAI Press.

Gaucher, R. (1989). The Canadian penal press: A documentation and analysis. *Journal of Prisoners on Prisons,* 2(1), 3–24.

Gaucher, R. (1991). Organizing inside: Prison Justice Day (August 10th)—a nonviolent response to penal repression. *Journal of Prisoners on Prisons,* 3(1&2), 93–110.

Gaucher, R. (1993). Editor's introduction. *Journal of Prisoners on Prisons,* 5(1), 1–3.

Gehring, T. (1992). Correctional teacher skills, characteristics, and performance indicators. *Issues in Teacher Education,* 1(2), 22–42.

Gerth, H. B., & Mills, C. W. (1964). *Character and social structure.* New York: Harcourt, Brace and Co.

Gilbert, D. (1991). These criminals have no respect for human life. *Social Justice,* 18(3), 71–83.

Giroux, H. A. (1988). *Teachers as intellectuals: Toward a critical pedagogy of learning.* New York: Bergin & Garvey.

Giroux, H. A., & Freire, P. (1987). Series introduction. In David Livingstone & Contributors, *Critical pedagogy and cultural power.* New York: Bergin & Garvey.

Goffman, E. (1961). *Asylums.* Garden City, NY: Anchor Books.

Goldin, C., & Thomas, J. (1984). The cooperative model in correctional education: Symbol or substance? *Adult Education Quarterly,* 34(3), 123–134.

Gonzales, L. (1986, February). The new Alcatraz. *Chicago Magazine,* pp. 121–148.

Goodman, E. (1992, January 3). Clemency for prisoner 81-G-0098. *Boston Globe,* editorial section.

Gosselin, L. (1982). *Prisons in Canada.* (P. Williams Trans.) Montreal, Que.: Black Rose Books. (Original work published 1977.)

Griffin, C. (1991). A critical perspective on sociology and adult education. In J. Peters, P. Jarvis, & Associates (Eds.), *Adult education: Evolution and achievement in a developing field* (pp. 259–281). San Francisco: Jossey-Bass.

Griffin, E. (1993). Breaking men's minds: Behavior control and human experimentation at the federal prison in Marion, Illinois. *Journal of Prisoners on Prisons,* 4(2), 17–28.

Habermas, J. (1984 & 1987). *The theory of communicative action* (Vols. 1 & 2). (T. McCarthy, Trans.). Boston: Beacon Press. (Original work published 1981.)

Hartnagel, T., & Gillian, M. E. (1980). Female prisoners and the inmate code. *Pacific Sociological Review,* 23(1), 84–104.

Hauerwas, S. (1981). *A community of character.* Notre Dame, IN: University of Notre Dame Press.

Hawkins, G. (1983). Prison labor and prison industries. *Crime Justice: An Annual Review of Research,* 5, 85–127. Chicago: University of Chicago Press.

Hoare, Q., & Smith, G. (Eds.). (1975). *Selections from the prison notebooks of Antonio Gramsci*. New York: International Publishers.

Ichheiser, G. (1970). *Appearances and realities: Misunderstanding in human relations*. San Francisco: Jossey-Bass.

Ignatieff, M. (1978). *Just measure of pain: The penitentiary in the industrial revolution, 1750–1850*. New York: Pantheon.

Illinois Department of Corrections (IDOC). (1991, January). *Insight into corrections*. Springfield, IL: IDOC.

Inniss, L., & Feagin, J. F. (1989). The black "underclass" ideology in race relations analysis. *Social Justice, 16*(4), 13–34.

Irwin, J. (1980). *Prisons in turmoil*. Boston: Little, Brown and Company.

Jacobs, J. B. (1976). Stratification and conflict among prison inmates. *Journal of Criminal Law and Criminology, 66*, 476–482.

Jenkins, H. D. (1994). Mandatory education. *Journal of Correctional Education, 45*, 26–29.

John Howard Association Report. (1986). *An uneasy calm: The U.S. penitentiary at Marion*. Chicago: John Howard Association.

Johnson, R. (1976). *Culture and crisis in confinement*. Lexington, KY: D.C. Heath.

Jones, R. L. (1992). A coincidence of interests: Prison higher education in Massachusetts. *Journal of Prisoners on Prisons, 4*(1), 3–20.

Jones, R. L., & d'Errico, P. (1994). The paradox of higher education in prison. In M. Williford (Ed.), *Higher education in prison: A contradiction in terms?* (pp. 1–16). Phoenix, AZ: The Oryx Press.

Jose-Kamfner, C. (1990). Coming to terms with existential death: An analysis of women's adaption to life in prison. *Social Justice, 17*(2), 110–125.

Karier, C., Violas, P., & Spring, J. (1973). Academic freedom and the public school teacher, 1930–1960. In P. C. Violas (Ed.), *Roots of crisis: American education in the twentieth century* (pp. 163–176). Chicago: Rand McNally.

Keller, R., & Sbarbaro, E. (1995). *Crises in corrections: Contemporary readings*. Albany, NY: Harrow & Heston.

Knights, W. (1981). Moral education and teaching practice: Heuristic or hidden curriculum? *National Conference on Prison Education Proceedings*. Victoria, BC; University of Victoria, 321–345.

Knights, W. (1989). Culture in the bureaucracy: The university in prison. *Yearbook of Correctional Education* (pp. 61–78). Burnaby, BC: Institute for the Humanities, Simon Fraser University.

Kohlberg, L. (1984). *Essays on moral development*, Vol. 2, *The psychology of moral development*. San Francisco: Harper & Row.

Kornbluh, R. (1972). *An IWW anthology*. Ann Arbor: University of Michigan Press.

Kraft, W. F. (1993). Wholistic character formation. *Journal of Correctional Education, 44*, 86–91.

Kuttab, J. (1988). The children's revolt. *Journal of Palestine Studies, 68* (Summer), 26–35.

Lauen, R. J. (1990). Community corrections: Getting involved. In *The state of corrections proceedings American Correction Association Annual Winter Conference 1989*. Laurel, MD: American Correctional Association.

Lawrence, D. W. (1994). The scope and diversity of prison higher education. In M. Williford (Ed.), *Higher education in prison: A contradiction in terms?* (pp. 32–51). Phoenix, AZ: The Oryx Press.

Legere, B. J. (1914). The red flag in the Auburn prison. *International Socialist Review*, 15, 337–341.

Lewis, A. (1967). *Gideon's trumpet*. New York: Random House.

Linebaugh, P. [Anonymous]. (1982). Credit to the parties in Brixton: Malcolm X Day at Attica. *Midnight Notes: Computer State Notes*, Spring, 41–43.

Livingston, D. W. (1987). Introduction. In D. W. Livingston & Contributors, *Critical pedagogy and cultural power* (pp. 1–14). South Hadley, MA: Bergin & Garvey.

Livingston, D. W., & Contributors. (1987). *Critical pedagogy and cultural power*. South Hadley, MA: Bergin & Garvey.

MacLean, B. (1986). State expenditures on Canadian justice. In B. MacLean (Ed.), *The political economy of crime: Readings for a critical criminology*. Scarborough, ON: Prentice-Hall Canada.

MacLean, B. D. (1991). Master status, stigma, termination and beyond. *Journal of Prisoners on Prisons*, 3(1&2), 111–118.

MacLean, B. D. (1992). Post-secondary education in the prison: Cognitive and moral development or social control? *Journal of Prisoners on Prisons*, 4(1), 21–28.

MacLean, B. D., & Milovanovic, D. (Eds.). *New directions in critical criminology*. Vancouver, BC: Collective Press.

Macmurray, J. (1977). *Conditions of freedom*. Toronto, ON: Toronto Mission Press.

Malcolm X. (1966). *The autobiography of Malcolm X*. New York: Grove Press.

Malcolm X. (1970). *Malcolm X on Afro-American history*. New York: Pathfinder Press.

Manly, H. (1993, November 19). A legacy of hope lives at Norfolk Prison. *Boston Globe*, p. 31.

Mann, W. E. (1967). *Society behind bars: A sociological scrutiny of Guelph reformatory*. Toronto: Social Science Publishers.

Marcuse, H. (1966). *One dimensional man: Studies in the ideology of advanced industrial societies*. Boston: Beacon Press.

Martin, B. (1982). The Massachusetts correctional system: Treatment as an ideology for control. In T. Platt & P. Takagi (Eds.), *Punishment and penal discipline: Essays on the prison and the prisoners' movement* (pp. 156–164). San Francisco: Crime and Social Justice Associates.

Martin, K. T. (1976). A brief history of prisoner education. In M. V. Reagen & D. M. Stoughton (Eds.), *Schools behind bars: A descriptive overview of correctional education in the American prison system* (pp. 31–48). Metuchen, NJ: Scarecrow Press.

Martinson, R. (1974). What works?—Questions and answers about prison reform. *The Public Interest*, 35, 22–54.

Marx, K. (1959). Theses on Feuerbach. In L. F. Feuer (Ed.), *Marx and Engels basic writings on politics and philosophy* (pp. 243–245). Garden City, NY: Anchor Books.

Matsueda, R. L., Piliavin, I., Gartner, R., & Polakowski, M. (1992, December). The prestige of criminal and conventional occupations: A subcultural model of criminal activity. *American Sociological Review*, 57, 752–770.

Matza, D., & Sykes, G. M. (1961). Juvenile delinquency and subterranean value. *American Sociological Review*, 26, 712–719.

Mauer, M. (1990, February). Young black men and the criminal justice system: A growing national problem.Washington, DC: The Sentencing Project.

Mauer, M. (1992). *Americans behind bars: One year later.* Washington, DC: The Sentencing Project.

McCollum, S. G. (1989). Mandatory literacy for prisons. In S. Duguid (Ed.), *Yearbook of correctional education* (pp. 121–128). Burnaby, BC: Institute for the Humanities, Simon Fraser University.

McCollum, S. G. (1990). Mandatory programs in prisons: Let's expand the concept. In S. Duguid (Ed.), *Yearbook of correctional education* (pp. 159–164). Burnaby, BC: Institute for the Humanities, Simon Fraser University.

McLaren, P., & Leonard, P. (1993). Editors' introduction. Absent discourses: Paulo Freire and the dangerous memories of liberation. In P. McLaren & P. Leonard (Eds.), *Paulo Freire: A critical encounter* (pp. 1–7). London: Routledge.

McLuhan, M. (1967). *The medium is the message.* New York: Bantam Books

"McNeil/Lehrer News Hour." (1985, June 16). "Prison Business." TV segment from Minneapolis affiliate. Produced by S. Levinson.

Melville, S. (1972). *Letters from Attica.* Great Neck, NY: Felix Morrow Publisher.

Merton, R. K. (1938). Social structure and anomie. *American Sociological Review, 3,* 672–682.

Merton, R. K. (1957). *Social theory and social structure.* New York: Free Press.

Messner, S. F., & Rosenfeld, R. (1994). *Crime and the American dream.* Belmont, CA: Wadsworth.

Michalowski, R. J. (1985). *Order, law and crime.* New York: Random House.

Milakovich, M. E., & Weiss, K. (1975). Politics and measures of success in the war on crime. *Crime and Delinquency, 21*(1), 1–10.

Mills, C. W. (1963). Language, logic and culture. In I. L. Horowitz (Ed.), *Power, politics, and people: The collected essays of C. Wright Mills* (pp. 423–438). London: Oxford University Press.

Mills, C. W. (1970). *The sociological imagination.* New York: Oxford University Press.

Morin, L. (Ed.) (1981a). *On prison education.* Ottawa, ON: Ministry of Supply and Services Canada.

Morin, L. (1981b). Inmate right to education. In L. Morin (Ed.), *On prison education* (pp. 23–33). Ottawa, ON: Ministry of Supply and Services Canada.

Morin, L. (1981c). On the place of values education in prison. In L. Morin (Ed.), *On prison education* (pp. 158–184) Ottawa, ON: Ministry of Supply and Services Canada.

Moton, D., Aylward, A., & Thomas, J. (1985, Winter). Pedagogical innovation and cognitive interests: A critical view. *New England Sociologist, 44–57.*

Moughrabi, F. (1992). Israeli control and Palestinian resistance. *Social Justice, 19*(3), 46–61.

Nabokov, P., & MacLean, M. (1980). Ways of native running. *Co-Evolution Quarterly,* (Summer), n.p.

Nettler, G. (1978). *Explaining crime.* New York: McGraw Hill.

Newton, H. P. (1973). *Revolutionary suicide.* New York: Harcourt Brace Jovanovich.

Northcut, N. (1976). Adult performance level. In C. Klevins (Ed.), *Methods and materials in continuing education.* New York: Klevins Publishers.

Norton, M. (1984, February 15). Prison no barrier to students' education. *Minnesota Daily*, pp. 1, 13.

Ontario Institute for Studies in Education. (1979, February). *Report to the Solicitor General of Canada concerning the education program of the Canadian Corrections System*. Phase two. No publisher.

Pallas, J., & Barber, B. (1980). From riot to revolution. In T. Platt & P. Takagi (Eds.), *Punishment and penal discipline: Essays on the prison and the prisoners' movement* (pp. 146–154). San Francisco: Crime and Social Justice Associates.

Parenti, M. (1986). *Inventing reality: The politics of the mass media*. New York: St Martin's Press.

Parker, J. (1984). In search of a real analysis: CBAE leaders response to Collins critiques. *Adult Education Quarterly*, 34(2), 105–110.

Patterson, O. (1982). *Slavery and social death: A comparative study*. Cambridge, MA: Harvard University Press.

Pfohl, S. (1985). *Images of deviance and social control: A sociological history*. New York: McGraw-Hill.

Platt, T., & Takagi, P. (Eds.) (1980). *Punishment and penal discipline: Essays on the prison and the prisoners' movement*. San Francisco: Crime and Social Justice Associates.

Rabinow, P. (1984). *The Foucault reader*. New York: Pantheon Books.

Ratner, R. S., & Cartwright, B. (1990). Politicized prisoners: From class warriors to faded rhetoric. *Journal of Human Justice*, 2(1), 75–92.

Reiman, J. (1990). *The rich get richer and the poor get prison* (3rd ed.). New York: Macmillan.

Rogers, J. A. (1967, 1970, & 1972). *Sex and race* (Vols. 1–3). St. Petersburg, FL: H. M. Rogers Publisher. (Original work published 1940, 1942, & 1944).

Ross, R. (1981). Cognition and crime: In search of a link. *Proceedings, National Conference on Prison Education*. Victoria, BC: University of Victoria and Canadian Association for Adult Education in cooperation with the Correctional Service of Canada, 279–290.

Ross, R., & Fabiano, E. (1985). *Time to think: A cognitive model of delinquency prevention and offender rehabilitation*. Johnson City, TN: Institute of Social Sciences and Arts.

Rothman, D. (1980). *Conscience and convenience: The asylum and its alternatives in progressive America*. Boston: Little Brown.

Rusche, G., & Kirchheimer, O. (1968). *Punishment and social structure*. New York: Russell & Russell.

Rutherford, A. (1986). *Prisons and the process of justice*. Oxford, England: Oxford University Press.

Ryan, T. A., & McCabe, K. A. (1993). The relationship between mandatory vs. voluntary participation in a prison literacy program and academic achievement. *Journal of Correctional Education*, 44, 134–138.

Schaller, J. (1981). Normalizing the prison work environment. In D. Fogel & J. Hudson (Eds.), *Justice as fairness: Perspectives on the justice model* (pp. 219–234). Cincinnati, OH: Anderson.

Schmitt, R. (1983). *Alienation and class*. Rochester, VT: Schenkman Books.

Schwartz, G. M., & Koch, C. A. (1992). U.S. Department of Education's correctional education initiative. *Issues in Teacher Education*, 1(2), 100–108.

Scollard, B. (1975, April–May). *NEPA news: The voice of the North East Prisoners Association*, III(4), n.p.

SCWPP. (1974). Course schedule, 1994–95. Cover.

Seashore, M. J., & Haberfield, S. (1976). *Prisoner education: Project Newgate and other college programs*. New York: Praeger.

Sherman, L., & Smith, D. (1992). Crime, punishment and stake in conformity: Legal and informal control of domestic violence. *American Sociological Review*, 57, 680–690.

Shor, I. (1980). *Critical teaching and everyday life*. Montreal: Black Rose Press.

Shor, I. (1992). *Empowering education: Critical teaching for social change*. Chicago: University of Chicago Press.

Shor, I. (1993). Education is politics: Paulo Freire's critical pedagogy. In P. McLaren & P. Leonard (Eds.), *Paulo Freire: A critical encounter* (pp. 25–35). London: Routledge.

da Silva, T. T., & McLaren, P. (1993). Knowledge under siege: The Brazilian debate. In P. McLaren & P. Leonard (Eds.), *Paulo Freire: A critical encounter* (pp. 36–46). London: Routledge.

Silva, W. (1994). A brief history of prison higher education in the United States. In M. Williford (Ed.), *Higher education in prison: A contradiction in terms?* (pp. 17–31). Phoenix, AZ: The Oryx Press.

Simon, R. I. (1992). *Teaching against the grain: Texts for a pedagogy of possibility*. New York: Bergin & Garvey.

Solicitor General of Canada. (1990). *Annual Report 1988–1989*. Ottawa, ON: Minister of Supply and Services Canada.

Sorokin, P. (1970). *Social and cultural dynamics*. Boston: Porter Sargent Publisher.

Spring, J. H. (1972, March/April). Education and the rise of the corporate state. *Socialist Review*, 2, 72–101.

Stanford, J. S. (1991). A brief cross country review of facts and figures on relevant environmental factors—The Canadian perspective. In *International symposium on the future of corrections: Program*. Ottawa, ON: Correctional Service of Canada.

Steurer, S. J. (1991). Inmates helping inmates: Maryland's peer tutoring reading academies. In S. Duguid (Ed.), *Yearbook of correctional education* (pp. 133–139). Burnaby, BC: Institute for the Humanities, Simon Fraser University.

Sutherland, E. H., Cressey, D. R., & Luckenbill, D. (1992). *Principles of criminology* (11th ed.). Dixon Hills, NY: General Hall.

Sykes, G. M. (1958). *The society of captives*. Princeton, NJ: Princeton University Press.

Sykes, G. M., & Messinger, S. L. (1960). The inmate social system. In Conference Group on Correctional Organization (Ed.), *Theoretical studies in the social organization of the prison* (pp. 5–48). New York: Social Science Research Council, Pamphlet no. 15.

Tannenbaum, F. (1938). *Crime and community*. New York: Ginn and Company.

Taylor, I., Walton, P., & Young, J. (1973). *The new criminology*. New York: Harper Torchbooks.

Taylor, J. M. (1994). Appendix one: Pell grants for prisoners. In M. Williford (Ed.), *Higher education in prison: A contradiction in terms?* (pp. 167–172). Phoenix, AZ: The Oryx Press.

Terry, D. (1992, September 13). More familiar, life in a cell seems less terrible. *New York Times*, pp. 1, 3.

Thio, A. (1975). A critique of Merton's anomie theory. *Pacific Sociological Review*, 18, 139–158.

Thomas, J. (1983). Teaching sociology in unconventional settings: The irony of maximum security prisons. *Teaching Sociology*, 10, 231–250.

Thomas, J., Mika, H., Aylward, A., & Blakemore, J. (1991, March). Exacting control through disciplinary hearings: "Making do" with prison rules. *Justice Quarterly*, 10, 37–57.

Thompson, E. P. (1978). *The poverty of theory and other essays*. London: Merlin Press.

Tifft, L. (1979). Coming redefinitions of crime: An anarchist perspective. *Social Problems*, 26, 392–402.

Torres, C. A. (1993). From the pedagogy of the oppressed to a luta continua: The political pedagogy of Paulo Freire. In P. McLaren & P. Leonard (Eds.), *Paulo Freire: A critical encounter* (pp. 119–145). London: Routledge.

Tough, A. (1981). *Learning without a teacher: A study of tasks and assistance during adult self-teaching projects*. Toronto, ON: OISE.

Turner, J. H., & Starnes, C. E. (1976). *Inequality: Privilege and poverty in America*. Santa Monica, CA: Goodyear Publishing.

Vold, G., & Bernard, T. (1986). *Theoretical criminology*. New York: Oxford University Press.

Walker, R. "Hakim." (1992, November 27). Suit filed against prison officials: Unfair labor practices. *The Mirror*, 106(8), p. 3.

Wall Street Journal/The Roper Organization. (1987, February). *The American dream: A national survey*. New York: Dow Jones & Co.

Weiss, R. P. (1987). The reappearance of the "ideal factory": The entrepreneur and social control in the contemporary prison. In J. Lowman, R. S. Menzies, & T. S. Palys (Eds.), *Transcarceration: Essays in the sociology of social control* (pp. 272–290). Aldershot, England: Gower.

Werner, D. R. (1990). *Correctional education: Theory and practice*. Danville, IL: Interstate.

Williamson, G. L. (1992). Education and incarceration: An examination of the relationship between educational achievement and criminal behavior. *Journal of Correctional Education*, 43, 14–22.

Wilson, J. Q. (Ed.). (1983). *Crime and public policy*. San Francisco: Institute for Contemporary Studies.

Wordsworth, W. (1902). *Poems of Wordsworth* (Vol. 2). New York: P. F. Collier & Sons.

Wotherspoon, T. (1986). Prison education and fiscal crisis. In B. D. MacLean (Ed.), *The political economy of crime* (pp. 166–176). Scarborough, ON: Prentice-Hall.

Ya'ari, E. (1989, October). Israel's prison academies. *The Atlantic*, 264, pp. 22–27, 30.

Zeitlin, I. M. (1968). *Ideology and the development of sociology theory*. Englewood Cliffs, NJ: Prentice-Hall.

Zinn, H. (1980). *A people's history of the United States*. New York: HarperCollins.

Index

Contributors

GAY BELL teaches English as a Second Language to adults in Toronto, Ontario, and is a writer who has been working with the Prisoners Justice Day Committee of Toronto to facilitate writers in prison getting their work out to a larger public.

MICHAEL COLLINS is a Professor of Adult Education at the University of Saskatchewan. His work on education program development and evaluation in prisons informs his concept of adult literacy. He is a founding member of the Emma Lake Summer Institute for Prison Educators and the author of *Adult Education as Vocation: A Critical Role for Adult Educator* (1991).

PETER CORDELLA is an Assistant Professor in the Department of Sociology and Criminal Justice at St. Anselm College, New Hampshire. Among his recent work is "Reconciliation and the Mutualist Model of Community" in *Criminology as Peacemaking* (1991), edited by Richard Quinney and Hal Pepinsky. He was on the faculty of Boston University's prison education program and a board member of the Massachusetts Council on Prison Education from 1985 to 1992.

HOWARD S. DAVIDSON is an Assistant Professor of Continuing Education at The University of Manitoba. He has taught basic reading and math skills to adults incarcerated in a forensic psychiatric hospital and provincial prison, and he has taught sociology for Boston University's prison education program. He is the founder of the *Journal of Prisoners on Prisons* and was its editor from 1988 to 1993.

KARLENE FAITH, a native of Saskatchewan, has been a human rights activist since her youth, and she has worked with prisoners in various countries. Currently with the Criminology Faculty at Simon Fraser University in British Columbia, she is the author of *Unruly Women: The Politics of Confinement and Resistance* (1993).

DANTE GERMANOTTA, a Professor Emeritus of Curry College, founded and coordinated the Curry College Justice Education Program at Walpole Prison. He was a founding member of the Massachusetts Council on Prison Education, serving as its president from 1984 to 1993. He was an early member of the International Conference on Prison Abolition and has written articles and book reviews on prison issues.

THERASA ANN GLAREMIN: "I am a strong women with a beautiful human spirit. If it was not for being wrongfully convicted, I would not have gotten an education. I continue to heal from systemic abuse with the love and support of my family and friends."

PETER LINEBAUGH was educated in Cattaraugus, London, Bonn, Frankfurt, and Karachi, Pakistan. He has been a Fullbright Scholar in Brazil and a Fellow of the Max Planck Institute, Göttingen. He is currently teaching in the History Department, University of Toledo. He is the author of *The London Hanged* (1993).

JUAN A. RIVERA, no. 86-A-3200, has served ten years of a ten year to life prison term in New York State. During this time, he has acquired an AAS in business administration and a BS in the integrative major, with concentrations in psychology and social work. He tutors for Marist College, and in his leisure time he instructs both a Puerto Rican history class and the Consciencia Study Program.

EDWARD SBARBARO teaches sociology and criminology in the Colorado state prisons and is coordinator of advising for the Regis University prison program. He is coauthor of *Prison in Crisis: Contemporary Readings* with Robert Keller and is currently studying federal crime legislation.

JULIAN STONE has taught law classes at MCI-Norfolk, Northeastern Correctional Center, Old Colony Correctional Center, and Bay State Correctional Center.

JIM THOMAS is a professor of Sociology/Criminal Justice at Northern Illinois University. In addition to his work on prison education, he has written about prison culture, prison litigation, and the death penalty. His interests also include technology and social control.

ROBERT P. WEISS is Associate Professor and Chair of the Department of Sociology, State University of New York at Plattsburg. Over the past twenty-five years, he has taught high school and college in the prison education programs of five states, and in 1982–1983 he was director of the University of Houston/Texas Department of Corrections Ramsey Unit College Program. His publications have been on the history of punishment, the privatization movement in corrections, and the historical development of private policing. He also guest edited a special issue of *Social Justice* (1991) on the twenty-year anniversary of the Attica prison rebellion.

ISBN 0-89789-347-6

9 0000>

9 780897 893473

HARDCOVER BAR CODE